A PSYCHOLOGY OF EARLY SUFI SAMĀᶜ

This book explores the psychology of altered states among the early Sufis. It examines *samāᶜ*, i.e. listening to ritual recitation, music and certain other aural phenomena, and its effect in inducing unusual states of consciousness and behaviours. The focus is on the earliest personalities of the Islamic mystical tradition, as found in texts from the tenth to the twelfth centuries CE.

These unusual states are interpreted in the light of current research in Western psychology, and also in terms of their integration into historical Islamic culture.

A Psychology of Early Sufi samāᶜ provides new insights into the work of five Sufi authors, and a fresh approach to the relation between historical accounts of altered states and current psychological thinking.

Kenneth S. Avery is a specialist in Sufi studies and Persian literature. He is a musician and a recent PhD graduate in Islamic Studies from the University of Melbourne.

ROUTLEDGECURZON SUFI SERIES

Series Editor: Ian Richard Netton
Professor of Arabic Studies
University of Leeds

The RoutledgeCurzon Sufi Series provides short introductions to a variety of facets of the subject, which are accessible both to the general reader and the student and scholar in the field. Each book will be either a synthesis of existing knowledge or a distinct contribution to, and extension of, knowledge of the particular topic. The two major underlying principles of the Series are sound scholarship and readability.

BEYOND FAITH AND INFIDELITY
The Sufi poetry and teaching of Mahmud Shabistari
Leonard Lewisham

AL-HALLAJ
Herbert W. Mason

RUZBIHAN BAQLI
Mysticism and the rhetoric of sainthood in Persian Sufism
Carl W. Ernst

ABDULLAH ANSARI OF HERAT
An early Sufi master
A.G. Ravan Farhadi

THE CONCEPT OF SAINTHOOD IN EARLY ISLAMIC MYSTICISM
Bernd Radtke and John O'Kane

SUHRAWARDI AND THE SCHOOL OF ILLUMINATION
Mehdi Amin Razavi

PERSIAN SUFI POETRY
An introduction to the mystical use of classical poems
J.T.P. de Bruijn

AZIZ NASAFI
Lloyd Ridgeon

SUFIS AND ANTI-SUFIS
The defence, rethinking and rejection of Sufism in the modern world
Elizabeth Sirriyeh

REVELATION, INTELLECTUAL INTUITION AND REASON IN THE PHILOSOPHY OF MULLA SADRA
An analysis of the al-hikmah al-ʿarshiyyah
Zailan Moris

DIVINE LOVE IN ISLAMIC MYSTICISM
The teachings of al-Ghazali and al-Dabbagh
Binyamin Abramahov

STRIVING FOR DIVINE UNION
Spiritual exercises for Suhraward Sufis
Qamar-ul Huda

A PSYCHOLOGY OF EARLY SUFI SAMĀʿ
Listening and altered states
Kenneth S. Avery

A PSYCHOLOGY OF EARLY SUFI SAMĀ‘

Listening and altered states

Kenneth S. Avery

RoutledgeCurzon
Taylor & Francis Group
LONDON AND NEW YORK

First published 2004
by RoutledgeCurzon
2 Park Square, Milton Park,
Abingdon, Oxon
OX14 4RN

Simultaneously published in the USA and Canada
by RoutledgeCurzon
270 Madison Avenue, New York, NY 10016

RoutledgeCurzon is an imprint of the Taylor & Francis Group

Typeset in 10/12pt Times by Graphicraft Limited, Hong Kong
Printed and bound in Great Britain by TJ International Ltd,
Padstow, Cornwall

British Library Cataloguing in Publication Data
A catalogue record for this book is available from the British Library

Library of Congress Cataloging in Publication Data
A catalog record for this book has been requested

ISBN 0–415–31106–3

CONTENTS

ACKNOWLEDGEMENTS

My introduction to the world of the Sufis was through an extraordinary teacher and mystic who was a tutor in Semitic studies at the University of Sydney in the 1970s and 1980s. Brian Parker held informal classes in Persian, and as soon as I learned the basic grammar, we began reading the easier parts of ʿAṭṭār's famed biographical collection. The journey which began over twenty years ago has culminated in this book.

In September 2000, the substance of the present study was presented as a PhD thesis at the University of Melbourne. I wish to thank Abdullah Saeed for his generous support during the period of my candidature, and for his constant encouragement and guidance. I also wish to thank Anthony Johns of the Australian National University for his thorough critique of the manuscript.

ABBREVIATIONS

E.I. *The Encyclopaedia of Islam*, new edition, ed. H.A.R. Gibb et al., Leiden: E.J. Brill, 1960–

Iḥyā' Al-Ghazālī, Abū Ḥāmid Muḥammad, *Iḥyā' 'Ulūm al-Dīn*, 4 vols, Cairo: Matba'ah Mustafā al-Bābī al-Halabī wa-Ulādah bi-Misr, 1939.

Kashf Al-Hujwīrī, Alī b. 'Uthmān al-Jullābī, *Kashf al-Maḥjūb*, ed. V.A. Zhukovski, Tehran: Amīr Kabīr, 1336 a.h.s. (reprint).

Luma' Al-Sarrāj al-Ṭūsī, Abū Naṣr 'Abdallah b. 'Alī, *The Kitāb al-Luma' fī 'l-Taṣawwuf*, ed. R.A. Nicholson, London: Luzac and Co, 1914 (1963 reprint).

Mcd. D.B. Macdonald, 'Emotional Religion in Islam as affected by Music and Singing. Being a Translation of a Book of the Iḥyā' 'Ulūm ad-Dīn of al-Ghazzālī with Analysis, Annotation and Appendices' in *Journal of the Royal Asiatic Society*, 22, 1901, pp.195–252 and 705–48; and 23, 1902, pp.1–28.

MSM 'Aṭṭār, Farīd al-Dīn, *Muslim Saints and Mystics: Episodes from the Tadhkirat al-Auliya'*, translated by A.J. Arberry, London: Routledge and Kegan Paul, 1966 (1979 reprint).

Nich. Al-Hujwīrī, Alī b. 'Uthmān al-Jullābī, *The Kashf al-Maḥjūb*, Translated by R.A. Nicholson, Leiden: E.J. Brill, and London: Luzac and Co, 1911 (1982 reprint).

Ris Al-Qushayrī, Abū 'l-Qāsim 'Abd al-Karīm, *Al-Risālat al-Qushayrīya fī 'Ilm al-Taṣawwuf*, ed. Ma'ruf Zarīq and 'Alī Balṭajī, Beirut: Dār al-Jīl, no date.

T.A. 'Aṭṭār, Farīd al-Dīn, *Tadhkiratu 'l-Awliyā*, ed. R.A. Nicholson, 2 vols, London: Luzac and Co, Leiden: E.J. Brill, 1905–7.

T.S. Al-Sulamī, Abū ʿAbd al-Raḥmān, *Ṭabaqāt al-Ṣūfīya*, ed. by Nūr al-Dīn Sharība, second ed., Cairo: Maktaba ʾl-Khānijī, 1969.

Source works in Arabic and Persian are referred to by volume (if more than one), page, and line(s); thus: *Iḥyāʾ* II.180.3–5 = *Iḥyāʾ* vol.2, p.180, lines 3–5.

1

INTRODUCTION

About the year 900 CE a group of scholars met in Baghdad. As they discussed various academic points, one among them, Abū 'l-Ḥusayn al-Nūrī, remained silent. Suddenly he stood up and began to recite four verses of love poetry. His recitation had such an overpowering effect that all those present went into a frenzy of delight and ecstasy.

Nūrī was not a scholar at heart, but an ecstatic Sufi mystic. It is thus not surprising that he chose to upset a scholarly assembly and turn their dry proceedings into an occasion of *samā*ʿ.

The emergence of a mystical and spiritual path in Islam in the second and third centuries after the Prophet Muhammad presents us with a striking phenomenon. On the one hand it is clear that there was an organic development of piety and asceticism, of meditation on the Qurʾān, and an experience of the overpowering majesty of God coupled with the feeling of incapacity on the part of humankind as His servants. This development was deeply impressed by the centrality of the Qurʾān as the foundation of all Muslim life and faith. In both its doctrinal teaching and the ritual of its recitation, the Holy Book inspired the piety and introspection of those who sought God. The notion of a covenant between God and humankind (Qur. 7.172) became central to much Sufi doctrine and practice, allied with the idea of the 'friends' of God and His love for them.

Yet on the other hand it is also clear that this spiritual movement in Islam mirrored to some extent the ascetic and mystical traditions of Christianity in Syria and Egypt, where the two religions overlapped. The very word *ṣūfī*, if derived from the Arabic word for wool (*ṣūf*), reflects the wearing of ascetic woollen garments characteristic of eastern Christian monks. The Christian anticipation of Sufism may also be reflected in doctrinal and practical areas: the emphasis on God's love, the adaptation of Greek neo-Platonist philosophy, the progress of the mystic through a hierarchically staged path, the espousal of poverty, and so on.[1]

However this may be, an ascetic and spiritual movement emerged during the early years of the Abbasid empire (from the middle second/eighth century), partly as a reaction to perceived hypocrisy and shallowness in mainstream religion and its wealthy supporters. This development crystallised around a number of charismatic and revered individuals who came to be honoured as friends of God, as shaykhs or spiritual masters. These individuals attracted to themselves younger or less experienced seekers of God. As yet, no formal orders or 'brotherhoods' existed; the relations between master and seeker were of a personal and informal basis. These early Sufi groupings sought to define and articulate their experience of asceticism and their understanding of Qur'ānic spirituality.

Though these individuals remained deeply pious and integrated into the practice of the Sharia or revealed law of Islam, their ascetic leanings and their stress on extra devotional activities led to inevitable differences and at times conflict with mainstream expressions of the faith. The personal and charismatic quality of the early Sufis also meant that individual doctrines and teachings emerged with much diversity. One archetypal example of these tendencies is in the figure of Abū Yazīd al-Bisṭāmī (d.261/874), an ascetic from Khurāsān in north-east Iran. He describes his mystical experiences in the form of symbolic journeys or flights of the spirit, based largely on the famous 'ascent' journey of the Prophet alluded to in the Qur'ān and embellished by later writers. In Iraq meanwhile, the movement came to centre around the most famous figure of early Sufism, Junayd (d.297/910). An outwardly conservative adherent of the Sharia, he was yet a profound teacher and writer about mystical unitary experience, which he expressed in allusive and obscure language.

These two personalities and their teachings represent two divergent tendencies which came to be characterised as the 'sober' and the 'intoxicated' paths of the Sufi way. Junayd, an influential and inspiring teacher, was also the supreme example of a 'sober' mystic. Although he had a charismatic personality and attracted many disciples, he tried to steer a course for his Sufi contemporaries away from public confrontation with critics and hostile authorities. He sought only private disclosures of those teachings, experiences or behaviours which were likely to upset non-mystics. This cautious approach of Junayd's attempted to maintain the mystical dimension as part of mainstream belief and practice, from which the Sufi movement was in danger of breaking away. Two centuries later the great scholar and mystic Abū Ḥāmid al-Ghazālī (d.505/1111) consolidated this 'sober' approach by his integration of Sufi thought with mainstream Ashʿarite theology.

In contrast to this 'sober' path was the path of the 'intoxicated', those who chose irreverent or antinomian attitudes and practices unacceptable to mainstream Islam. One of these tendencies was the *malāmatī* way, those who sought to bring blame on themselves by their apparently irreligious behaviour. By concealing their true devotion and showing outward disrespect for piety, they brought upon themselves condemnation from ordinary believers and authorities alike. As well as Bisṭāmī, other 'intoxicated' Sufis include the infamous Manṣūr al-Ḥallāj, who was executed amid political intrigue and charges of blasphemy in 309/922. Unlike Junayd, with whom he once studied, Ḥallāj was not afraid to speak openly and in confrontation with authorities about his inner unitary experience. A contemporary of Ḥallāj was Abū Bakr al-Shiblī (d.334/946), whose outrageous behaviour led to detention in a mental asylum, and who declared that his 'madness' saved him from Ḥallāj's fate.

A feature of the 'intoxicated' Sufis was their public demonstration of altered state experience, an outward show of their 'intoxicated' state, brought about by intense ascetic deprivation, meditations and rituals. During such occasions they would speak openly about their experience and their beliefs, though often these ecstatic utterances would be incomprehensible or seem blasphemous to others.

These unusual states were sought after because they were seen as signposts or way stations on the path of the mystic's goal of divine unitary experience. Due to their sometimes ecstatic and blissful nature, these states were also interpreted as manifestations of divine love and mercy.

By the third and fourth centuries of the Islamic era (ninth and tenth centuries CE) techniques and rituals had developed for the generation of altered state experiences both individually and in a social setting. Such techniques were not restricted to the 'intoxicated' Sufis but seem to have been fairly widespread. For mainstream Islam, however, and particularly for those who disapproved of the Sufis, such practices were frowned upon and regarded as unacceptable 'innovations' from the path laid down by the Prophet.

One of the techniques used to induce altered states was that of aural stimulation: chanting, listening to music, poetry, or the recitation of the Qur'ān. In a ritual or social setting, at first among a private group of seekers, later in larger and more public settings, this practice became known as *samāʿ* ('listening' or 'spiritual concert').

The practice of *samāʿ* is clearly an extension of the more basic practice of *dhikr* ('remembrance [of God]' or ritual chant and praise). The Qurʾān itself prescribes the constant remembrance and praise of God, and all these ritual activities have as their source the recitation of the Qurʾān.[2]

Such practices could lead to the heightening of spiritual awareness culminating in various types of ecstasy, alterations of the psyche, and spontaneous physical reactions. The physical and psychological impact of chanting and recitation, especially with the accompaniment of music, was powerfully effective, far beyond the semantic force of the words being heard. J. Spencer Trimingham reminds us that music, chant and recitation 'not only has mystical power to draw out the deepest emotions, but also, when co-ordinated with symbolic words and rhythmical movements, has power over man's will'.[3]

As well as these more or less ritualised practices, early Sufi writings also remark on the effects of informal or casual aural stimuli. A chance hearing of words, song or poetry in a crowded place, the cry of a street vendor, or a 'misheard' sound or utterance could also act as a powerful trigger for altered state experiences.

The focus of this book is on these two types of *samāʿ* – the formal ritual activity, and the informal, casual or chance occasions mentioned in early Sufi writings. Attention is directed to the heightened awareness and spiritual states associated with 'listening'. The first task of the book is the description of these altered states as found in various texts from the formative period of Sufi literature. Secondly, an attempt is made to interpret these unusual states and behaviours in the light of contemporary psychological research.

The concept of *samāʿ* has a wide range of meanings, as will be discovered in the Sufi texts discussed below. Jean During, whose *Musique et extase* is one of the few recent works devoted to this topic, introduces the subject in the following way:

> Samāʿ, which literally means 'audition', denotes, in the Sufi tradition, spiritual listening, and more particularly listening to music with the aim of reaching a state of grace or ecstasy, or more simply with the aim of meditating, of plunging into oneself, or as the Sufis say, to 'nourish the soul'. It thus operates in a mystical concert, of spiritual listening to music and songs, in a more or less ritualised form.[4]

During's study is largely concerned with the later developments of *samāʿ*, particularly those of the Mevlevi order associated with

Jalāl al-Dīn Rūmī (d.672/1273), and writers influenced by the famous Andalusian Sufi, Ibn al-ʿArabī (d.638/1240). The period before the seventh/thirteenth century, however, saw a much more diffuse, less formalised practice of *samāʿ*. Trimingham, in his work on the Sufi orders, maintained that it is difficult to give details about these practices during this early period, 'apart from the singing of mystical poems to induce ecstasy'.[5] This view needs some modification: a close examination of the texts from this period shows that a variety of practices were operating; some developed into more formal rituals, while others may have been abandoned. It is true that certain details are lacking, but it will be shown in later chapters that we can provide a clearer picture of the personalities and practices involved. Moreover, the picture from these centuries can be seen quite adequately without the need for an interpretative overlay provided by the Ibn al-ʿArabī school.

During's definition of *samāʿ*, while emphasising the musical and ritual aspects of the practice, is too narrow for the purposes of this book. A broader concept of *samāʿ* is needed because it includes a wider field of auditory events described in the source texts. Many of the instances of 'listening' in the Sufi writings studied here are not found in formal, ritual situations; nor is music or poetry always involved. As mentioned above, many of the auditory phenomena which give rise to altered states are chance occurrences, such as street cries, songs or overheard speech. Even these everyday events can produce a profound psychological effect in the receptive listener.

It is this effect, this special awareness or ecstasy associated with 'listening', which is the focus of the present work. The term 'altered states' best summarises the range of psychological changes and physical behaviours being considered. The source texts indicate that it is not simply a matter of becoming entranced or enraptured by hearing music or poetry, a common enough occurrence in many cultures. It is a more intense and overwhelming experience which affects the whole mind/body; it is longer lasting, and may involve profound physical and mental changes.

In cross-cultural and psychological studies, this experience of altered states is known to occur in a variety of situations. It has similarities and parallels with trances of various kinds, epileptic-like behaviours, Tourette's syndrome, glossolalia ('speaking in tongues' seen in some charismatic Christian circles), and other 'hyperaroused' states.[6] The psychology and cross-cultural perspective on these altered states is an emerging discipline, with much progress being made in recent years. In Sufi studies little attention has been paid to these phenomena, and the task of the present work is to help redress this situation.

The chosen sources for this study stem from the formative period of Sufi writings, the fourth/tenth to the sixth/twelfth centuries. This period was one of the most creative and productive in the history of Sufism.[7] Some of the texts from these centuries contain important materials dealing with *samāʿ* and altered states. Chapter 2 of the book provides an overview of these sources, a summary of their relevant contents, and discussion of their arguments, as appropriate. Many of the source texts are poorly represented in English translation, and they are not readily accessible. The second chapter thus provides the necessary framework for the topic as a whole.

Chapter 3 considers the issue of language and semantics. The first question addressed is the use of the widely ranging term *samāʿ* in the source texts. The semantics of other important words are considered, particularly in their use as mystical terminology, and in expressing highly diffuse concepts. The purpose of this chapter is to throw light on the particular language and idiom used by our chosen authors. Understanding Sufi psychology involves breaking through this language barrier as far as possible.

The following three chapters, 4, 5 and 6, form the core subject matter of the book. These chapters deal with the psychological aspects of *samāʿ*, analysing numerous accounts of unusual behaviours and altered states evoked by listening. The behaviours are collated according to their characteristics and discussed in the light of modern psychological and cross-cultural understandings of altered states. An attempt is made to discover whether there is a common pattern in these states, whether there is a typical psychological condition associated with *samāʿ*.

In Chapter 6 the Sufi writers are examined for their view of the nature and explanation of the states they describe. This is done to avoid over-reliance on modern, Western psychological research to explain the phenomena, research which often has a cultural and religious, or rather, anti-religious, bias. The Sufi writers speak for themselves as to how they regard these altered states, and how they are integrated into their religious and cultural framework.

Chapter 7 considers the utterances attributed to various Sufi personalities as they speak ecstatically about their experience of altered states. The work by Carl Ernst on ecstatic sayings is exemplary in approaching these statements, though Ernst's book deals with a slightly different phenomenon.[8]

After the psychological aspects of *samāʿ* have been considered, Chapter 8 looks at the ritual and sociological issues arising from this practice. The texts provide some incidental information about the group behaviours and ritual contexts associated with formal *samāʿ* concerts. This enables us to construct a picture of the group dynamics and organisation of Sufi communities from these early centuries, at least as far as their participation in *samāʿ* is concerned. The picture thus formed is not complete in all its details, as most of the information is incidentally recorded along with other matters which were considered more important. However, there are few other witnesses to these sociological details from the early years of Sufi life. The chapter also compares the behaviours and rituals of the source texts with those witnessed in more contemporary situations, mainly relying on the excellent musicological fieldwork of Regula Qureshi.[9]

Chapter 9 presents a case study of two of the most important and frequently mentioned Sufis in the source texts. These two ecstatic personalities, Nūrī and Shiblī, both lived in the third/ninth and fourth/tenth centuries, and were associated with the famous school of Junayd in Baghdad, a group which had a profound impact on the course of Sunni mysticism. Both Nūrī and Shiblī were known as practising ascetics and mystics of very great renown. This study looks at their lives as a whole, and the importance of *samāʿ* and altered states in their mystical experience.

There are several methodological challenges associated with an investigation of the type attempted here. The most outstanding is the distance in culture and time between the age when the Sufi texts were written, and the present. The language difficulty has been mentioned above, reflected, for instance, in the use of specialised idiom known only to initiates of the Sufi path.

What is more problematical is the extent to which the modern reader can understand the state of mind of individuals through a purely textual approach. This is perhaps more of a difficulty than the usual historiographical problem of reliance on written sources. The problem in this work is that we are dealing with the most inaccessible of experiences, of a highly personal and often ineffable nature. Some would argue that one cannot approach the minds of people from written texts only, as does Eric Sharpe in relation to religious studies: 'States of mind, and their verbal expressions, are tenuous things, and in reality hardly accessible to later investigators'.[10] In defence of the approach of this book, however, it must be said that thought processes or states of mind are not the object of inquiry here. It is not possible to venture this far; rather, the object of our search is the outward manifestation of states of mind, resulting behaviours, actions, physical signs and ecstatic sayings, which are a legitimate source of information. These outward manifestations are worthy of consideration as they often provide sufficient detail to make their study informative, and to give some notion of deeper processes involved. It is often not possible to inquire any further than this, however, and speculation about mental states is kept to a minimum in our analysis. What is provided by these outward manifestations is a pattern of behaviours which may indicate a particular condition not considered before in this cultural context. Moreover, this condition may be comparable to those already under scrutiny in contemporary Western psychology or cross-cultural studies.

This leads to an important consideration, namely that the present work takes an experiential approach to the subject under study. It is the experience and reaction of individuals in their encounter with altered states that is the primary evidence considered in this book. Though there is mediation through written texts, the accounts recorded are the nearest we can approach these unusual phenomena. The evidence being studied is not that of a belief system, or mystical symbolism. Important though these may be, these latter inevitably involve further layers of mediation and a greater distancing from the data of personal encounters with altered states.

This broadly phenomenological method also means that the subject under discussion is taken seriously and considered a worthy area of inquiry. It would be a simple exercise to rationalise or explain away the present subject, particularly from the point of view of behaviourist or materialist psychology. Many religious phenomena may be explained away by an approach which is hostile to the basic assumptions and understandings of religious experience. Yet this serves only to confirm the researcher's inadequate frame of reference. By seriously considering the phenomena under study, the investigator can enter more fully into the subject, and gain a more thorough appreciation of its importance.

The methodology adopted here may also appear to take a literal and naïve interpretation of the texts and the narratives they contain. This can hardly be avoided, since the facts behind every story or biographical anecdote cannot be ascertained. On the other hand, many of the accounts of the deeds and sayings of these early Sufis are stories which had to happen. Paradigmatic of their experience and actions, these are powerful narratives, and the factual issue is not an overriding concern.

Finally, as this study is the first to deal in detail with this aspect of the early Sufis, there are some inevitable shortcomings. This is so particularly since the study of altered states is an evolving area in Western psychology. If there is some uncertainty in the present work, it is shown in my taking a largely descriptive approach, first surveying the field and gathering the initial evidence. As the psychology of altered states develops, further research will yield more comprehensive outcomes.

Notes

1 Julian Baldick, *Mystical Islam: An Introduction to Sufism*, London: I.B. Tauris, 1989, p.15.
2 Ian Richard Netton, *Sufi Ritual: The Parallel Universe*, Richmond: Curzon Press, 2000, pp.12–13.
3 J. Spencer Trimingham, *The Sufi Orders in Islam*, Oxford: Clarendon Press, 1971, p.195.
4 Jean During, *Musique et extase: L'audition mystique dans la tradition soufie*, Paris: Albin Michel, 1988, p.13.
5 Trimingham, op. cit.
6 The writings of Oliver Sacks provide a good introduction to these phenomena (see bibliography).
7 Caesar E. Farah, 'The Prose Literature of Sufism', in M.J.L. Young et al. (eds) *The Cambridge History of Arabic Literature: Religion, Learning and Science in the ʿAbbasid Period*, Cambridge: Cambridge University Press, 1990, pp.56–8.
8 Carl W. Ernst, *Words of Ecstasy in Sufism*, Albany, NY: State University of New York Press, 1985.
9 See the various articles listed in the bibliography.
10 Eric J. Sharpe, *Comparative Religion: A History*, second edition, La Salle: Open Court, 1986, p.72.

2

SAMĀʿ IN EARLY SUFI LITERATURE: AN OVERVIEW

The formative period of Sufi literature (from the fourth/tenth to sixth/twelfth centuries) saw the emergence of a variety of writings from Sufi authors in many parts of the Islamic empire.[1] Several different styles and genres were adopted, primarily of a descriptive, didactic or biographical nature. Often highly creative, these writings reflected the spiritual development of the Sufi path at the forefront of Islamic piety and asceticism within politically and socially turbulent times.

Our choice of texts was made on the basis of relative importance and value among foundational Sufi writings. The texts studied here are acknowledged as being highly influential, and in some cases definitive, within the prose literature of early Sufism. The chosen sources also represent some of the different genres of literature which have survived from this period. There are examples of reference literature, namely the *Kitāb al-Lumaʿ* (*Book of Splendours*) of Abū Naṣr al-Sarrāj (d.378/988), the oldest work of its kind; and the famous *Risāla* (*Treatise*) of Abū ʾl-Qāsim al-Qushayrī (d.465/1072). Also chosen for study is ʿAbd al-Raḥman al-Sulamī's (d.412/1021) biographical *Ṭabaqāt al-Ṣūfīya* (*Generations of the Sufis*), again the oldest and most exemplary work of its kind.

These early Arabic works of reference and biography found worthy successors in the Persian context, with ʿAlī b. ʿUthmān al-Hujwīrī (d. circa 465/1072), whose *Kashf al-Maḥjūb* (*Revealing the Veiled*) was an 'original' development from Arabic predecessors. A century later, Farīd al-Dīn ʿAṭṭār (d. circa 617/1220) wrote his famed *Tadhkirat al-Awliyāʾ* (*Memorial of the Saints*), transforming the earlier Arabic biographies into colourful hagiographies.

At the centre of all these varied works, however, lay the most illustrious and monumental of mainstream Sufi writings, Abū Ḥāmid al-Ghazālī's (d.505/1111) *Iḥyāʾ ʿUlūm al-Dīn* (*Revival of the Religious*

Sciences). The chapter on *samāʿ* from this famous book provides the touchstone for much of the discussion in the present study.

With the possible exception of Ghazālī's *Iḥyāʾ*, many of these Arabic and Persian works are largely inaccessible to the English reader. There are German translations of Qushayrī's *Risāla* and Sarrāj's *Lumaʿ*, both by Richard Gramlich. A small portion of ʿAṭṭār's *Tadhkirat* has been translated into English by A.J. Arberry,[2] and R.A. Nicholson translated most of Hujwīrī's *Kashf*,[3] though a number of significant portions are omitted.

The aim of the present chapter is to present a summary of those sections of the chosen texts relevant to our topic. This does not involve lengthy translation, but rather a synopsis and some analysis where needed. The chapter also outlines the life and writings of each author. This overview provides the basis for discussions and analysis concerning 'listening' and altered states among the early Sufis.

The Kitāb al-Lumaʿ of Abū Naṣr al-Sarrāj

The earliest and most fundamental source for the study of many topics in early Islamic mysticism is the definitive reference work, the *Kitāb al-Lumaʿ fi ʾl-Taṣawwuf* (*Book of Splendours concerning the Sufi Way*).[4] This comprehensive and wide-ranging text was written in the late fourth/tenth century by the Sunni ascetic and scholar, Abū Naṣr ʿAbdallāh b. ʿAlī b. Muḥammad b. Yaḥyā al-Sarrāj al-Ṭūsī (d.378/988). Richard Gramlich, in the introduction to his German translation of the *Lumaʿ*, states that it is the oldest extant guide to Sufism. As such, it is an indispensable source of early Islamic piety, and a mine of information which would otherwise have been lost.[5] It has a clear apologetic purpose 'to set forth the true principles of Sufism and to show by argument that they agree with, and are confirmed by, the doctrines of the Koran and the Apostolic Traditions', as argued by Nicholson in the introduction to his edition of the Arabic text.[6]

As for the author's biography, the details are rather sparse. Sarrāj originated in Ṭūs in Khurāsān, but little is known of his early education or his teachers. It appears from his writings that he sought out many Sufi masters and visited their schools on his extensive travels throughout the Abbasid empire. His concern was to collect their teachings and to document their way of life. One example of this is his mention of travelling to Bisṭām to ascertain the true facts concerning the teaching and reputation of Abū Yazīd al-Bisṭāmī

(d. circa 261/874), the celebrated mystic to whom he devotes several chapters of his work.[7]

The Persian biographers surnamed Sarrāj 'the Peacock of the Poor' (*ṭāʾūs al-fuqarāʾ*), and both Hujwīrī in his *Kashf al-Maḥjūb* and ʿAṭṭār in his *Tadhkhirat al-Awliyāʾ* tell of the extent of his asceticism in the following anecdote. Arriving in Baghdad at the start of Ramadan, he was given a private chamber in the Shūnīzīya mosque and was appointed to superintend the other dervishes. During the nightly prayers he would recite the Qurʾān five times. Each night a servant brought a loaf of bread to his chamber, but on the feast day at the end of the month Sarrāj departed and the servant found all thirty loaves untouched. ʿAṭṭār also relates the story of his face being unharmed by a fire when he was thrown onto it in a state of ecstasy.[8] Sarrāj died in Ṭūs in 378/988. The date of composition of the *Kitāb al-Lumaʿ* is not known, but it is certainly the result of many years' preparation and collecting of materials, and represents the work of a mature mind.

The *Lumaʿ* is less a treatise than a thematic collection of Sufi remembrances, teachings, traditions and etiquette. Nicholson argues that Sarrāj's reserve in not promulgating his own interpretations and viewpoints is to be welcomed. It allows for a more historically valuable document, and gives a unique insight into the crucial formative years of Sufi practice.[9]

As noted above, the apologetic character of the work is foremost in the author's mind. Since the Sufi path is bound to the spirit of the Prophet and the Sunna, and since the Sufis have a strong position among Islamic teachers, all religious knowledge thus derives from three sources: the Qurʾān, the Prophetic Traditions, and the mystical gnosis of the 'saints' or friends of God. Part of this apologetic character also shows itself in Sarrāj's endeavour to rebuff critics of the Sufis, of whom there were many, and to correct erroneous views about Islamic mysticism.

The historical need to defend Sufism is explained by A.J. Arberry as arising in the fourth/tenth century, following the scandal of the trial and execution of the outspoken radical, Manṣūr al-Ḥallāj (d.309/922). Sufi groups felt themselves more under fire than ever from more conservative mainstream Muslims. Many prominent thinkers were accused of being a *zindīq*, 'freethinker', a general term of abuse covering many allegedly impious beliefs or actions. The need to regroup and defend the legitimacy of Sufi practice was keenly felt, and it is Sarrāj whom we have to thank for a masterly work of apology.[10]

His writing is not wholly uniform or consistent, but this is expected in a *collectanea* derived from varying sources. Sarrāj's usual method is to intersperse collections of sayings or traditions with authoritative citations as required, yet with a minimum of editorial interpretation. Gramlich observes that Sarrāj is not like Ghazālī who puts forward his own masterly thoughts to which other quotes are subordinate. Rather, he is a guide who speaks through the collected thoughts of others.[11] On the other hand, Sarrāj is not simply a conduit, or a collector of fragments, writing in the style described by Louis Massignon as the 'anecdotal atomism' of early Muslim historiographers.[12] There is an overall pattern to his writing, based on his acknowledged apologetic purpose. He is down to earth, factual, and methodical as a relater of traditions, but also a good storyteller who writes in a lively fashion.

The apologetic and polemical style of the whole work is evident in the particular chapters on *samā*ʿ, entitled *Kitāb al-Samā*ʿ (*Book of Audition*). Sarrāj endeavours to defend the practice of ritual concert among the Sufis, and he argues for its legitimacy against those who would outlaw it in Muslim society. Moreover, he attempts to show that it was approved by the Prophet and his companions, and that it is thus conformable to mainstream Islam. This is the main purpose of the *Kitāb al-Samā*ʿ.

In addition, though, Sarrāj wishes to give some indication of the actual practice of *samā*ʿ among the Sufis. He describes the various 'stages' through which the receptive listener moves, what is appropriate for some but not for others, and the varying responses in terms of physical or emotional reactions and altered states of consciousness.

Nicholson has provided an English abstract of the contents of Sarrāj's work as a whole, including the *Kitāb al-Samā*ʿ, and there is no need to duplicate it here.[13] However, some aspects of Sarrāj's work deserve consideration not given elsewhere, in order that his contribution to the discussion of *samā*ʿ is better understood. The following analysis will address his polemical and apologetic style, as well as surveying his arguments. Some attempt will also be made to consider Sarrāj's purposes, and to understand the arguments he tries to counter.

An analysis of Sarrāj's *Kitāb al-Samā*ʿ

At the outset the author proceeds straight into the defence of *samā*ʿ as a ritual or formal practice of Qurʾān recitation, the chanting of sacred formulae and poetry. Without any prologue he begins a spirited argument against the conservative and legalistic opponents of these activities.

The beauty of the human voice

The first chapter of the *Kitāb al-Samāʿ* deals with the view that the human voice is a thing of beauty and a divine gift; it is thus pleasing to God when it is heard (*Lumaʿ* 267.13ff.) It is clear from the chapter that this latter point is contentious, though Sarrāj does not say so explicitly. He argues against those who declared the use of the human voice in recitation to be unlawful. Such anti-*samāʿ* polemic was known in Sarrāj's day, and indeed this contention has a long history in Islamic writings. It is contained, for example, in the third/ninth century work, *Dhamm al-Malāhī* (*The Censure of Pastimes*), by Ibn Abī al-Dunyā (d.281/894), which rails against singing and recitation. Ibn Abī al-Dunyā regards these as the 'amulet of fornication', which 'decreases shame, increases desire, and destroys manliness, and verily it takes the place of wine and does what drunkenness does'.[14] Such arguments were known to Sarrāj, else his strong polemic in defence of *samāʿ* would have little purpose.

The author opens his case with citations from the Qurʾān and various *ḥadīth*s, as is the usual practice in such presentations, but what is noteworthy is that three of the *ḥadīth*s have doubtful authenticity.[15] It seems that Sarrāj attempts to marshal as much evidence as he can to support his case, even if there is some doubt about the reliability of the evidence.

The well-established *ḥadīth* that the Prophet said: 'Beautify (the recitation of) the Qurʾān with your voices!'[16] gives an occasion for Sarrāj to provide his first extended explanation in an otherwise long series of citations (*Lumaʿ* 268.10–18). The necessity for an explanation of this sacred Tradition is evident in its implication that the uncreated Book can be beautified and enhanced by created human voices. Sarrāj offers two solutions, first suggesting that it means to embellish one's own recitation of the Qurʾān by raising the voice, improving one's intonation, and the like. A second, rather curious interpretation is to suggest that the statement is an example of syntactic transposition, the intended meaning being: 'Beautify your voices with (recitation of) the Qurʾān.' This obviates the problem mentioned above, but despite the author citing another example of such transposition in the Qurʾān, it remains a somewhat forced explanation. By running counter to the usual syntactic order for no other reason, it appears as a post hoc solution to a difficulty. This is evidently a well-known interpretation of this *ḥadīth*, since it is in this form that Hujwīrī cites it in his *Kashf al-Maḥjūb* (Nich. p.399).

It is noteworthy that a hierarchy of evidence is brought to bear in Sarrāj's process of argumentation. First Qur'ānic citations, then references drawn from sacred Tradition, and the third rung lower in this series is the sayings of scholars (*al-ḥukamā*ʾ). This hierarchy concurs with Sarrāj's description of the three sciences of religion, as outlined in the first chapter of the *Kitāb al-Luma*ʿ, and also illustrates his consistent use of triadic constructions in descriptions and explanations.[17]

In the present case, however, it could be argued that the hierarchy continues downward. Sarrāj next cites the therapeutic effects of sounds, as used for example in the treating of melancholia by 'the ancients' (*al-awā*ʾ*il*). This refers to Greek physicians, notably Hippocrates and the Pythagoreans, as argued by Amnon Shiloah with regard to a similar reference in Ibn Hindū's (d.410/1019) *Kitāb Miftāḥ at-Ṭibb* (*Book of the Key to Medicine*).[18] The medical writings of the Greek 'ancients' were translated into Arabic two centuries before Sarrāj's time. Moreover, the philosopher Al-Kindī (d.250/865) and the enigmatic fourth/tenth century group known as the *Ikhwān al-Ṣafā*ʾ (*Brethren of Purity*) held firm beliefs in the therapeutic power of music.[19]

The lowest rung on this ladder of evidence deals with the animal world, namely the beneficial effect of the cameleer's voice in urging and soothing tired camels. Sarrāj recounts a charming narrative about a camel master being ruined by a slave cameleer's enchanting voice. The slave urged on the tired camels with their heavy loads in a state of enchantment until they died of exhaustion (*Luma*ʿ 270.3–271.3). The anecdote is recounted with charm and realism, telling of the *wajd* or 'ecstasy' experienced by the beasts. This attractive story illustrates the essential humanism of Sarrāj, and anticipates the dramatic effects of music and poetry on the human soul described in the following chapters.

The nature of samāʿ

The second chapter of the *Kitāb al-Samā*ʿ consists of a series of quotations from various Sufis about the nature and benefits of *samā*ʿ. As a development from Chapter 1 where the beauty of the human voice is considered, the notion of *samā*ʿ is extended in this next chapter. There is no explicit attempt at defining the concept, but one may infer that it means more than simply 'listening' to a voice or music. For example, it involves communal gatherings in places such as mosques, and certain ritualised activities, though these are never formally detailed.[20] Equally important for the Sufis quoted in this chapter, it is the listener's response which constitutes an essential aspect of *samā*ʿ. The altered state of consciousness which 'listening' can bring about and the ensuing spiritual benefits are vital elements for the Sufis' engagement in this activity.

It is in this way that the concept of *samā*ʿ begins to merge with that of *wajd*: 'ecstatic response or experience'. One is the natural concomitant of the other. Clear differentiation between the two was probably not in the minds of the early Sufis, as is borne out by the statements in this chapter. One example will suffice: on being asked about *samā*ʿ, Dhū ʾl-Nūn (d.246/861) replied: 'It is the arrival of Truth which arouses hearts toward the Truth; one who listens to it truthfully is confirmed in that Truth, but one who listens to it sensually becomes an unbeliever' (*Luma*ʿ 271.8–10). Ghazālī's comment on this in the *Iḥyā*ʾ shows the overlap of *samā*ʿ and *wajd*: 'It is as if he (Dhū ʾl-Nūn) asserted that *wajd* is the arousal of hearts toward the Truth, and this is what one discovers of it on its arrival, i.e. the arrival of *samā*ʿ, since he calls *samā*ʿ the arrival of Truth' (*Iḥyā*ʾ II.289.7–8).

The legal status of **samā**ʿ

The third chapter in Sarrāj's work (*Luma*ʿ 273.4–277.15) addresses the question of the legal permissibility of *samā*ʿ. The narrower definition of this practice is used here, that of listening to recitation or music, rather than the more inclusive mystical and spiritual dimensions covered in the previous chapter. Many of the arguments advanced here are similar to those used by other writers on this subject, and Ghazālī repeats several of Sarrāj's arguments in his *Iḥyā*ʾ.[21]

The author uses a hierarchy of arguments in descending order of authority, similar to the structure seen in Chapter 1. Evidence is cited from the Qurʾān as the highest source of authority, then from *ḥadīth* and *sunna*, and finally from 'scholars and legal authorities'.

In the Qurʾān there is scant direct reference to the topic in question, but several favourable allusions are confidently arrayed by our author. The verses referring to His signs being 'in your own selves' (Qur. 41.53 and 51.21) are interpreted to mean being present in the five senses. The sense of hearing distinguishes between pleasant and unpleasant sounds just as sight distinguishes between beautiful and ugly. When this is juxtaposed with the verse: 'the harshest of sounds is without doubt the braying of the ass!' (Qur. 31.18), there is an implied commendation of beautiful sounds. The third line of argument is the Qurʾānic description of the sensual delights of paradise. These include the houris who sing constant praises to God. If the rendering and hearing of praises is an activity sanctioned in paradise, it must therefore be sanctioned in this world. The drinking of wine, on the other hand, is permitted in paradise, but specifically forbidden in this world. This is unlike the practice of *samāʿ*, against which no specific condemnation is made.

The next level of evidence comes from the *ḥadīth* and *sunna* of the Prophet and his companions. Sarrāj cites sacred Traditions which tell of the Prophet allowing singing and playing of music in his presence, and the companions reciting poetry. The Prophet's statement that 'Wisdom is sometimes found in poetry'[22] is quoted as evidence for the sanctioning of poetry recitation. This being so, it is argued that recitation with embellishments, lengthening of vowels and the addition of music is similarly sanctioned.

The final series of evidence comes from 'a large group of leading scholars and legal thinkers' who allow *samāʿ*.

Sarrāj concludes the chapter by stressing that *samāʿ* is permissible provided no corrupt intention is involved. He also adds the proviso that none of the 'proscribed' musical instruments should be used, i.e. those instruments used by 'vain or superficial people' (*ahl al-bāṭil*), and prohibited in sacred Traditions.

The effects of samāʿ

In the next chapter (*Lumaʿ* 277.16–279.21) Sarrāj analyses to some extent the effects of *samāʿ* on Sufi adepts. He concentrates on the types of 'states' aimed for and experiences sought after, as far as these can be described. There is a sense of abstraction in some of these descriptions, and a theoretical tone in parts of this chapter. As far as these experiences can be explained, they are inevitably idealised and systematised so that any immediacy and real-life characterisation is lost. Such systematisation appears evident in the first section of this chapter where several classifications by Sufi theorists are presented in neat, triadic categories. One example suffices to illustrate the contents of this chapter. Abū Yaʿqūb al-Nahrajūrī (d.330/941–2) is quoted as using a threefold classification of those affected by *samāʿ*. One group are physically moved by the force of the 'moment' of *samāʿ*; one group are noted for their silence and stillness; and a third group, 'the weakest', are thrown to the ground by their experience. This characterisation by physical reactions may show that such motor effects are highly indicative, so that all listeners fall into one of these groups based on their behaviour.

Qurʾān recitation

The fifth chapter of the *Kitāb al-Samāʿ* deals with those whose *samāʿ* involves listening to Qurʾān recitation (*Lumaʿ* 280.1–283.6). Sarrāj begins the discussion with a series of citations from the Qurʾān and the Prophet about the value of reciting the Book.

The author then outlines two aspects of Qurʾān listening which he considers important. The first is the value of paying close attention to what is heard, not only with the ears but also with the heart. Sarrāj then alludes to the great power of hearing the Book, noting that people have lost consciousness, or died, or lost the power of their limbs from listening to its recitation.

Sarrāj relates a number of stories involving prominent Sufis which exemplify aspects of the Qurʾān's power. These episodes which contain examples of the physical effects of *samāʿ* will be discussed in the chapters on psychology later in this book.

Poetry and the Qurʾān

The next chapter continues the theme of the previous one, for although it deals ostensibly with listening to secular poetry, it also has much to say about Qurʾān recitation (*Lumaʿ* 283.7–285.10).

Sarrāj claims that authority for listening to secular poetry is given by the Prophet in his statement: 'Wisdom is sometimes found in poetry.' He goes on to argue that those who listen to poetry recitation are showing respect for the Holy Book. By adhering to the doctrine of the uncreatedness of the Qurʾān, these people maintain its superiority by not embellishing it with human melodies. In line with this argument, the author states that human passions ought not to be encouraged or satisfied by melodic recitation of the Qurʾān. Rather, these passions are better served by poetry which in its nature has an affinity to human sensitivities and is better able to rouse human passions. The Qurʾān, on the other hand, has an affinity with 'reality or the real nature of things'.

There is some inconsistency in Sarrāj's basic argument in this chapter, that there is mutual exclusivity between the divine and human realms, between the uncreated Book and created melodies or poetry. The author claims that even a small portion of the Qurʾān revealed in its 'real nature' to human hearts can burst these hearts apart. Yet it is possible to recite the Qurʾān often, and to find no sensitivity or emotion in one's heart unless it is performed with a beautiful voice or melodies. The argument continues that some people consider the emotional response to arise from the Qurʾān's innate power and beauty, but if this were the case, these effects would be present at every reading of the Book.

Sarrāj's answer to this difficulty is what was mentioned above concerning emotions being in affinity with base human passions. These are readily aroused by sensuous melodies and poetry, while the Qurʾān, being on a higher plane, does not so easily cause this arousal.

Both aspects of this argument, however, cannot be maintained. The alleged power of the Qurʾān to 'burst' human hearts sits poorly with the author's acknowledgement that one can recite it many times without apparent emotional effect. The argument also comes close to undermining the Qurʾān's superiority and separateness from secular poetry.

In fairness to Sarrāj, however, it is difficult to conceive of a more persuasive argument here. Ghazālī encounters the same difficulty while employing a similar argument in the *Iḥyāʾ*.[23]

The author argues on a firmer basis in concluding that embellishing the Qurʾān with chants and melodies makes it more attractive to ordinary believers, contrary to those scholars who disapprove of this practice. The Holy Book's message is thereby made more palatable for people to hear and understand.

Sufi novices

The seventh chapter (*Lumaʿ* 285.11–288.8) consists of two apparently unrelated sections. The first part is a series of stories from various sources relating to the dramatic effect of listening to 'recollection' (*dhikr*) or verse. In each of these narratives a person is affected by an altered state, such that sudden death ensues. These accounts will be discussed more fully in the chapters on psychology later in this book. In the second section of the present chapter Sarrāj describes a number of conditions and prerequisites for novices who wish to practise *samāʿ*. He lays down these conditions as a miniature 'rule' for novices under the direction of their shaykh.

No reason is given for the juxtaposition of these two unrelated topics. However, in comparing Hujwīrī's *Kashf al-Maḥjūb* (Nich. pp.407–8), a similar series of stories is preceded by warnings to novices. We might suppose that Sarrāj is prefacing his 'rule' for novices with a clear warning of the dangers of unprepared listening. This is confirmed by the fact that the narratives mostly involve young disciples as those most profoundly affected by *samāʿ*, and thus those most in need of expert guidance by their shaykh.

Sarrāj presumes some advancement along the Sufi path as a condition for the practice of *samāʿ*. Certain types of understanding are assumed, as is the need for maturity in asceticism and renunciation, such as not being 'stained' with love for the world, and not having the desire for human company.

When these conditions are met, some listening is allowed, namely that which is suitable for penitence, humility and fearfulness, and which urges toward right conduct and striving. This would preclude most secular material, and would largely restrict the listener to appropriate religious texts. Sarrāj states explicitly that listening for pleasure is forbidden, as this would distract the listener from his service of God. If such conditions are not met, the novice should withdraw from *samāʿ*, except for recollection of God and chanting His praises.

Sufi adepts

The eighth chapter (*Lumaʿ* 288.9–292.9) contains a variety of subjects loosely connected with various Sufi adepts or masters. Some aspects of *samāʿ* are given further exposure, and the subject of resulting rapture or ecstasy is mentioned in several narratives. Since these stories all have a strong psychological component, discussion of their content will be held over for later in this book.

Sufi masters

The two preceding chapters dealt with aspects of *samāʿ* relating to an ascending order of participants: first novices, then adepts of middle ranking. Now we deal with those who have reached the highest levels, literally 'the choice of the choice and the people of perfection', as Sarrāj's heading describes them.

Four main arguments are advanced in this chapter (*Lumaʿ* 292.10–294.19), using a combination of biographical narratives with editorial comments. The first argument is that those who have advanced to higher phases of 'consciousness' (*ḥāl*, pl. *aḥwāl*) rarely display outward signs of being affected by such states. The usual signs for beginners are kinetic, such as involuntary movements of limbs, trembling and agitation. The Sufi masters rarely display such signs, and their 'state' remains one of calm and stillness, this lack of movement being regarded as superior.

This leads directly to the next argument, that the adept's 'state' and presence of heart remains the same before, during and after the *samā*ʿ session. This is the corollary to the superiority of the state of stillness outlined above.

The next argument follows logically, that adepts are not distracted by any physical or sensual interference in their quest for recollection of mind. An illustrative anecdote is related of Mimshādh al-Dīnawarī (d.299/912), who claimed that all the musical instruments in the world would not distract his inner state. Sarrāj goes on to argue that their passions have been so refined that adepts do not delight in beautiful sounds. Their intent is single minded, their hearts and qualities purified, and their human natures offer no resistance (*Luma*ʿ 294.2–8).

There are obvious dangers in this line of reasoning which could undermine the author's overall purpose in advocating the value of *samā*ʿ. If the Sufi masters find that no sound is distracting, and if they find no delight in listening, then participation in these activities can be seen as a hindrance, or superfluous. At the more advanced stages of Sufi practice, the need for external stimuli to heighten consciousness, such as that provided by *samā*ʿ, is not required at all. It is legitimate only in the early stages where external aids might be seen as effective, though somewhat artificially so. Sarrāj does not actually mention this difficulty, but other writers do. Hujwīrī, for example, specifically states: 'Audition is the viaticum of the indigent: one who has reached his journey's end hath no need of it' (Nich. p.405).

Given these implications in his reasoning, it is to Sarrāj's credit that he advances the final argument which follows logically. *samā*ʿ may be unnecessary to the masters, yet the author lists a number of reasons for their involvement in listening sessions: to give support to their brothers, to teach and guide, and to support those from other fraternities through their integrity and strength of purpose.

samāʿ *and wisdom*

The topic of the tenth chapter (*Luma*ʿ 295.1–296.11) is the relationship between *samā*ʿ and *ḥikma* ('wisdom, wise sayings'). Sarrāj argues that wise sayings are able to stir strong feelings in the heart. Moreover, there are influences from the transcendent world, such as those encountered in words of wisdom, or other *samāʿ*, which act subconsciously on one's heart. The author claims that *samāʿ* is not merely beautiful sound to be enjoyed, but is a type of *ḥikma* which can have a powerful and beneficial influence on hearts.

An anecdote mentioned by Sarrāj is noteworthy partly for its repetition by later authors.[24] A person asks Junayd at what stage one should regard God's praise and blame as being the same. One of Junayd's companions, evidently misunderstanding the question and regarding it as foolish, answers: 'When he is put in the asylum and shackled with fetters!' Junayd gently rebukes this interjector by answering that it is when he knows for certain that he is a created being. The force of this reply is shown by the questioner then sighing with a groan, probably as a physical indication of a dissociative reaction.

The author then enters into his main argument, claiming that wise sayings are able to stir up strong feeling (*wajd*) in the inner self, or a burning in the heart. This is a similar function claimed elsewhere for music and recitation.

Sarrāj continues by stating that 'there are things encountered by hearts, when they are pure, that impinge upon them from the Unseen world, whether audible or visible perceptions. If these (perceptions) correspond (to what is in the heart) their influence is strong, but if they are contrary and obstructive, they are weak . . . Sometimes recollections are renewed for (those who receive them) in what they hear, and visible perceptions are clarified for them time after time. This increase of clarity is renewed for them in listening to wise sayings and attending to their subtleties' (*Lumaʿ* 295.16–296.4). This is a difficult passage in Sarrāj's text, but it seems that he is alluding to some sort of reawakening of hidden knowledge. This may refer to the events of the 'day of Alast', the primordial covenant between God and humankind (Qur.7.172). Abū Bakr al-Kalābādhī (d.385/995) writes in a similar vein in his *Kitāb al-Taʿarruf* (*Book of Knowledge*):

> 'Abū Muḥammad Ruwaym said: 'The people heard their first *dhikr* [recollection of God] when God addressed them, saying, "Am I not your Lord?" This *dhikr* was secreted in their hearts . . . So when they heard the (Sūfī) *dhikr*, the secret things of their hearts appeared, and they were ravished . . .'[25]

As well as the allusion to hidden knowledge, there may also be a reference here to notions very similar to the archetypes of neo-Platonist philosophy. Titus Burckhardt argues that *dhikr* can mean 'memory' in the neo-Platonist sense of reflected knowledge of archetypes, and also the traditional 'mention'. This double aspect is important in that it connects the sonorous practice of invocation with the evocation of essential truths or knowledge of the divine Word.[26]

That *samā*ʿ and *dhikr* are not meaningless incantation and sonorous melodies is reinforced by the author's citing of *ḥikma* as a vehicle of *samā*ʿ along with Qur'ānic recitation, poetry and recollection. This illustrates the juxtaposition of *dhikr* with the Divine Word.

Sarrāj concludes that what is important is the heart's encountering the strong emotion or ecstasy of sacred recollection. It is reawakening the secreted knowledge of the 'day of Alast', or the evoking of essential truths which causes ecstasy and burning of the heart.

Psychology of samāʿ

In this next chapter (*Luma*ʿ 296.12–298.10), various topics mentioned earlier are given further elaboration. The main subject taken up later in this chapter concerns the transformation which listeners undergo on hearing poetry. In Chapter 9 Sarrāj mentioned a type of projection taking place from the Sufi's 'momentary state of mind' onto the particular sounds or words being heard. Here the author mentions that the original message may remain intact, but is so transformed in interpretation that it takes on a completely new aspect, its secular meaning becoming one of religious significance.

Sarrāj begins, however, by presenting a short summary of the psychological process which culminates in ecstatic utterance: 'When (listeners) hear things which correspond to their momentary experience (*al-waqt*), the hidden tendencies of their hearts are intensified; their hearts cannot contain this and they begin to give expression to their strong emotion (*wajd*)' (*Luma*ʿ 296.15–17). As these ecstatic utterances are likely to occur during the practice of *samā*ʿ, the author continues: 'It does not occur to their mind the intention of the poet in his poetry, or the purpose of the speaker in what he says' (*Luma*ʿ 296.18). Sarrāj concludes the chapter with several narratives illustrating this last statement.

Opponents of samāʿ

This is the final chapter of the *Kitāb al-Samā*ʿ (*Luma*ʿ 298.11–300.13), and it consists of simply listing the reasons why some people disapprove of the practice of *samā*ʿ. Given the author's clear endorsement of the practice, it is surprising that he does not offer a spirited defence against its detractors. This shows the fair-mindedness of Sarrāj in giving scope for his opponents to state their case openly.

The first reason for disapproval is the claim that the early leaders of Islam opposed the practice. In fact many of the same arguments from *ḥadīth* cited by opponents of *samā*ʿ are also used by supporters in its defence. For example, Abū Bakr's censure of the singing girls in the Prophet's presence is seen by opponents of *samā*ʿ to be conclusive evidence of its disapproval.[27] Ghazālī and others, however, see this same *ḥadīth* as supportive of singing, since the Prophet himself allowed it to continue. A similar situation with other sacred Traditions leads Arthur Gribetz to comment that such disputation 'does not resolve the controversy conclusively due to the subjective nature of the interpretations involved'.[28]

The second, third and fourth reasons concern the alleged frivolity of the practice, for young people and novices, for those who seek pleasure, and for the ordinary believers who may gain a false impression of the sincerity of the Sufis. The fifth reason for not practising *samā*ʿ is simply because one's peers do not, and association with those of a different outlook is to be avoided. Sixth, there is the *ḥadīth* that one should not concern oneself with things which have no value for salvation, or which are not expressed duties or obligations.

The final reason offered is perhaps the most forceful of all, namely that *samā*ʿ is not needed by those with advanced mystical consciousness. Such Sufis enjoy complete control over their minds and thus have no need for external stimulation by sound which may interfere with their constant inner 'converse' (*Luma*ʿ 300.5–12). Aspects of this argument were mentioned in an earlier chapter, and the implications not developed there are now fully articulated. If outside influences have no effect on them, it follows that aids such as *samā*ʿ are not needed for reaching higher mystical states. As mentioned earlier, this tends to devalue the practice of *samā*ʿ, since it is really only of use to novices and the inexperienced.

When viewed as a whole, the *Kitāb al-Samā*ʿ attempts a vigorous justification for the practice of *samā*ʿ among the Sufis. Sarrāj sets forth his apology in a meticulous and painstaking way. His exposition is carefully arranged and systematically presented in an attempt at a serious rebuttal of those opposed to *samā*ʿ. The heat generated by this controversy, as outlined by Gribetz, was considerable, and it is to our author's credit that his defence is well reasoned and unaffected by emotive pleas. This is particularly commendable when compared with anti-*samāʿ* writings such as Ibn Abī al-Dunyā's *Dhamm al-Malāhī*, where the lack of these reasoning qualities is conspicuous.

It has been noted that Sarrāj often uses hierarchies of evidence and argument, in a quasi-legal fashion, stating his case from the Qurʾān, then from the Traditions, and finally from noted scholars or Sufis. Such triadic argumentation is a constant feature of the author's work, lending an air of balance and order to his exposition. At times, however, an object under discussion or a certain group of people are divided into three classes or types. It seems that the author sometimes forces the subjects under scrutiny into triadic categories which are almost certainly artificial.

The Qurʾān is an important source of support for Sarrāj's arguments, more perhaps due to theological exigencies than as a valuable source of evidence. There are very few direct Qurʾānic references to the subject matter, but verses are cited with the least possible connection in order to provide authoritative support for the author's case.

With the use of evidence from the Traditions, every possible reference is again used to bolster the case that the Sufis are conforming to early Islamic piety.

The use of evidence from scholars and prominent Sufis is by far the most frequent, usually taking the form of illustrative anecdotes from the lives of the Sufi masters or scholars. Although these narratives do not have the same authoritative status as *ḥadīth*, there is a large collection from which to draw, and thus the author is able to select the most relevant for his purposes. Indeed there are many sections of the work which consist of a series of narratives with little bridging material or editorial comment. On the whole this proves a very effective means of advancing the author's case, especially as these vignettes from the lives of the Sufi masters are often vigorous and full of colour, supplying much interest to the text. On occasion, however, some of the anecdotes prove more baffling than illuminating, and call for explanations which the author does not provide.

The *Kitāb al-Samāʿ* is a well-constructed and well-argued piece of writing. It is often lively and colourful, thanks to the quality of the narratives. As for the effect of Sarrāj's writing, judging by later authors on the subject, it is clear that it had a positive impact. His arguments are often reused or restated, by Ghazālī in his

Iḥyāʾ, for example, where Sarrāj is acknowledged (*Iḥyāʾ* II.297.20ff), and in the earliest Persian prose text on Sufism, Hujwīrī's *Kashf al-Maḥjūb*.

An analysis of Sarrāj's *Kitāb al-Wajd*

Immediately following the *Kitāb al-Samāʿ*, there is a further substantial section of Sarrāj's work entitled *Kitāb al-Wajd* (*The Book of Ecstatic Experience*) (*Lumaʿ* 300.14–314.18). This section discusses in detail certain aspects of the concept of *wajd*, 'ecstatic experience or trance'. This subject is intimately connected with *samāʿ*, and in Ghazālī's *Iḥyāʾ* the two topics are dealt with as one. The following analysis focuses on those parts of the *Kitāb al-Wajd* which are relevant to the discussions of this book.

The concept of wajd

The first chapter (*Lumaʿ* 300.14–302.10) deals with a number of different definitions and statements concerning the nature of *wajd*. Several Sufi masters are quoted with their varying notions about the subject. None of these statements provides a strict lexical definition applicable in different contexts. Rather, the chapter unfolds more like a large canvas upon which various artists add their own touches of colour. In the end there is a collected impression, added piece by piece, giving a better understanding of the subject, though perhaps not describable as an integral whole.

A lengthy comment attributed to Junayd comes nearest to a definition or lexical equivalent. Junayd considers *wajd* to be 'encountering, finding' (*al-muṣādafa*), and he provides an almost philological argument for this by glossing several Qurʾānic usages of the root *wajada* with equivalents from *ṣadafa*, form III. Junayd adds that 'all which the heart encounters of grief or joy, that is *wajd*. God has made it known concerning hearts that they observe and understand, and that is *wajd* for them' (*Lumaʿ* 301.5–6).

Junayd's concept of *wajd* is simply 'what the heart encounters', whether in terms of emotional attributes (grief or joy), or of intelligible knowledge. This accords with the concept of *qalb*, 'heart', as the organ of gnosis and of emotion. This notion of 'encountering' spiritual truths removes the need for more ebullient concepts such as 'ecstasy', 'emotive excess', 'passion', and so on, and is consistent with Junayd's well-known 'sober' approach. This stands in contrast to the most frequent English equivalent of *wajd* as 'ecstasy'.[29]

Attempted ecstatic experience

The second and third chapters (*Lumaʿ* 302.11–306.3) discuss the theme of *tawājud*, 'simulating or attempting ecstatic experience'. Sarrāj uses theoretical discourse as well as relating several narratives about prominent Sufis. Without detailing these stories, their common argument is the similarity of such 'simulated' experience with the genuine type, especially since the famous Sufi masters experienced such ecstasy in their lives.

Physical effects of wajd

The fourth chapter of the *Kitāb al-Wajd* (*Lumaʿ* 306.4–308.2) deals with some of the overpowering physical effects felt by Sufis in their experience of *wajd*. A narrative is related of Junayd and Sarī al-Saqaṭī (d.253/867) in which these two masters debate whether *wajd* can produce such insensitivity to pain that a person can be struck by a sword and not feel its effect. There follows a discussion similar to one touched on earlier in the *Kitāb al-Samāʿ* over the external signs of the trance state.

The fifth chapter (*Lumaʿ* 308.3–309.18) continues this last topic of discussion in more detail. The whole of this chapter is a digest of the subject as argued by a certain Abū Saʿīd b. al-ʿArābī (d.341/952) in his (now lost) *Kitāb al-Wajd*. The discussion is of scant interest in the present context, partly because it is treated in a purely dogmatic fashion, but also since it adds little light on the physical and psychological effects at issue.

wajd *according to Abū Saʿīd b. al-ʿArābī*

The final chapter (*Lumaʿ* 310.1–314.18) is a more general discussion of *wajd* summarised from the work of Abū Saʿīd b. al-ʿArābī. The author begins in a psychological vein, mentioning various feelings or states of mind which can arouse ecstatic experience and which may accompany it. These include 'disquieting recollection', 'fears', 'regret', 'remorse', and so on. This is instructive in the light of modern research which shows a correlation between anxiety and stress states and the onset of altered state or dissociative behaviours.[30]

Very soon the author reverts to a more theological tone in describing the onset of *wajd*: 'encounters of . . . the inner with the inner, and the Unseen with the Unseen, and the secret heart with the secret heart . . .' (*Lumaʿ* 310.6–7). Among these abstract discussions, however, there are some valuable insights to be gained. For example, the author speaks of the sudden onset of the trance state: 'This state is not known before its arrival and there is no familiar habituation with it because of its rapid passing when it occurs, so that it is like a totally instantaneous occurrence. The joyous state (thus produced) is not fulfilled when it occurs, so there remains regret at its passing' (*Lumaʿ* 310.14–16). The author goes on to speak of the physical effects, loss of control over the movement of one's limbs, and so on, and the great power and force of the onset. Furthermore: 'Every occurrence is an extraordinary experience (*mustaghrab*)' (*Lumaʿ* 310.18). The force and power is so terrible that were it not for God's grace, the subject would not be able to bear it, and they would lose reason and soul. For some subjects there remains partial memory of the experience, and knowledge gained thereby can be used as proof of its validity.

Abū Saʿīd b. al-ʿArābī, through the medium of Sarrāj, proceeds to ponder at length the ineffability of this topic: 'How can one describe something which has no description other than itself, and to which no witness can testify other than itself? . . . this is similar to the case of love (*maḥabba*) and yearning (*shawq*) and nearness (*qurb*); all this is too subtle for description, and its essence is not apprehended except by one who experiences it' (*Lumaʿ* 313.7–8; 12–13). The remainder of this chapter continues in this fashion, often expressing in eloquent terms the indescribability of such mystical experience, and the futility of trying to understand this subject without direct and immediate knowledge.

With such a limit placed on the value of the discussion, Sarrāj completes the subject of *samāʿ* and *wajd*. The earlier portion of Sarrāj's work has greater value intrinsically, and also for the purposes of the present book. Our discussion will thus draw much more from the earlier part of the work.

The writings of Abū ʿAbd al-Raḥman al-Sulamī

A generation later than Sarrāj comes the important Sufi hagiographer and theorist, Abū ʿAbd al-Raḥman al-Sulamī. His writings are perhaps not as fundamental for our present topic as his illustrious predecessor's, but Sulamī's contibution is nevertheless important. One of his major works, the *Ṭabaqāt al-Ṣūfīya* (*Generations of the Sufis*), is a ground-breaking biographical collection which formed the basis for many later writings of a similar nature in both

Arabic and Persian. As such, it contains many anecdotes of the Sufi masters which contain valuable information on the subject of *samāʿ*.

Again the details of Sulamī's biography are rather sparse.[31] He was born in Nishapur in 325/937 or 330/942, into a pious family, studying under his maternal grandfather, Ismāʿīl b.Nujayd al-Sulamī (d.366/976). Ibn Nujayd was a leading *malāmatīya* figure, and a renowned *ḥadīth* scholar. Sulamī's mother was also inclined toward the Sufis, and thus the youth gained a thorough traditional education from an early age.

He studied *ḥadīth* with some of the leading authorities of the time, and became a specialist in his own right. He travelled extensively in search of Traditions, as far away as the Hijāz, Cairo, Iraq, as well as the Persian-speaking areas of the empire. He also learned the principles of Ashʿarī theology, and in law adhered to the Shāfiʿī school, which in fourth/tenth century Nishapur had many links with the Sufi way.

One of his many pupils was Abū ʾl-Qāsim al-Qushayrī (d.465/1072), who also wrote important works on Sufism, which we will consider later. Sulamī built a small *khānaqāh* or lodge in Nishapur, which became renowned during his lifetime, and he was buried there in 412/1021.

Nūr al-Dīn Sharība, in the introduction to his edition of the *Ṭabaqāt*, argues that Sulamī began his writing career around AH 350.[32] His renowned commentary on the Qur'ān, the *Ḥaqāʾiq al-Tafsīr* (*Realities of Interpretation*), was probably written at the end of the 370s; the *Tārīkh al-Ṣūfīya* (*History of the Sufis*) in the 380s, and the *Ṭabaqāt al-Ṣūfīya* near the end of the fourth/tenth century.

The *Ṭabaqāt* is a collection of biographical traditions concerning the Sufi masters, their lives and their sayings. It was not the first such work of this genre in Islamic literature, but its great importance lies in the fact that virtually all earlier works of Sufi biography have been lost to us. It is a treasury of the opinions and interpretations of the Sufis, and of the stories concerning their lives and characters. His work also influenced later writers in this genre, many of whom rely heavily on Sulamī. Thus, Abū Nuʿaym's *Ḥilyat al-Awliyāʾ* (*Embellishment of the Saints*) Qushayrī's *Risāla* (*Treatise*), and Jamī's *Nafaḥāt al-Uns* (*Breaths of Intimacy*) all show their debt to the *Ṭabaqāt*.[33]

Etan Kohlberg argues that Sulamī seems to have had two distinct aims. First, his task was to defend Sufism against its many critics, and second, to spread knowledge of Sufism among the general public as well as the Sufis themselves. In this, there is little difference from the aims of Sarrāj in writing the *Lumaʿ*.[34]

Sharība argues that what distinguished the Nishapur school of Sufi writers from their Baghdad counterparts was their more objective style of authorship.[35] This is characterised by their restraint from giving personal opinions and interpretations on the subjects being discussed. This is certainly the case with Sulamī's *Ṭabaqāt* where he seldom expresses his own view. He is content to be a faithful compiler, transmitting the materials he has collected intact and without obvious personal interpretation. The serious 'Traditionist' quality of Sulamī's work also shows itself in the structure of each Sufi biography, which consists of a series of stories or sayings arranged in the usual fashion of *ḥadīth* literature. Each pericope carries a full *isnād* or chain of transmission authorities, unless there are several with the same *isnād*, in which case various abbreviations are used. Each Sufi biography, or rather 'tradition', is also preceded by a *ḥadīth* of the Prophet. This identification with the Prophet's words and deeds imprints the stamp of legitimacy to what follows.

samāʿ and *wajd* in the *Ṭabaqāt al-Ṣūfīya*

The *Ṭabaqāt al-Ṣūfīya* is a collection of Sufi traditions and not a systematic treatise. As such, references to *samāʿ* and altered states are scattered throughout the book, often in isolated incidents relating to the lives of the masters. Because of the character of Sulamī's writing, moreover, there is no unified line of argument or approach to the topic. Some of the references to the subject in question are positive and supportive of the practice, while others are inimical, depending on the individual views of the Sufi being quoted.

It should be noted also that most of the references to *samāʿ* in the *Ṭabaqāt* are different from the many anecdotes, stories and sayings contained in Sarrāj's *Kitāb al-Lumaʿ*. Al-Sulamī evidently used different sources for his collection of traditions from that of Sarrāj.

The following survey is a compilation of the various references to *samāʿ* and related topics, as they occur in order throughout the *Ṭabaqāt*, with some comments as appropriate.

1 *Ṭabaqāt al-Ṣūfīya* (*T.S.*) 60.7–12: Ḥārith al-Muḥāsibī (d.243/857) was present at a *samāʿ* concert when a *qawwāl* (professional reciter) chanted some verses about the sadness of leaving one's homeland and one's beloved. Ḥārith arose in ecstasy and

cried out so that all those present were moved with compassion for him.

2 *T.S.* 116.6–117.2: Abū Ḥafṣ al-Naysābūrī (d.265/879) would not mention the name of God heedlessly or without due honour and respect. When he mentioned God, his state (*ḥāl*) would change such that all those present would be aware of the change. Some sayings of his during such occasions are recorded.

3 *T.S.* 119.3–5: Abū Ḥafṣ had a companion who frequented *samāʿ* sessions, where he would weep and tear his clothes. Abū Ḥafṣ is reported to have said that everything should be done to save the man from this activity. (These last two pericopes suggest that Abū Ḥafṣ was a Sufi of the 'sober' school, rejecting the excesses of ecstatic activity, but himself deeply sensitive to the extraordinary states induced by *samāʿ*.)

4 *T.S.* 195.7–8: Samnūn b. ʿAbd Allāh (d. circa 300/913) is reported to have cried out (perhaps indicating an altered state) and said: 'If only humankind would cry out due to the force of His *wajd* in love of Him, to fill what lies between East and West with crying out!'

5 *T.S.* 202.12–13: ʿAmrū b. ʿUthmān al-Makkī (d.291/904) is reported to have said that there can be no explanation of the nature of *wajd* as it is a mystery (*sirr*) of God with His true believers.

6 *T.S.* 204.11–205.6: An incident is related of al-Makkī in which he visits a sick young follower in Isfahan. A *qawwāl* accompanies al-Makkī and recites some verses. The sick youth recovers and al-Makkī explains that the signs of his recovery preceded the recitation, thus indicating its divine source. Had there been no sign of recovery before the recitation, this would have indicated its evil source.

7 *T.S.* 239.8–11: Abū ʾl-ʿAbbās b. Masrūq al-Ṭūsī (d. circa 298/910) was asked about listening to poetical quatrains. He replied that our hearts do not learn obedience naturally but by application and appropriation. Listening to quatrains aids the harmonisation of outward and inward, strengthens one's mental state (*ḥāl*) and helps to perfect knowledge.

8 *T.S.* 240.8–14: Abū ʾl-ʿAbbās once walked with Junayd through one of the alleys of Baghdad. A singer was reciting some fragments of verse. Junayd began to weep bitterly, and picking up on some of the words of the singer, he reflected in poetic fashion on his failures: 'O Abū ʾl-ʿAbbās, how good are the stages of concord and familiarity, and how lonely are the states of

antipathy! I never cease to yearn for the origin of my desire, with a keen path, and terrors as my steed, desirous to attain my goal! But look at me now during times of indolence; I yearn for past times!'

9 *T.S.* 299.15–16: Abū 'l-Ḥusayn al-Warrāq (d. before 320/932) is reported to have said that the way to God is difficult for one who does not come upon it with overwhelming enthusiasm (*wajd*) and passionate desire (*shawq*).

10 *T.S.* 328.9–15: Abū Ḥamza al-Khurāsānī (d.290/903) heard one of his companions censuring another for being overcome by *wajd* and showing his inner state in a gathering where there were opponents of *samāʿ*. Abū Ḥamza told him to stop his scolding, for *wajd* obliterates distinctions, makes all places one, and all eyes one. One should not be censured for being overcome by *wajd* which is involuntary. He then recited a verse of Ibn al-Rūmī (d.283/896).

11 *T.S.* 329.7–9: Abū ʿAbd Allāh al-Ṣubayḥī (d.?) is reported as saying that *samāʿ* (meaning the recitation of poetry) which speaks plainly is welcome; *samāʿ* which uses allusions is feigning, but the subtlest *samāʿ* is that which is obscure except for the one hearing it (i.e. one hearing and being emotionally affected by it).

12 *T.S.* 330.10–12: Abū ʿAbd Allāh also said that when *wajd* is genuine it should be upheld and defended; no one should be allowed to speak disparagingly of an altered state (*ḥāl*).

13 *T.S.* 331.1–2: Abū ʿAbd Allāh also said that the most complete form of fear is that which takes on the characteristics of *wajd*, not from loss of something hoped for or desired. (Presumably, the characteristics of *wajd* alluded to here are physical changes of state, trembling, etc., which are also characteristic of a state of fear.)

14 *T.S.* 356.13–15: Abū ʿAlī al-Rūdhabārī (d.322/934) is asked about listening to musical instruments. The questioner says that he considers it lawful, for he has reached a stage where differences in states of consciousness (*aḥwāl*) do not affect him. Abū ʿAlī replies that the questioner has reached somewhere, by God!, but that place is Hell!

15 *T.S.* 375.3–6: Abū Bakr al-Kattānī (d.322/934) comments on the various types of *samāʿ*. For ordinary people, it is 'following natural inclinations'; for initiates, it is desire and fear; for friends of God (*awliyāʾ*), it is a vision of benefits and grace; for knowers

(*al-ʿārifīn*), it is direct witnessing; for the 'people of Truth' (*ahl al-ḥaqīqa*), it is revelation and witnessing; and each one of these has their own place and ranking.

16 *T.S.* 375.9–13: Al-Kattānī is also reported as saying that the listener to *samāʿ* ought to find more than just refreshment – it causes *wajd*, or yearning, or being overwhelmed, which destroys every settled and familiar notion.

17 *T.S.* 432.14–16: Abū ʿAmrū al-Zujjājī (d.348/960) was asked about *samāʿ*. He replied that the state (*ḥāl*) of someone who needs the stimulation of *samāʿ* is inferior. *samāʿ* is the weakest of states (presumably meaning it induces the weakest of states). If the *ḥāl* is strengthened, continues Abū ʿAmrū, there is surely no need for *samāʿ* and the sounds of musical instruments.

18 *T.S.* 498.4–6: A rather enigmatic statement from Abū ʿAbd Allāh al-Rūdhabārī (d.369/980) to the effect that *dhawq* (taste, or direct experience) is the first thing felt by a person in ecstasy (*al-muwājīd*). When slanderous people (*ahl al-ghība*) drink of this experience, they go astray (or: lose their reason); when people of the Presence drink, they live happily.

19 *T.S.* 500.10–19: Rūdhabārī speaks at length about *samāʿ*. There are three aspects to its secret: the eloquence of its expression, the subtlety of its meaning, and the soundness of its method. (This evidently refers to *samāʿ* as poetry recitation.) Similarly with melody, there are three aspects: fineness of nature, performance, and correct rhythm. One who is sincere in his *samāʿ* has three aspects to his secret: knowledge of God, fulfilling one's dues, and integrity of intentions. The place where one listens requires three qualities: sweet air, good lighting, and decorum; and the absence of three things: the contrary distractions, people who are ashamed, and those who seek pleasure or amusement. One hears from three groups: the Sufis, the poor, and those who are friends of them. One hears in three ways: by love, by *wajd*, and by fear. Movement comes about through three things: pleasure (*ṭarab*), fear, and *wajd*. Pleasure has three signs: dancing, clapping, and joy; fear has three signs: weeping, striking with the hand, and sighs; *wajd* has three signs: absence, bewilderment (*iṣṭilām*), and crying out. (This is almost a miniature 'rule' concerning the practice of *samāʿ*, where there is a somewhat artificial use of threefold categories).

20 *T.S.* 512.12–14: Abū Qāsim al-Rāzī (mid fourth/tenth century) is quoted as saying that there is a great danger in *samāʿ* unless

one has sufficient knowledge, a genuine altered state of consciousness (*ḥāl*), and *wajd* which is overwhelming, and not indulged in for pleasure.

The issues arising from these references to *samā*ʿ and *wajd* in the *Ṭabaqāt al-Ṣūfīya* will be dealt with later in the present work.

The minor writings of Sulamī

There are a few references to our subject in some of the other minor writings of Sulamī. In his *Jawāmi*ʿ *Ādāb al-Ṣūfīya* (*Collections of Sufi Manners*), a short work dealing with etiquette, there is a pericope devoted to a story about Ḥusayn al-Nūrī (d.295/908) which also appears in Sarrāj's *Kitāb al-Luma*ʿ.[36] The basis of the story is Nūrī's inability to enter into ecstasy at a *samā*ʿ session, and his recital of some love poetry which causes all those present, himself excluded, from entering into an ecstatic state. Sulamī uses this story as an example of the Sufi masters keeping things hidden, not disclosing the real nature of their altered states, and their use of metaphor rather than plain language.

The other minor work of Sulamī where there is a significant reference to our subject is the *Kitāb al-Arba*ʿ*īn fī ʾl-Taṣawwuf* (*Book of Forty Traditions concerning the Sufi path*).[37] This is a short pamphlet combining Sufi and *ḥadīth* elements, following the established custom of including forty Traditions in the one work, preceded by complete chains of transmission. Each *ḥadīth* is introduced by relating it to a Sufi custom, identified with the words and deeds of the Prophet, and thus ensuring its legitimacy.

The second last chapter of the *Kitāb al-Arba*ʿ*īn* is titled 'Concerning the permissibility of *samā*ʿ'. In this chapter the *ḥadīth* referring to ʿĀʾisha is related, of the Prophet entering her home on a festival day when there were two singing girls present. Abū Bakr enters and rebukes the music, but the Prophet allows the performance because of the festival. This Tradition is also cited by Sarrāj and Ghazālī as evidence of Prophetic support of the practice of *samā*ʿ, while Abū Bakr's rebuking is cited by opponents of the practice as evidence of disapproval.[38]

These scattered references to *samā*ʿ in the writings of Sulamī are included without any editorial additions from the compiler. There is a generally positive tone to these references, however, and the last example is included in a compilation of Sufi customs which claims

Prophetic approval. This suggests that Sulamī was favourably inclined toward the practice, as does his general tolerance displayed in the *Ṭabaqāt* toward the spectrum of Sufi customs and behaviours. Sulamī's writings are a valuable source of information about early Sufi tradition concerning our subject area, and they provide worthwhile materials for discussion later in our study.

Qushayrī and his *Risāla*

Also originating from Khurāsān, two generations later than Sulamī came a famous pupil of his, Abū ʾl-Qāsim al-Qushayrī.[39] A scholar and mystical theorist, Qushayrī is best known for his apologetic summary of Sufi teaching and terminology, the *Risāla* (*Treatise*).

Born in 376/986 into a property owning family in Ustuwāʾ, he only began his religious education in earnest after visiting Nishapur for business reasons. He met the Sufi shaykh, Abū ʿAlī al-Daqqāq, and became a disciple, later marrying his daughter and succeeding the master on his death in 405/1015. Meanwhile, Qushayrī had learned Shāfiʿī law in Ṭūs, and studied Ashʿarī theology with scholars in Nishapur. Performing the pilgrimage, he studied *ḥadīth* in Baghdad and the Hijāz, and began teaching this on his return to Nishapur in 437/1046.

During the next decade he was involved in theological struggles in Nishapur between the Ḥanafī and Ashʿarī-Shāfiʿī factions. At one point an uprising led to his imprisonment for some weeks in 446/1054. Two years later he was summoned by the Caliph al-Qāʾim (d.467/1075) to teach *ḥadīth* in Baghdad. On returning to Khurāsān he settled in Ṭūs to avoid his Ḥanafī opponents, now dominant in Nishapur. When the vizier Niẓām al-Mulk (d.485/1092) temporarily restored the balance between the factions, Qushayrī returned to Nishapur, where he died in 465/1072. He was buried in the institute where he had taught, the Madrasa al-Qushayrīya.

Of his writings, most are devoted to mystical topics, such as a voluminous Qurʾān commentary, *Laṭāʾif al-Ishārāt* (*The Subtleties of Guidance*), written before 410/1019. The very short *Arbaʿ Rasāʾil fī ʾl-Taṣawwuf* (*Four Treatises on the Sufi Way*) is a collection of three brief treatises on mystical topics, followed by a didactic poem of 39 verses. His most famous work, however, is the *Risāla*, written in 438/1046. In many ways it follows the pattern of Sarrāj's *Lumaʿ*, being apologetic and defensive of the legitimacy of Sufi teaching and practice, and also providing explanations of characteristic terminology and concepts. Some of the material in the *Risāla* is also derived from the *Luma*ʿ, though Qushayrī's discussions are not as detailed or extensive as those found in Sarrāj's work.

The book begins with a short introductory section on the principles of unitary experience (*tawḥīd*), a fundamental doctrine of Sufism. This is followed by a substantial section devoted to technical terms, explaining Sufi concepts and vocabulary. The main section of the book follows, building from the preceding chapters into a fully developed exposition of Sufi theology along conceptual lines. This section on the 'stages' of the Sufi path begins with *tawba* (repentance), *mujāhada* (struggle), and so on through the characteristic theological topics, ending, it so happens, with *samā*ʿ.

A third section of the book recounts matters relating to visions, miracles and special states of the Sufi masters. The final section of the book provides a biographical survey of 83 Sufi masters, some notices only a few lines in length, others amounting to several pages. In this section the style of his teacher Sulamī is evident, with the pattern of the *Ṭabaqāt al-Ṣūfīya* being adopted. A short notice is given with the full name of the person, his/her associates or teachers, sometimes the date of death, but little else. This is followed by a number of quotations or teachings ascribed to the master, sometimes in the form of *ḥadīth* reports with transmission details.

In his introduction to the *Risāla*, Qushayrī openly acknowledges the apologetic aim of his writing.[40] The Sufi movement having fallen into disrepute, and being publicly slandered by opponents from many sides, Qushayrī felt the need to rebuff false accusations and mistaken notions about the Sufi path. In addition to this task of defence and apology, Qushayrī also aimed to correct erroneous teachings which had misguided many aspirants of the path. By explaining its true doctrines, he helped to strengthen disciples on the path, and to rebut the false allegations of opponents. His solid defence of the Sufi way on Ashʿarī principles prepared the ground for the later and more brilliant work of Ghazālī.

The chapter on *samā*ʿ in the Risāla

The chapter on *samā*ʿ in Qushayrī's work is not extensive, some fourteen octavo-sized pages in the edition consulted.[41] It appears as the last chapter of the main section on 'stages', which is really an exposition of Sufi theology and practice, presented thematically.

Stylistically, the author's writing resembles that of Sarrāj. There are generous quotations from traditional sources, the Qur'ān, *ḥadīth*, and Sufi masters, interspersed with the author's own opinions and arguments, and with generous quotes from Qushayrī's own master, Abū ʿAlī al-Daqqāq. The author's personal comments do not dominate, however. He is content to allow the revered sources to take centre stage by presenting them with a minimum of editorial interpretation.

Qushayrī begins with quotations from the Qur'ān which purportedly refer to *samāʿ*, and are supportive of the practice. The vague applicability of these verses and their remote connection to *samāʿ* is apparent in all these quotations, as we have noted above with Sarrāj. The main concern of the author, however, is to argue for a cautious acceptance of the practice. He claims that listening to poetry with melodies and music is generally 'permissible' (*mubāḥ*) by religious law, provided nothing repulsive or unlawful is heard, and that free reign is not given to desires or idle amusement (*Ris*. 336.4–10).

That the Prophet and his first followers are known to have listened to recitation provides a further reason for its acceptability. Listeners should apprehend poetry for its morally uplifting qualities, increasing the desire for obedience and remembrance of God's provision for His servants. The author argues that *samāʿ* is a 'recommended' or 'rewarded' (*mustaḥabb*) act for religious purposes, though 'voluntary' (*mukhtār*) rather than obligatory as far as revealed law is concerned.

The author mentions certain *ḥadīth*s concerning the Prophet's acceptance of *samāʿ* and Qur'ānic recitation. Those involving ʿĀ'isha and her acceptance of the singing servant girls are given prominence by Ghazālī in his treatment of the subject. Qushayrī on the other hand is more restrained and offers a plain summary account (*Ris*. 337–8).

Many sayings and narrative anecdotes of the Sufi masters are presented, some more or less verbatim from Sarrāj's account. There is no particular conceptual order to these quotations, which fill the remainder of the chapter. The sayings are almost always supportive of *samāʿ*, or they proclaim certain dogmatic points. The narrative accounts are also illustrative of some phenomenological aspects of the practice in its social setting, or in its effect on the lives of the Sufi masters.

There is no discernible underlying argument which links together this diverse material. It is presented as a collection from varying sources, with very little structure imposed by the author. This contrasts with Sarrāj's basically conceptual arrangement, and more particularly with Ghazālī's highly ordered and carefully argued presentation using similar source material.

While many of the sayings and narrative accounts are similar to those of Sarrāj's *Lumaᶜ*, perhaps being derived from this earlier source, there are some which show interesting differences. One notable example is the account of Dhū 'l-Nūn's arrival at Baghdad and his participation in a *samāᶜ* session. In Sarrāj's version, Dhū 'l-Nūn rises in ecstasy, and then falls down again, perhaps in a type of faint. Another participant in the ceremony imitates the behaviour of the visiting master, but Dhū 'l-Nūn reprimands him for his pretence of ecstatic behaviour (*Lumaᶜ* 289.20–290.7). In Qushayrī's account there is no mention of the other participant at all, while Dhū 'l-Nūn's fall causes blood to trickle from his forehead, but without his actually touching the ground! (*Ris.* 344.4–9.)

The differences in these accounts could have been formed at any number of points, particularly in their pre-literary stages, as oral transmission of these traditions preceded their written versions. Sarrāj's earlier account is not necessarily more trustworthy, but a modern reader would probably give priority to the earlier version because of its precedence.

Qushayrī's reliance on the earlier work of Sarrāj is not often mentioned, but at one or two points he specifically quotes Sarrāj as his source for some material (*Ris.* 345.11). It seems also that other sources, written or oral, were used by the author in his compilation, since some of the material preserved by Qushayrī is not found elsewhere.

Qushayrī's chapter on *samāᶜ* does not compare favourably with that of his predecessor, Sarrāj. The work tends to lack some direction and purpose, and shows less than a keen interest in the topic. The fact of its relative brevity also leaves one with a sense of dissatisfaction with Qushayrī's work. It has limited value beyond reinforcing the earlier writing of Sarrāj, though it does provide a second version of similar source material. It required the genius of Ghazālī to produce a masterful rewriting and development of these sources in new and fruitful directions.

Ghazālī and the *Iḥyāʾ ᶜUlūm al-Dīn*

With Ghazālī and his major work, the *Iḥyāʾ ᶜUlūm al-Dīn* (*The Revival of the Religious Sciences*), we arrive at the zenith of Sufi writings on *samāᶜ*. Not only does Ghazālī encompass all that was written earlier on the subject, but he transforms his source material into a masterly work by the extraordinary genius of his mind.

Sulamī was recognised as a diligent collector of Sufi *ḥadīth* and biography; Sarrāj and Qushayrī are valuable sources of early lore and traditions, moulded partly by their editorial oversight. In Ghazālī, however, we read the distilled arguments and reflections of a master philosopher, rhetorician, theologian and teacher who guides, persuades and impels us by the force of his reason to see the truth of the subject. His chapter on *samāʿ* and *wajd* in the *Iḥyāʾ* is not a mere collection of sayings gleaned from the Sufi masters; it is a powerful argument for the legitimacy and the value of these practices, carefully reasoned, and the result of long deliberation. What Ghazālī has to say on this subject is always enlightening, and his arguments in favour of the value of *samāʿ* are comprehensive and attractive. His work is the culmination of Arabic writing on the subject at least for the formative period of Sufism.

The details of Ghazālī's life are well known, and easily accessible; they do not need repetition here.[42] It suffices to say that it was during the period of his retirement from teaching at Baghdad, in the years 488/1095–499/1106, that he composed his great work, the *Iḥyāʾ ʿUlūm al-Dīn*. During this period of his life, following a critical breakdown, and his voluntary departure from his distinguished teaching post, he resided in Damascus and Ṭūs, though also undertaking several other journeys, including a pilgrimage to Mecca. Having regained the certainties of faith and knowledge which he lost during his period of crisis, he spent many years as a recluse, living in poverty, and spending most of his time in meditation and spiritual disciplines.

The writing of the *Iḥyāʾ* in approximately the last decade of his life, therefore, represents the author at his most mature and reflective stage. The *Iḥyāʾ* is encyclopaedic in its contents, being a 'complete guide for the devout Muslim to every aspect of the religious life – worship and devotional practices, conduct in daily life, the purification of the heart, and advance along the mystic way'.[43]

The lengthy chapter on *samāʿ* and *wajd*, titled *Kitāb Ādāb al-Samāʿ waʾl-Wajd* (*The Book of Manners concerning Listening and Ecstasy*), covers some thirty-six and a half pages in the folio Cairo edition used for this study.[44] The chapter is found in the second volume of the *Iḥyāʾ* which deals with *ʿādāt* or social customs.

What distinguishes this treatment of the subject from earlier writers is not so much the materials used – these are largely the same as with Sarrāj and Qushayrī – but the masterly way in which the author deals with the issues. At every point the reader encounters the clear, logically based arguments of the mature philosopher who is in complete control of his subject. He writes in an engaging and very readable style, his lack of formality perhaps being due to the fact that Arabic was his adopted, rather than first, language.[45] He also shows himself as a great teacher and orator who is able to demonstrate and persuade by his arguments. In the chapter on *samā*ʿ, the reader is brought into contact with a powerful intellect, not with a mere compiler of traditions. One of the most attractive aspects of the *Iḥyā*ʾ is to watch this intellect at work, and to witness the creative way in which familiar materials are transformed by Ghazālī's rationality and spirituality into something profound and original.

In the following analysis, the chapter on *samā*ʿ from the *Iḥyā*ʾ is treated thematically, rather than in the order presented by Ghazālī. There is also some reference to other writers on the subject, and their differences from Ghazālī's approach.

The legal focus of Ghazālī

It is clear that the *Iḥyā*ʾ builds on the work of Ghazālī's predecessors, such as Sarrāj, who is acknowledged at one point (*Iḥyā*ʾ II.297.20). It is not surprising, however, that given his legal and dialectical training and inclination, Ghazālī is more concerned with questions of the legal status and permissibility of *samā*ʿ, and the intricacies of the associated legal arguments. Whereas Sarrāj devotes only two short sections to the question of permissibility, Ghazālī takes up most of the first half of his whole discussion in dealing with this question. Even in the second part of the work, the question is never far from his mind, with occasional references to the legal aspects of *samā*ʿ appearing. Again, Sarrāj devotes the final chapter of his *Kitāb al-Samā*ʿ to listing reasons why some people disapprove of the practice. Ghazālī, on the other hand, engages these arguments head on, and attempts a vigorous rebuttal of these objections (*Iḥyā*ʾ II.282.7-end 284). This illustrates the dialectical commitment of the author, and his readiness to defend his principles and show up the weaknesses of his opponents at every opportunity.

There is a relatively short section dealing with the actual legality of *samā*ʿ near the beginning of the discussion (*Iḥyā*ʾ II.268.14–273.1). The author begins with an outline of the methodological requirements for determining such questions, namely the use of appropriate textual evidence and the use of analogous arguments.

The principal reasoning used for *samā*ʿ is that of the acceptability of beautiful sounds, which has textual corroboration in the Qurʾān and *ḥadīth*, both directly and indirectly by analogy. In this, Ghazālī follows similar lines to those laid down by Sarrāj. The acceptability of listening to beautiful sounds in nature, such as bird song, is extended to the sounds made by musical instruments. Such listening, furthermore, cannot be condemned simply because it gives pleasure, else all pleasurable activities would be prohibited. The author then digresses into a discussion of the prohibitions surrounding wine drinking, evidently to illustrate the reason for banning certain musical instruments because of their association with drinkers and drinking.

Singing and recitation of poetry is considered next, the main argument here being that since something spoken is acceptable or not because of its content, this is not altered by its being sung or declaimed. Arguments from *ḥadīth* are presented on the acceptability of recitation and listening to poetry.

As well as arguing strongly for the permissibility of *samāʿ*, Ghazālī is also forthright in cataloguing the situations where the practice is forbidden. It was noted above that Sarrāj outlined the prerequisites for listening on the part of novices. Ghazālī, however, takes a more systematic and proscriptive approach, setting out five specific situations where *samāʿ* is prohibited (*Iḥyāʾ* II.279.7–281.19).

The first situation is where the performer is a woman on whom it is unlawful to gaze, or a beardless youth. This is forbidden because of the fear of temptation occasioned by the performer's presence, not because of what is recited or sung.

The second occasion is where certain musical instruments are played, namely those associated with wine drinkers and *mukhannathīn*, usually referred to as 'effeminate artists'.[46]

The third situation involves the censorship of language used in recitation or singing. Obscene or indecent language is prohibited, as well as mocking or speaking falsely about God, the Prophet and his companions. The erotic introduction to the poetic genre of the *qaṣīda* is not prohibited, but the male listener ought to avoid the sin of applying its descriptions to a woman forbidden to him by law. Ghazālī goes on to say that one who is in love applies all amorous utterances to himself and his beloved, whether the latter is human or divine. By means of illustrative stories the argument is advanced that verse which gives rise to unintended interpretations cannot be banned. Rather, the onus is on the listener and the application or understanding of what is heard.

The fourth situation concerns the young person in whom desire and lust are strong, and who may be easily aroused by the erotic descriptions contained in poetry. Such desires are part of the forces of Satan, and hence *samāʿ* must not be allowed for these people.

The fifth occasion where it is prohibited is with the ordinary person who is not a Sufi but who listens simply for the sake of pleasure.

Ghazālī remarks on the difficulty of generalising in legal discussions about what is allowable and what is not. First, not every permitted action is allowed in excess, such as eating, which in excess becomes gluttony. Second, something permitted may on occasion do damage, hence it must be then prohibited. The example offered is the eating of honey, which in medieval medicine was not permitted if the person was feverish. Conversely, wine is normally forbidden, but is allowable if a person is choking and there is nothing else available. The author states that all such generalisations in legal terms have exceptions, and hence *samāʿ* with its restrictions conforms to this pattern.[47]

The epistemological emphasis

There are several occasions in the chapter on *samāʿ* where Ghazālī digresses to raise questions of epistemology and the nature of knowledge. The discussion of these issues shows the underlying philosophical inclination and purpose of Ghazālī's writing.

Following a discussion of ecstatic states and the perception of those who encounter them, the author makes a brief digression on the topic of perception in general (*Iḥyāʾ* II.277.25-end). He recognises the difficulty of the person who is 'dull, who has a hard heart (and) is forbidden the pleasure of listening'; such a person is amazed at the pleasure of listening and the effect it can produce. Similarly, those who lack a particular faculty wonder at the pleasure that faculty can give. The reason for this is that pleasure is a type of perception which requires intelligence and the power of perceiving. Thus if the latter is incomplete, the pleasure resulting from this perception cannot be imagined. Ghazālī offers some examples from the five senses and the power of reasoning, and concludes: 'Likewise is the experience of listening in the heart. Following from the arrival of sound at the ear, it is perceived by an inner sense in the heart; one who does not possess this (inner sense) inevitably finds no pleasure in it.'

In another section where the author discusses the mystical state of *fanāʾ* or 'passing away' from ordinary experience, he presents a brief outline of the intimacy experienced by one who is 'immersed' in mystical knowledge (*Iḥyāʾ* II.288.11–16). One who is infatuated with what one 'sees', such as the Sufi experiencing *wajd*, does not pay heed to the means of seeing, the 'eye' or 'heart', because of this state of immersion. Similarly, the drunkard has no knowledge of drunkenness, or the epicure of pleasure, inasmuch as neither can dispassionately describe the drunkenness or pleasure in terms of causes and effects. Ghazālī seems to maintain that such intimate knowledge is different to knowledge *about* something, i.e. of the dispassionate, 'scientific' variety. One who learns something intimately is shown that knowledge by that thing alone. Moreover, it is often a momentary state; knowledge comes like a flash of lightning which does not last. If this flash did continue it would overwhelm human faculties, such as happened to Abū ʾl-Ḥusayn al-Nūrī who eventually died as a result of being overwhelmed by *wajd*.

What is interesting about this short discussion is the way in which knowledge is related to revelation or to mystical insight rather than to mundane 'scientific' or empirical learning. Ghazālī is certainly not discounting the latter, but he advocates a more passionate, intimate and thoroughgoing insight into nature which can only be gained by direct experience, and is similar to the insight gained by revelation. The notion of the lightning flash of insight has a curiously modern aspect to it, as this is one of the current ways of describing the creative process of scientists and mathematicians.[48] It is also noteworthy that Ghazālī takes such a refreshingly modern view on the perennial question of the object–subject dichotomy in epistemology.

Qurʾānic recital and the arousal of emotion

Ghazālī raises a most important question concerning the fact that often the recital of the Qurʾān fails to elicit an emotional response in a listener, whereas the recital of secular poetry readily achieves this. It was noted above that Sarrāj dealt with this issue to some extent in the *Lumaʿ*, but Ghazālī devotes considerably more space to an explanation of why this occurs (*Iḥyāʾ* II.293.15–298.15).

As a preliminary answer to this question, the author cites numerous instances where the Prophet and his companions did indeed experience *wajd* or 'emotion' at the recital of the Qurʾān. A number of anecdotes are also related concerning some of the prominent Sufis who similarly experienced ecstasy. Most of these anecdotes are similar to those related by Sarrāj in the *Lumaʿ* and need not be of concern here. Ghazālī notes that the main point to these illustrations is that 'one who has a spiritual sense is not devoid of emotion while listening to the Qurʾān' (*Iḥyāʾ* II.295.9).

Approaching the question directly as to why listening to the Qurʾān sometimes has no effect, Ghazālī cites seven reasons.[49]

First, the Qurʾānic verse recited may not accord with the listener's state of mind, unlike secular poetry which is designed to arouse emotion. Allied to this is the fact that many parts of the Qurʾān are legal or prescriptive texts which obviously do not provoke an emotive response. Surprisingly, however, the author argues that even prosaic texts can arouse *wajd* if one considers legal passages, for instance, in the light of God's providence for His creatures, and so on.

Second, the Qurʾān is often a memorised text and as such has less effect than a verse of poetry heard for the first time.

Third, poetry is metrical, which provokes more effect than the non-metrical Qurʾān.

Allied to this are the fourth and fifth reasons, the recital of secular poetry using melodies in certain keys, and their support by various rhythmic means.

Sixth, secular song may not accord with a listener's state of mind, leading him to reject and disregard the song. This cannot be allowed with the Qurʾān which must appeal to all people. Ghazālī seems to imply that the addition of meter, rhythm and melody enhances poetry's appeal to those receptive to it. Conversely this means that those who are not receptive will reject or dislike the poetry. In the case of the Qurʾān this cannot be allowed, nor can individual interpretation or application of meaning be permitted on these grounds.

The seventh reason, the essence of Ghazālī's argument according to K. Nelson,[50] is directly attributed to Sarrāj. Ghazālī summarises the earlier writer's statement that the Qurʾān is uncreated, and revelation of the least part of it to created hearts produces bewilderment. Poetry and music, on the other hand, being created, have a relationship with our human passions and qualities which they can easily arouse.

As was mentioned in the analysis of Sarrāj's use of this argument, there are real problems in this division between created and uncreated texts. The alleged power of the Qurʾān to have such overwhelming effects is problematical when the issue under discussion is its failure to elicit emotive responses. There is here a highlighting of the fact that secular poetry plays upon human emotions without the Qurʾān being able to elicit responses appropriate to its status as an inspired text. This seventh reason of Sarrāj's is a somewhat forced argument with special pleading, however theologically necessary.

In concluding this discussion, Ghazālī relates a story of Abū ʾl-Ḥusayn al-Darrāj's (d.320/932) meeting with Yūsuf b. al-Ḥusayn al-Rāzī (d.304/916–7). Yūsuf weeps at the recital of a verse of secular poetry after a whole morning's recital of the Qurʾān had failed to elicit any response from him. To explain this, and to summarise his argument, Ghazālī states:

> When hearts are inflamed by the love of God, an unusual verse rouses in them what the recitation of the Qurʾān does not. This is because of the metre of the verse, and its affinity with human nature . . . As for the Qurʾān, its construction transcends literary styles and modes, and is thereby weakened; nor does it share in the human faculties
>
> (*Iḥyāʾ* II.298.9–12)

Fadlou Shehadi in his analysis of this aspect of Ghazālī's thought makes the appealing argument that there was an antagonism on the part of some more conservative writers toward singing and music. This may have been due to the competitive edge which these forms of *samāʿ* had over recitals of the Qurʾān. This seems to be reflected even in Ghazālī, who was not so conservative, by the lengthy section devoted to the question of why secular recitation has such emotive effects.[51]

The decorum of 'listening' sessions

Ghazālī includes in his discussion of *samāʿ* a section on *ādāb* ('manners, decorum') of listening sessions (*Iḥyāʾ* II.298.18–302.12). This enables us to gain some insight into the practices at such sessions, and some knowledge of the participants' behaviour and activities. Ghazālī's brother Majd al-Dīn (d.520/1126) has left a valuable account of the conduct of a *samāʿ* ceremonial in his short treatise, *Bawāriq al-Ilmāʿ* (*Gleams of Guidance*). The section on *ādāb* in the *Iḥyāʾ*, however, though not attempting a detailed description, is just as significant for its incidental details. It throws light, for instance, on the practice of dancing and tearing one's clothes during trance. This allows us indirectly to gain a better picture of such sessions.

Ghazālī begins his discussion with an explanation of Junayd's saying that 'Listening requires three things . . . the (appropriate) time, place, and companions.' Ghazālī emphasises the need for a quiet place without other activities, and the need for like-minded companions who are not ostentatious; otherwise it is better to refrain from the practice.

A second rule concerns the readiness and suitability of novices or young people for *samāʿ*. There are several reasons which make some members of the Sufi community unsuitable. Some only perceive the outward signs of the Sufi path, and have no inclination or 'taste' for *samāʿ*; with these people it is just a waste of time. Those whose passions are still strong ought not to be allowed to participate since it is a mere gratification of desires for them. Those who are ignorant of spiritual and theological knowledge ought to be forbidden because they may gain false and heretical understandings of the spiritual matters revealed during *samāʿ*. Moreover, anyone whose heart is preoccupied by worldly concerns or who listens solely for pleasure ought to be prevented from participating.

The third rule is a short list of etiquette for listeners. Among the elements noted are the need for attentiveness, stillness, silence, and sitting with bowed head. One should not look at others, clear the throat, yawn, clap, dance or talk. If one is overcome by *wajd* resulting in involuntary movements, one should return to a quiet state as soon as this passes. Ghazālī makes a digression to discuss these involuntary movements during ecstasy, claiming that the intensity of the overwhelming experience does not necessarily correspond to the amount of observable physical activity. Rather, the most perfect form of trance is that which produces complete stillness.

The fourth rule continues this theme, arguing that restraining oneself from ecstatic activity or from weeping is acceptable, but so is dancing and weeping, provided there is no deception or pretence in these activities. The tearing of garments, however, is not acceptable unless it is done involuntarily. One reason for this prohibition is that the act of tearing garments is wasteful of precious cloth, yet if tearing yields pieces of cloth which can be used for mending other garments, then it is acceptable!

The final rule relates to obtaining the assembly's approval and consent for whatever activities are carried out, and also following the particular group's customs. Ghazālī mentions, for example, that some groups remove all their turbans when a person goes into trance and loses their turban; others remove outer garments when someone tears their garment and it falls off. This is done for the sake of comradeship and politeness. Similarly, one should not dance if this activity is disapproved by the group, and so on.

This section on the decorum of *samāʿ* adds much detail to our knowledge of the practice of this activity. It is often the incidental details that provide us with valuable information which is otherwise passed over by authors concerned with other issues.

This short survey does not exhaust the variety of contents and arguments in this remarkable chapter of Ghazālī's *Iḥyāʾ*. An attempt has been made, however, to illustrate the quality of argument and the types of issues dealt with by the author.

Hujwīrī and the *Kashf al-Maḥjūb*

The previous writings on *samāʿ* considered in this study were all written in Arabic; the two remaining works to be discussed, however, are both in Persian. The first of these, the *Kashf al-Maḥjūb* (*Revealing the Veiled*), is the oldest and most authoritative treatise on the Sufi path in the Persian language.

The author of the *Kashf* was ʿAlī b. ʿUthmān al-Jullābī al-Hujwīrī, a fifth-century mystic who died in about 465/1072.[52] Hujwīrī was a native of Ghazna, but spent the last years of his life in Lahore, where he wrote his only surviving book. The details of his life are mostly drawn from incidental references in the *Kashf*. He appears to have travelled widely, like Sarrāj and Sulamī before him, meeting many Sufi masters and paying homage to the shrines of those who had died. He was taken as a prisoner to Lahore, and lamented the loss of his library in Ghazna while he was composing the *Kashf*.

The work itself is similar in structure to Sarrāj's *Lumaʿ*; indeed, it appears that Hujwīrī modelled his book on the former. Written in the later years of the author's life, it answers questions posed by a certain Abū Saʿīd al-Hujwīrī (d.?). It is a systematic treatise, aiming to present a complete system of Sufi doctrines and practices. Hidayet Hosain explains that 'Before giving his own opinion, the author usually examines the opinions of earlier writers on the subject, refuting them if necessary; these discussions of the problems of mysticism are illustrated by examples drawn from the writer's own experience.'[53]

Unlike Sarrāj, there is less of the apologist in Hujwīrī; the work was not composed in order to persuade sceptics, but to teach aspiring Sufis. There is nevertheless a great reliance on the earlier work of Sarrāj, as well as on the writings of Sulamī and Qushayrī.

The section on *samāʿ* is a lengthy chapter which comes at the very end of the work. In substance, there is a great similarity with Sarrāj's *Lumaʿ*, as many of the illustrative stories and quotations from authorities are identical. Hujwīrī's editorial style is also like that of Sarrāj, with the exception that there is more reliance on personal experience and a greater offering of personal opinions.

A further difference is the author's more circumspect view of *wajd* and the more emotive or excessive activities associated with *samāʿ* such as dancing, tearing of garments, etc. Though he accepts the practice in general, he is cautious about any excesses which might denigrate its value. His view of *samāʿ* as a whole may perhaps be summed up in the statement, attributed to Hujwīrī's own shaykh, that it is 'the viaticum of the indigent: one who has reached his journey's end hath no need of it' (Nich. p.405).

samāʿ in the *Kashf al-Maḥjūb*

The chapter on *samāʿ* begins with a short section in which Hujwīrī argues for the superiority of the sense of hearing in the religious domain. One comes to know the necessity of belief through hearing both the Qurʾān and the Prophetic Traditions. Oral tradition and the speech of the prophets is primary to faith, and superior to the importance of sight, of witnessing, or of miracles.

Hujwīrī then expounds on the value of hearing the Qurʾān, as the most beneficial type of *samāʿ*. In this, he follows the lines laid down by Sarrāj, drawing on arguments largely from *ḥadīth*.

The next section deals with the permissibility of listening to secular poetry, which Hujwīrī approves of, based on Prophetic example. Listening to erotic imagery, however, is regarded as forbidden, on the analogy that hearing a description of something unlawful is itself unlawful. For Hujwīrī, this is a black and white situation, and there is no hint of the more subtle interpretation advanced by Ghazālī in the *Iḥyāʾ*. For Ghazālī, erotic imagery is acceptable provided it is applied to a lawful spouse, or used with reference to mystical love.

Hujwīrī next deals with the acceptability of hearing beautiful voices, and hence melodies and music. Again there is a similarity with Sarrāj's earlier arguments, such as the effect of the cameleer's song on his beasts, and the therapeutic effect of pleasant sounds. The author also allows the use of musical instruments provided no evil or frivolous intention is present.

In a chapter dealing with the principles of *samāʿ* (Nich. pp. 402ff), Hujwīrī uses a binary distinction between those who listen to the spiritual meaning, and those who listen to the physical sound. This is based on the principle that when a person's temperament is evil, what he hears will be evil, and vice versa. Numerous illustrations of this tenet are provided by the author, including the saying attributed to Dhū ʾl-Nūn that *samāʿ* is 'a Divine influence (*wārid al-ḥaqq*) which stirs the heart to seek God: those who listen to it spiritually (*ba-ḥaqq*) attain unto God (*taḥaqqaqa*), and those who listen to it sensually (*ba-nafs*) fall into heresy (*tazandaqa*)' (Nich. p.404).

Hujwīrī describes the various stages of the Sufi path, as beginners, those in the middle, and the advanced, each with corresponding stages of *samāʿ* activity. The beginner's temperament is 'nowise capable of (enduring) the word of God, but is overpoweringly impressed by the descent of that spiritual reality, so that some lose their senses in audition (*samāʿ*) and some die . . .' (Nich. p.407). Some illustrative stories are offered, illustrating 'crisis' outcomes for those inexperienced in dealing with the effects of *samāʿ*.

Reflecting the structure of Sarrāj's *Kitab al-Samāʿ*, Hujwīrī concludes his discussion with an outline of the reasons why some Sufis disapprove of the practice of *samāʿ*. Thus Prophetic Tradition is cited, along with other arguments familiar to us from Sarrāj. There is also the argument not encountered before that *samāʿ* can be a demonic instrument. Abū ʾl-ʿAbbās al-Ashqānī (d. mid-fifth/eleventh century) is quoted as saying that he witnessed a *samāʿ* assembly where he saw naked demons dancing among the others and breathing on them so that they 'waxed hot' (Nich. p.412).

wajd and related topics in the Kashf

Hujwīrī offers a rather abstract discussion on the nature of *wajd* and *wujūd*, claiming that the former is 'grief' or loss of the object of desire, while the latter is 'finding' or attainment to the object. This is an astute binary distinction, recalling Qushayrī's dichotomy of *basṭ* and *qabḍ*,[54] or the more common 'hope' (*rajāʾ*) and 'fear' (*khawf*), such categories being useful for their theoretical neatness. Whether this provides an adequate description of the effects of *samāʿ* and accounts for the narratives related in the source materials is another question. Many of the phenomena recorded in Sarrāj and Sulamī cannot be categorised in this simple binary way.

Hujwīrī briefly describes *tawājud* as 'taking pains to produce *wajd*', and he goes on to approve of this behaviour. Dancing (*raqṣ*) and 'gazing at youths' are proscribed by Hujwīrī as forbidden activities (Nich. p.416). The practice of tearing one's garments is approved by the author, first on the basis of its practical usefulness: the torn cloth can be reused. In addition, it can be seen as a gift to the performer, or used as a blessing, much like a holy relic.

Hujwīrī concludes the discussion as a whole by outlining a number of rules on the conduct of *samā*ʿ sessions. These include several organisational requirements, such as the need for a spiritual director to be present, that there be no uninitiated people present, that the performer be respectable, and so on. There are also a number of 'controlling' conventions mentioned, aiming at keeping the performance and the participants ordered and restrained. For example, one must allow the impact of ecstatic states to proceed smoothly, without interference from others, and without disturbing other participants. The author concludes by warning about the dangers of *samā*ʿ, and its possible corrupting influence, especially on young people. With a short prayer for himself, the author swiftly ends this discussion, and his book as a whole.

The value of Hujwīrī's contribution does not at first appear to be great. It certainly has not the originality and profundity of Ghazālī's writing, nor the breadth and detail of Sarrāj. Nevertheless, there is value in some of the editorial contribution and original arguments put forward by the author. The extent of this contribution will be seen later in the present study where issues raised by all the source writers will be discussed. Moreover, though there is some repetition of material found in Sarrāj and Qushayrī, the small differences in detail are often noteworthy, as is the way in which Hujwīrī adds his own explanation to incidents which are related without editorial additions in the earlier sources.

ʿAṭṭār and the *Tadhkirat al-Awliyā*ʾ

The final source used in this study is the famous biographical work by the Persian poet, Farīd al-Dīn ʿAṭṭār. The *Tadhkirat al-Awliyā*ʾ (*Memorial of the Saints*) is justly known as one of the principal works of early Sufi biography and hagiography; it is a storehouse of folklore, deeds, sayings, doctrines and miracles attributed to the early masters.

The details of ʿAṭṭār's life are rather sketchy; there is no scholarly consensus on the dates of his birth and death, the latter being placed from 586/1190 to 627/1230.[55] It is certain, however, that he lived most of his life in Nishapur, and that he followed the profession of pharmacist/doctor, having a shopfront in the city where he attended to his patients. Few other reliable details can be gleaned from his numerous writings, as they are works of religious allegory and poetry, containing very few topical references.

Most of ʿAṭṭār's works are religious poems using the structure of rhyming couplets known as *mathnawī* form, and containing mystical subject matter. The best known of these is the *Manṭiq al-Ṭayr* (*Speech of the Birds*), an allegorical poem dealing with the Sufi path to God as the quest of thirty birds for the mythical royal bird, the *sī-murgh* ('thirty birds').

The *Tadhkirat al-Awliyāʾ* is ʿAṭṭār's only prose writing, being a work of hagiography, a memorial to the lives, deeds and words of the early Sufi masters. ʿAṭṭār lists his reasons for writing the work, most having to do with the benefits gained from remembering the words and deeds of the Sufi 'friends of God'. The pious motives of his writing probably explain the numerous miraculous and legendary accounts which he includes in the *Tadhkirat.* The factual accuracy of his biographies was not a matter of concern for such a writer as ʿAṭṭār. The *Tadhkirat* cannot be judged by modern standards of historiography; it is often much more liberal in dealing with the fantastical elements in the lives of the Sufis than its predecessors, such as Sulamī's *Ṭabaqāt*.

This presents a problem for our intended use of the *Tadhkirat* as a source for phenomenological accounts of the experience of *samāʿ*. ʿAṭṭār can so freely recount fantastical and miraculous events as part of the daily fare of the Sufis. How much less cautious will he be to include accounts of dissociation and altered states of consciousness caused by *samāʿ*. This is likely to present a problem for most of the sources looked at so far; but the fact of ʿAṭṭār's excess in the use of the miraculous makes it much more acute in his case.

There are various answers to this problem. First, it is inevitable that some exaggeration or 'gilding' will occur in hagiographies where modern notions of historical accuracy are quite misplaced. Whatever distortion takes place, however, the fact that there are other, earlier sources mitigates this difficulty, at least in the case of ʿAṭṭār. Related to this is our ability to generalise from particular instances. The more examples of the phenomenon of altered states found in the sources, the more evidence we have to distil the common and more universal elements which are important for our discussions. Exaggerated or fantastical phenomena will tend to be eliminated in this way, as the more common experiences will tend to be the more trustworthy.

Moreover, despite this liberality as regards the miraculous, it is of note that in dealing with the phenomena of *samāʿ* and altered states, ʿAṭṭār is remarkably cautious. In what could be seen as an avenue where the miraculous and supernatural could have full scope, he is notably circumspect. As will be shown later in specific instances, ʿAṭṭār does not let his imagination loose in this area. He is inclined to write with restraint and subtlety, a fact which argues for the credibility and trustworthiness of his narratives.

Some of the sources of ʿAṭṭār's biographies can be traced; for example many of the narratives are found in the earlier works considered in the present study. There is a great deal of material in the *Tadhkirat*, however, which cannot be traced further back. The author appears to have had access to individual writings of the Sufis, directly or through quotations, and to other oral and written source materials.

In terms of the style of the work, it is noted for its entertaining and lively character, which suggests that it was meant for a wide audience. Iranian scholars comment on the simplicity, directness and 'sweetness' of the language used, in this regard quite unlike the florid and verbose style often associated with later Persian writers.[56]

The form of each biography maintains a standard pattern. There is first a short encomium of the Sufi, often in rhymed prose, followed by a generally chronological account of life events, usually by means of narrative anecdotes, often dramatic and full of colour. This is usually followed by a series of sayings attributed to the person. Finally there is a narrative surrounding the events of their death, and dreams about the deceased related by others, explaining how they fare in the next world. There are a few exceptions to this pattern, most notably in the case of Abū Yazīd al-Bisṭāmī, where there is an extended account of his *miʿrāj* or symbolic ascent journey, with ʿAṭṭār's explanation.

The parts of the *Tadhkirat* of value for our subject are often short, isolated fragments of sayings about *samāʿ* or *wajd*, or longer anecdotes involving altered states and other such experiences. There is no sustained or thematic presentation of the subject, owing to the biographical nature of the work. This being the case, there is little value in listing here the scattered references to *samāʿ*. These will be presented in the body of the present study, particularly in reference to the psychological discussions.

Notes

1 For an overview of this literature see Caesar E. Farah, 'The Prose Literature of Sufism', in M.J.L.Young et al. (eds), *The Cambridge History of Arabic Literature: Religion, Learning and Science in the ʿAbbasid Period*, Cambridge: Cambridge University Press, 1990, pp.56–75.

2 Farīdu'ddīn 'Aṭṭār, *Muslim Saints and Mystics: Episodes from the Tadhkirat al-Auliya'* transl. A.J. Arberry, London, Boston and Henley: Routledge and Kegan Paul, 1966 (1979).
3 Alī b. 'Uthmān al-Jullābī al-Hujwīrī, *The Kashf al-Mahjūb*, transl. R.A. Nicholson, Leiden: E.J. Brill, and London: Luzac and Co, 1911 (1982).
4 ed. R.A. Nicholson, London: Luzac and Co, 1914 (1963).
5 Richard Gramlich, *Schlaglichter über das Sufitum. Abū Naṣr as-Sarrāğs Kitāb al-luma' eingeleitet, übersetzt und kommentiert*, Stuttgart: Franz Steiner Verlag, 1990, p.5.
6 *Kitāb al-Luma'*, ed. Nicholson, English introduction, p.v.
7 *Luma'*, pp.380–90.
8 *Kashf*, p.323, and 'Aṭṭar, Farīdu'ddīn, *Tadhkiratu 'l-Awliyā*, ed. R.A. Nicholson, London: Luzac, and Leiden: E.J. Brill, 1905–7, vol.2, pp.182–3.
9 *Luma'*, English introduction, p.viii.
10 A.J. Arberry, *Sufism: An Account of the Mystics of Islam*, London: Allen and Unwin, 1950 (1979), p.66.
11 Gramlich, op.cit., p.22.
12 Louis Massignon, *The Passion of al-Hallāj*, abridged, ed. and transl. H. Mason, Princeton, NJ: Princeton University Press, 1984, p.xxii.
13 *Luma'*, English abstract, pp.69–77.
14 J. Robson (ed.), *Tracts on Listening to Music*, London: The Royal Asiatic Society, 1938, transl. p.27, text p.49.
15 For details see Gramlich, op.cit., pp.391–2.
16 A.J. Wensinck, *Concordances et indices de la tradition musulmane*, Leiden: E.J. Brill, 1936–88, vol.3, p.436.
17 See further Svend Søndergaard, 'al-Sarrādj's use of triads in Kitāb al-Luma'' in E. Keck et al. (eds) *Living Waters*, Copenhagen: Museum Tusculanum Press, 1990, pp.347–52.
18 Amnon Shiloah, 'Ibn Hindū, le médecin et la musique' in A. Shiloah, *The Dimension of Music in Islamic and Jewish Culture*, Aldershot: Variorum, 1993, pp.449ff.
19 Amnon Shiloah, *Music in the World of Islam: A Socio-Cultural Study*, Aldershot: Scolar Press, 1995, pp.50ff.
20 See Junayd's statement in *Luma'* 272.4–5.
21 See K. Nelson, *The Art of Reciting the Qur'an*, Austin, TX: University of Texas Press, 1985, Chapter 3.
22 See Wensinck, op.cit., vol.1, p.419.
23 See Nelson, op.cit., pp.48–9.
24 'Aṭṭār, *T.A.* II.64.6–7. Ghazālī also repeats this story; in his account the man groans and dies! (*Iḥyā'* II.295.11–14).
25 Abū Bakr al-Kalābādhī, *The Doctrine of the Sūfīs*, transl. A.J. Arberry, Lahore: Ashraf, 1966 repr., pp.181–2.
26 Titus Burckhardt, *An Introduction to Sufi Doctrine*, transl. D.M. Matheson, Lahore: Ashraf, 1959 (1973), pp.71–2.
27 So Ibn Taymīya and others. See Arthur Gribetz, 'The samā' Controversy: Sufi vs. Legalist', *Studia Islamica*, LXXIV, 1991, especially pp.46ff.
28 Gribetz, op.cit., p.49.
29 Hans Wehr, *A Dictionary of Modern Written Arabic*, ed. J.M. Cowan, third ed., London: Harrap, 1976, p.1050.

30 Clare M. Lathers and Paul L. Schraeder (eds), *Epilepsy and Sudden Death*, New York, NY and Basel: Marcel Dekker, 1990, pp.418; 426ff; and John P. Kildahl, *The Psychology of Speaking in Tongues*, New York, NY: Harper and Row, 1972, p.57.
31 Biographical details are from Abū 'Abd al-Raḥmān al-Sulamī, *Jawāmi' Ādāb al-Ṣūfiyya and 'Uyūb al-Nafs wa-Mudāwātuhā*, ed. Etan Kohlberg, Jerusalem: Academic Press, 1976; and idem, *Ṭabaqāt al-Ṣūfīya*, ed. Nūr al-Dīn Sharība, Cairo: Maktaba 'l-Khānijī, 1969, pp.16ff.
32 *Ṭabaqāt*, op.cit., pp.29;49–50.
33 See Jawid A. Mojaddedi, *The Biographical Tradition in Sufism: The Ṭabaqāt Genre from al-Sulamī to Jāmī*, Richmond: Curzon Press, 2001.
34 Kohlberg, op.cit., p.8.
35 *Ṭabaqāt*, op.cit., p.49.
36 *Jawāmi'*, op.cit., pp.58–9. Cf. *Luma'* 304.18–305.7.
37 Hyderabad: Majlis al-'Uthmānīya, 1981.
38 Luma' 274.14ff; and Gribetz, op.cit., pp.46–7.
39 Biographical details are from the article by H. Halm in *E.I.*, vol.5, pp.526–7.
40 Abū 'l-Qāsim 'Abd al-Karīm al-Qushayrī, *Al-Risālat al-Qushayrīya fī 'Ilm al-Taṣawwuf*, ed. M. Zarīq and A. Balṭaljī, Beirut: Dār al-Jīl, no date, pp.35–8.
41 Ibid., pp.335–50.
42 See article by W.M. Watt in *E.I.*, vol.2, pp.1038–41.
43 Ibid., p.1040.
44 Cairo: Matba'a Mustafā al-Bābī al-Halabī wa-Ulāda bi-Misr, 1939, 4 vols.
45 Suggested by Margaret Smith in *Al-Ghazali the Mystic*, Lahore: Kazi Publications, no date, p.67.
46 See Amnon Shiloah, *Music in the World of Islam*, op.cit., pp.12–13.
47 See Fadlou Shehadi, *Philosophies of Music in Medieval Islam*, Leiden: E.J. Brill, 1995, pp.121–4 for a differing account of this topic.
48 See Paul Davies, *The Mind of God: Science and the Search for Ultimate Meaning*, London: Simon and Schuster, 1992, pp.144–5; 228–9.
49 This is more than those mentioned by K. Nelson, *The Art of Reciting the Qur'an*, op.cit., pp.48–9.
50 Ibid.
51 Shehadi, op.cit., p.126.
52 Biographical details are from the article by Hidayet Hosain in *E.I.*, vol.3, p.546; and from the preface of R.A. Nicholson's translation of the *Kashf*, op.cit., pp.xvii–xix.
53 Hidayet Hosain, op.cit.
54 See the discussion in R.C. Zaehner, *Mysticism Sacred and Profane*, Oxford: Oxford University Press, 1957 (1980), pp.85ff.
55 For the various arguments see the article by Hellmut Ritter in *E.I.*, vol.1, p.752; and F. de Blois, *Persian Literature: A Bio-bibliographical Survey*, London: Royal Asiatic Society, 1994, vol.5. part 2, pp.270–6.
56 See M. Qazwīnī in 'Aṭṭār, *Tadhkirat al-Awliyā'*, op.cit., vol.1, p.19.

3

THE LANGUAGE OF *SAMĀʿ* AND OTHER KEY CONCEPTS

In the source writings studied in this book, there are many descriptions of unusual religious and mystical experiences, as well as explanations of these phenomena. In order to understand the intentions of these writings, it is crucial that the reader has a clear knowledge of the language and vocabulary used by the various authors.

The unusual nature of the subject matter and its experiential character means that discussion of these phenomena will be fraught with difficulties. Writers in this field readily acknowledge this problem. William James, for example, in his classic *Varieties of Religious Experience*, cites ineffability as the first criterion of mysticism: 'The subject of it immediately says that it defies expression, that no adequate report of its contents can be given in words.'[1] Sarrāj acknowledges a similar situation in regard to his own discussion: 'How can one describe something which has no description other than itself, and to which no witness can stand other than itself?' (*Lumaʿ* 313.7–8). The subjective nature of these experiences also means that description in terms of ordinary language can only be partial and inadequate.

Given this situation, it is vital that the reader is equipped with some understanding of the vocabulary of the authors being studied. The subtleties of the language employed must be carefully weighed in order to appreciate more fully the meanings being conveyed.

There are several other reasons why a close study of the vocabulary and semantics of these writings is required. There are a number of key terms, such as *wajd*, *ḥāl*, *qalb*, which are crucial in understanding the nuances of Sufi writings. We cannot assume that these words mean what their usual signification would imply, particularly as the writings we are considering come from a period in the history of Sufism when a special vocabulary was still in the process of being developed.

The significance of this special terminology is noted by Qushayrī in his introduction to the section of his *Risāla* which deals with this subject. Qushayrī writes that all groups have special vocabulary which enables mutual understanding and unveils secrets for that group. Conversely, this vocabulary hides understanding from outsiders so that their language is unintelligible to opponents or others likely to misunderstand, and prevents their secrets being divulged. He goes on to assert that the truths expressed in special language are not assembled by artifice or devoted effort, nor from free usage, but are placed by God in people's hearts (*Ris.* 53). The importance of special terminology among the Sufis in the linguistic development of the early Islamic centuries has been documented in the well-known works of Louis Massignon and Paul Nwyia.[2] The scope of these earlier studies does not, however, extend to many of the materials being considered in this book.

It must also be acknowledged that the standard dictionaries of Arabic, both native and Western, do not generally include a discussion of usages peculiar to mystical writings. There is thus no recognised source or reference work which accurately gauges the vocabulary of the particular authors being considered here. This is why Nicholson, in his edition of the *Kitāb al-Lumaʿ*, included a glossary of unusual and special usages which is indispensable for reading the text. There also exist some specialised Sufi dictionaries, that of ʿAbd al-Razzāq al-Qāshānī (d.730/1330) being the best known.[3] Unfortunately, Qāshānī's work is of limited usefulness, owing to his particular view of the subject through the eyes of post-Ibn al-ʿArabī theosophy. Moreover, he usually takes no account of the historical and theological development of Sufi terminology.

This issue of historical development and a diachronic approach to language is important for our present purposes. The writers being considered all come from toward the end of the formative period of Sufi history. Thus their own particular terminology may differ quite markedly from that of quoted sources from an earlier period, where less standardised language may have been in use. There are also various doctrinal emphases reflecting various 'schools' where differing terminologies were used.

The special nature of the writings being considered here requires careful attention to the semantics involved. Even if we have an adequate picture of the semantic range of a particular word, we should not assume conformity to this range in all situations. It should always be kept in mind that the author, or the mystic uttering an ecstatic saying, may be extending the limits of his language in order to express an unusual experience or concept. In addition to this, we should also be aware of the possibilities of multivalence in the language being used. The significance of linguistic expression cannot be restricted to a single level of meaning. Indeed, one of the methods of inducing a dissociative reaction to *samāʿ* documented in the sources is through 'misunderstanding' a spoken phrase because of its multivalent or homophonic characteristics.

The less than adequate handling of mystical language in the standard dictionaries, and the tendentious approach of Sufi lexicons such as Qāshānī's means that a re-examination of linguistic sources is needed. In this study, the primary sources are of course the texts of the authors themselves. Second, there are a selection of dictionaries, native and Western, which need to be considered. The most important native dictionary used here is Ibn Manẓūr's (d.711/1311) *Lisān al-ʿArab*, which, in the words of John A. Haywood, 'aimed at fullness, not brevity, and which was the recognised exhaustive work even until modern times'.[4] The dictionaries of E.W. Lane and R. Dozy are the principal Western sources.[5] Third, there are some studies relating to the vocabulary of the Sufis, such as those of Massignon and Nwyia referred to above, and some other shorter articles.

Methodologically, the primary evidence of the source writings was considered first, with a listing of key words in their contexts, and a preliminary surmise of the meaning. This material was then examined in the light of the secondary sources, the dictionaries, glossaries, and other studies mentioned above. The resulting descriptions presented here are thus individual word studies relating to the semantic range of key concepts in the source writings.

samāʿ

The most obvious word to begin with is *samāʿ*, a verbal noun from root *s-m-ʿ*, and with the basic meaning of 'hearing', and by extension 'that which is heard'. This may apply, therefore, to singing, or any musical performance or other pleasant sound in which the ears take delight.[6] Thus poetry recitation, which is a type of singing, is included in this, as the *Lisān*[7] has it: 'all which the ear finds delightful of a beautiful sound (or voice) is *samāʿ*' (vol.8, p.165). From this we find its application to the Sufi tradition of musical concert, in a more or less ritualised form. Jean During explains that *samāʿ* is considered to be 'nourishment of the soul', a devotional practice which can induce emotional transport, states of grace, ecstasy, and revelations. During asserts that

> The very sense of the term *samāʿ* . . . suggests that it is actually listening which is spiritual, since music or poetry do not necessarily have a sacred nature. 'Hearing', on the other hand, can be applied to any sound, natural, artificial or artistic . . . (*samāʿ* is thus) a synonym of 'understanding', in other words, comprehension, acceptance and application of the Revelation, and the practice of *samāʿ*, beyond ecstacy or rapture, can be an unveiling of mysteries, a means of attaining higher knowledge . . .'[8]

This seems a highly diffuse definition of *samāʿ* which is specific to Sufi understandings of the term, but there is at least the basis of this understanding in the root sense of *s-m-ʿ*. Thus in the *Lisān* (vol.8, pp.162–4) the various configurations of the root often imply acceptance and action on what is heard, particularly in regard to 'hearing' God's word. If something is not accepted and acted upon, it is as though it were not heard. There is also the sense of 'understand and retain' in the usage of the imperative forms of the verb.

Sarrāj

The earliest author we are considering uses the term *samāʿ* rather less frequently than expected. In the first chapter of the *Kitāb al-Samāʿ*, for instance, the term is not used at all, whereas *sawt* ('sound, voice') and *naghma* ('voice, melody') appear almost as substitutes. Elsewhere, Sarrāj uses *samāʿ* only seldom, seeming to avoid this term, in contrast to Ghazālī who employs it frequently.

This may indicate that the author had in mind certain specific meanings for the term outside of which its use was inappropriate. Thus the common sense of 'hearing, listening' as a general term is seldom employed.

Sarrāj's usage of the term falls into two categories, the first referring to listening to poetry, to sonorous or beautiful sounds, and the communal activity of *samāʿ* concert which involves such 'listening'. The second category relates to the mystical aspects of the term, which may not necessarily involve communal activity or listening to audible sounds. This type of *samāʿ* may involve quiet converse with God, devotions leading to states of grace or to revelations, as well as the emotional transports associated with receiving audible or spiritual stimuli.

Examples of the first category, where the term is used in a mundane sense, include *Lumaʿ* 271.11 where *samāʿ* means 'listening to poetry'. Similarly at 277.1 the author refers to al-Shāfiʿī (d.204/820) as permitting *samāʿ* and the chanting of poetry (*al-tarannum biʾl-shiʿr*). The other sense of *samāʿ* in this category is that of communal concert, referred to at 272.4 where Junayd is quoted as saying that those who listen to *samāʿ* require three things: the (appropriate) time, place and companions. Similarly, at 288.18, 290.18 and elsewhere, there is mention of *samāʿ* where people are gathered and someone is reciting verse, whether a *qawwāl* (professional reciter) is mentioned or not.

The second category, where the term is used in a mystical sense, presents greater difficulty for semantic analysis. The precise concept which the author had in mind is often elusive, in accordance with the difficulties mentioned in the introduction to this chapter. The examples given below illustrate the nature of the problem.

Sarrāj first uses the term in the second chapter of the *Kitāb al-Samāʿ* where several 'definitions' are offered. Thus Junayd's statement that *samāʿ* is 'the arrival of the Truth which arouses hearts toward the Truth' (*Lumaʿ* 271.9) refers to the revelatory aspect of the concept, and its divine origin. The author quotes Abū Yaʿqūb al-Nahrajūrī (d.330/941–2) who speaks of *samāʿ* as 'a state which indicates a return to the mysteries (of the heart) after its being inflamed' (*Lumaʿ* 271.13–14). This is a subtle and ambiguous expression, but by no means unusual.

Less obscure usages of the term occur later where *samāʿ* is referred to by Abū Ḥusayn al-Nūrī as an ascetic practice, like prayer and other devotion, which defines the Sufi as such, and is preferable to social converse (*Lumaʿ* 272.12–13). This solitary practice cannot have anything to do with listening to poetry in a ritual setting, but rather is part of the ascetic's devotional converse with God. This is reinforced by the observation of al-Ḥusrī (d.371/982) that there is no value in *samāʿ* which ceases when the person listening to it stops hearing; it must be continuous (*Lumaʿ* 272.18–19). This is similar to *samāʿ* associated with listening to Qurʾānic recitation or *dhikr* as a devotional practice (*Lumaʿ* 280.2ff; 283.1ff).

A different notion of *samāʿ*, containing a more theoretical or abstract element, occurs in discussions about the classification of various stages attained by Sufis in this practice. Thus Abū ʿUthmān Saʿīd b. ʿUthmān al-Rāzī (d.298/910) is quoted as dividing *samāʿ* into three categories: first, novices and beginners who claim to experience more exalted states of consciousness than is really the case; second, the sincere (*al-ṣiddīqīn*) who seek an increase in their experienced states; and third, the sincere from among the knowers (*al-ʿarīfīn*) who are completely open to any divine impression during their devotion (*Lumaʿ* 277.17–278.3). There are several similar threefold classifications mentioned by Sarrāj; these categories divide the practitioners of *samāʿ* into various groups, rather than being indicative of differing shades of meaning in the concept itself.

Occasionally, however, *samāʿ* is referred to in a different sense as the highest of mystical attainments, similar to the concept of *fanāʾ* and the experience of *tawḥīd.* After speaking of the sublimity of this attainment, and its near ineffability, the author describes the highest *samāʿ* as being 'in God, and to God, and is from God, and is directed to God. Those who experience this are those who are at one with the true nature of things and have passed beyond the various states of feeling and have ceased acting and speaking . . .' (*Lumaʿ* 279.8–9). In another passage the author describes in less exalted language the notion of *samāʿ* as parallel with *wajd*, both of which, in the ideal practitioner, are more or less permanent states experienced with equanimity (*Lumaʿ* 293.15).

This overview of Sarrāj's usage of the term shows the great variety of senses which he allows for *samāʿ*. The use of the term falls into two main semantic areas: first, listening to poetry or recitation, and the communal concert associated with this, and second, as mystical converse, devotion, or revelation, and as an expression of the highest mystical experience. Within these broad areas, however, there are numerous distinctions, some of which are almost certainly lost to us now.

Sulamī

In considering the writings of Sulamī, a similar pattern of usage emerges; the term is not encountered frequently, but there is a large semantic range for the word *samāʿ*. There appears also a similar distinction between secular or mundane references, listening to singing or poetry, and communal concert, and the second category mentioned above of mystical reference involving devotional practices and influencing states of consciousness.

In the first category there is the simple use of *samāʿ* as 'hearing' a reciter's declamation of poetry (*T.S.* 205.5–6; 500.11). The term is then used by extension to refer to communal concert or listening sessions, as mentioned in *T.S.* 119.4; 239.8–10; and *Jawāmiʿ Ādāb al-Ṣūfīya*, sect.150. A further distinctive use of the term refers to the semantic or language component of the poetry or other recitation being heard. Abū ʿAbd Allāh al-Ṣubayḥī is quoted as saying that *samāʿ* which is 'plain' is welcome, that which is allusive is feigned, and the subtlest is that which is obscure or difficult except for the inspired listener (*T.S.* 329.7ff).

In the second category of mystical reference, there are again a number of discrete semantic differences evident. Abū Bakr al-Kattānī is quoted as listing various degrees of *samāʿ* corresponding with classes of Sufis: beginners, those near to God, those who know mysteries, and so on. Their *samāʿ* consists of fear or desire, visions of grace, revelation and seeing, and so on (*T.S.* 375.3–6). Kattānī is also quoted as saying that *samāʿ* is not simply 'refreshment' (*mustarwiḥ*), rather it should provoke emotion (*wajd*) or yearning (*shawq*), or a state of being overwhelmed, and it should destroy every fixed or learned notion (*T.S.* 375.9–11).

A rather enigmatic statement of Abū ʿAmrū al-Zujjājī accords to *samāʿ* the quality of being one of the 'weakest' of states since it requires stimuli (presumably of an aural nature) to provoke it; if it were stronger, it would not require listening or musical instruments (*T.S.* 432.14–16). This statement indicates a shift in meaning of *samāʿ* from 'listening' or 'something heard', to 'the state induced by that hearing'.

Qushayrī

With Qushayrī's *Risāla* there appears little advance on the usages outlined in the earlier sources. Since a good portion of the *Risāla* chapter on *samāʿ* is adopted more or less verbatim from Sarrāj, there are frequent overlaps and similarities, especially in relation to the many narratives and direct quotes from the early Sufi masters.

Those sections of the chapter which contain Qushayrī's own statements show a basic distinction between 'listening' or 'hearing' in an everyday sense, and the use of *samāʿ* as a special mystical term. For example, at the beginning of his discussion, Qushayrī states his overall position succinctly: that listening to poetry with beautiful music is permitted, given the usual conditions of its being in accordance with religious law (*Ris.* 336). This usage is the everyday sense of ordinary listening. The special sense of *samāʿ* is in evidence in a statement of Junayd's that in the covenant of Alast, 'the sweetness of listening to spiritual words was poured forth' (*Ris.* 340).

Many usages of the term appear to be in the everyday sense of listening to poetry or music, often implying listening in special sessions or concerts. In accordance with Qushayrī's adaptation of much of his material from Sarrāj, there is no perceptible semantic development associated with *samā*ʿ.

Ghazālī

The word *samā*ʿ is used frequently in Ghazālī's chapter on this topic in the *Iḥyā*ʾ. As well as a high frequency of usage, there is also a wide variety of meanings associated with the word. These fall into three main categories, with some subsections in the two latter categories, as summarised below:

The semantic range of *samā*ʿ in Ghazālī		
A		The simple physical act of hearing or listening.
B	(i)	The act of intentional listening to poetry or music, which may have legal consequences involving permissibility or prohibition, and often but not always associated with the following:
	(ii)	Specific *samā*ʿ concert sessions or gatherings.
C	(i)	A mystical concept involving 'hearing' associated with *ḥāl* (a transient 'state'); or as a Sufi conceptual term in a theoretical discussion.
	(ii)	A mystical concept including converse, revelation or knowledge from God.
	(iii)	The highest stage of understanding and ecstasy with the most intimate mystical knowledge.

Examples of usage A, the simple physical act of hearing, occur frequently in the first pages of Ghazālī's discussion (*Iḥyā*ʾ II.266.18, 20,22,25, etc. Mcd. pp.199–200) and throughout the chapter wherever this sense is required.

Usage B(i) occurs, naturally enough, in discussions of legal questions, particularly concerning the permissibility of listening to recitation or music (Thus *Iḥyā*ʾ II.266.27ff; Mcd. pp.201ff).

Examples of B(ii) are not very numerous; however, at *Iḥyā*ʿ II.287.10 (Mcd. p.713) there is the story of a certain Sufi who 'had not attended *samā*ʿ for many years', the evident meaning being 'communal concert or recitation session'.

Category C presents more intricate problems of definition and appraisal; it must be noted that the distinctions listed in the table above are only provisional. The evidence of context is often not sufficient to pinpoint accurately the author's intended sense. Given these caveats which apply particularly to this category C, there are a number of clear instances where the sense is transparent. For C(i), the term being used as a general mystical concept, Ghazālī writes of 'the Sufis and those philosophers who have considered the relation of *samāʿ* to the soul' (*Iḥyāʾ* II.289.5; Mcd. p.719), or 'the first step in *samāʿ* is understanding what is heard, . . . then this understanding has ecstasy as its fruit' (*Iḥyāʾ* II.285.1; Mcd. p.705).

Examples of C(ii) include references to mystical converse or revelation, not simply listening to a voice or music, even in Sufi concerts, but with a sense of the disclosure of knowledge, or a revelation of some sort from the divine source. Thus, Ghazālī relates a story concerning a young dervish who fainted and died upon hearing a verse recited, thinking that it was God speaking directly to him. In commenting on this, the author writes: 'The purport is that this man considered himself drowning at the time through his state (of consciousness) in relation to God Most High, and through the knowledge that he was too weak to be constant in the beauty of intimacy with God, and through grief at the changing of his heart and its turning from the laws of Truth' (*Iḥyāʾ* II.286.4–5; Mcd. p.709). Ghazālī goes on to argue that one whose *samāʿ* is from God requires a previous understanding of the nature of God so that the disclosures received do not lead to error or unbelief.

An example of C(iii), *samāʿ* as the highest stage of mystical experience, of understanding and ecstasy, occurs in Ghazālī's explanation of Nūrī's last ecstasy. Nūrī was present at a *samāʿ* session when he heard a verse which caused such an ecstatic reaction that he wandered about in a trance, repeating the verse to himself, and oblivious to the pain caused by his stumbling onto a thicket of sharp reeds. The injuries he sustained eventually led to his death some days later. Commenting on the incident, Ghazālī writes that 'this is the stage of those who are faithful in understanding (*fahm*) and ecstasy (*wajd*), and is the highest of these stages, for *samāʿ* through states (*aḥwāl*) is lower than the stages of perfection . . . which is that the subject should pass away totally from himself and his states' (*Iḥyāʾ* II.288.21ff; Mcd. p.717). In this way, Ghazālī describes Nūrī's *samāʿ* as an advanced stage of mystical experience and knowledge, a stage upon which he had elaborated earlier in the discussion. Ghazālī had described the *samāʿ* of 'one who has passed beyond states and stages' as heedless like the women who saw the beauty of Joseph (Qurʾān, Sūra 12), or like the drunkard who is completely immersed in his experience and oblivious to all description of it (*Iḥyāʾ* II.288.6ff; Mcd. pp.715ff).

Hujwīrī

In the earliest Persian author studied here, there is found a similar range of meanings for the term *samāʿ* as in Ghazālī's writings. This is not surprising, as similar sources were used by both authors, and Hujwīrī lived only slightly earlier in time than Ghazālī.

To use the same categorisation as that used above with Ghazālī, there are found examples of *samāʿ* indicating physical hearing of sounds, as in the chapter devoted to 'sounds and melodies' (*Kashf* 520.4ff; Nich. pp.399ff). *samāʿ* as a concept subject to legal consequences is also found quite frequently, in particular relating to the communal assemblies of the Sufis, and their organisation (*Kashf* 524.4ff, 544.16ff; Nich. pp.401–2 and 418–20).

Where the term is used in a mystical sense, there is inevitably more ambiguity in its reference. There is one slight difference with both Persian writers, Hujwīrī and ʿAṭṭār, from their Arabic counterparts. This is the use of the term *samāʿ*, often in association with the verb *kardan* ('to do, make'), and the noun *ḥāl* ('state'), to indicate ecstatic mystical experience. Thus Nicholson translates: 'Foolish aspirants to Sufiism, seeing the adepts absorbed in ecstasy during audition (*samāʿ*), imagined that they were acting from a sensual impulse . . .' (Nich. p.398; *Kashf* 519.14ff). The literal sense of the crucial phrase here, *mī kardand samāʿ bi-ḥāl*, indicates a closer conjunction between *samāʿ* and ecstasy than this translation affords. Thus rather than 'absorbed in ecstasy during audition', the sense is more 'absorbed in ecstatic listening'. This may seem only a minor point, but other examples of this usage of the term in both Persian writers indicate a distinct extension of meaning. In fact this sense of *samāʿ* is found without the addition of *ḥāl*, as in *Kashf* 521.2 (Nich. p.399): 'The nightingale became silent and went into ecstasy (*u-samāʿ mīkard*).'

There are other examples of the mystical sense of *samāʿ*, in line with the categorisation used for Ghazālī, but these are mostly repetitions of the same sources used in that work.

ʿAṭṭār

The term *samāʿ* is not used frequently in ʿAṭṭār's *Tadhkhirat*, but where it is, there is more evidence of the phenomenon noted above with Hujwīrī's writings. Thus, the term seems to indicate the effects of *samāʿ*, ecstatic reactions and experiences, as much as the 'listening' itself. There is thus a convergence of *samāʿ* with *wajd*, perhaps because of the close associations between the two in practice. For example, Junayd reports a dream in which he questions Iblīs about the opportunities he has for tempting people. Iblīs replies that he 'sees' people who 'fall into *samā*ʿ and *wajd*' (*T.A.* I.276.8). Similarly at *T.A.* II.32.7–10, Junayd explains physical reactions to *samā*ʿ (i.e. the phenomenon of *wajd*) as caused by remembering the joy of the covenant of Alast.

wajd

The term *wajd* and other derivatives from the same root, particularly *tawājud*, are of similar importance to the subject of this study as the previous *samā*ʿ. *wajd* is usually translated into English as 'emotion', 'ecstasy' or 'rapture', and these rather vague equivalents demonstrate the difficulty of finding precise and useful meanings for the word. While 'ecstasy' or 'rapture' may conjure up for us a set of behaviours indicating an unusual state of mind, or a feeling of exhilaration, this is often not what is meant by the use of *wajd* in Sufi writings. The behaviours indicated by *wajd* might include trembling, agitation, sweating, pallor, rigidity, spontaneous speech or crying out, fainting, and so on, and there is often no mention of joy or exhilaration. Such behaviours could well indicate to us a sudden onset of illness or seizure rather than what is normally understood by 'ecstasy'.

Instead of trying to find an English term which describes such behaviours adequately, it may be better to adopt a functional definition. In this way, a working definition of *wajd* might be those behaviours or physical signs resulting from the aural stimuli of *samā*ʿ in its various forms. This definition covers a wide range of behaviours which are associated in Sufi writings with listening to verse, music, sounds, or direct communication with the divine.

The Sufi writers themselves often preferred to 'derive' this word from the root *wajada* in the meaning of 'find, attain, discover, or know by experience'.[9] Ghazālī is representative in his definition of the term thus: 'These states are called in the language of the Sufis *wajd*, derived from *wujūd* ('finding, discovery' and 'encounter'); that is, one encounters in one's self states which were not encountered before listening to music or verse' (*Iḥyā*ʾ II.277.19–20 Mcd. p.229). Hujwīrī, finding other root meanings for the cognates *wajd* and *wujūd*, defines the former as 'grief' or 'pain', and the latter as 'finding' (the object of desire), detailing at length a bipolar explanation of mystical experience in these terms (*Kashf* 538.13ff; Nich. pp.413ff).

Such 'derivations' and attempts at etymology are ingenious, but are ultimately inaccurate, post hoc 'popular' etymologies. They do reveal, however, the way such terms were understood, and they shed some light on the areas of experience designated by these words. These two notions of 'finding' and 'grief', for example, recur often in Sufi discussions about *wajd*, the latter notion often surfacing as 'passion' or 'emotion' more generally. By this means, the physical or functional features outlined above are accounted for, while at the same time both these senses can be traced back to the root meaning of *wajada*.

Qushayrī offers a more grammatically informed approach to *tawājud* (usually meaning 'pretence at, or imitation of ecstasy'). He argues that the term involves 'seeking' or 'summoning' *wajd* by voluntary means; thus it is not a perfect form of *wajd*. For Qushayrī, *tawājud* is not a perfect attainment because it involves much striving and fabrication or pretence, and it remains far from being verifiable (*Ris*. 61).

Sarrāj

A similar approach to that of Ghazālī and Hujwīrī mentioned above is demonstrated in the relevant chapters of Sarrāj's writings. The only attempt at definition, such as that recorded of Junayd, is along the lines of Ghazālī's noted above: that of 'encountering' (*muṣādafa*; *Lumaʿ* 301.2). Yet in several places the 'emotive' aspect of *wajd* is brought to the fore. In a discussion about recitation of the Qur'ān, the author cites *wajd* in a series with *riqqa*, *ṣafā'*, and *taladhdhudh*, 'tenderness, serenity, and delight' (*Lumaʿ* 284.6–7). Elsewhere, *wajd* is juxtaposed with *riqqa* and *hayajān*, the latter meaning 'excitement, agitation', and the former in this case 'sensitivity' (*Lumaʿ* 296.7). Even more indicative of the emotive sense of this term is its use in parallel with *iḥtirāq*, 'burning', describing the arousing effect of some types of *samāʿ* on the heart (*Lumaʿ* 295.14).

These examples show part of the wide semantic range of *wajd*; there is also evidence to show that Sarrāj was aware of a more functional usage. In discussing his theory of what may be called sympathetic resonance, i.e. that *samāʿ* produces a sympathetic emotive response in the listener, the author states that: 'their hearts cannot contain this, and they begin to utter words due to their emotive response (*wajd*)' (*Lumaʿ* 296.16–17). This shows the term being characterised by its effects, in this case uttering words or sounds (*yanṭiqūn*) in an apparently involuntary fashion. Following a discussion of Junayd's explanation of *wajd* as 'encounter', Sarrāj offers his own contribution as follows:

> Do you not see that with one of those (experiencing this) he is quiet at first, and then he becomes agitated and begins to groan and sigh. There may be another who is stronger than this, and he is at rest during his experience, and nothing is evident of these (external signs).
>
> (*Lumaʿ* 301.9–11)

This goes part of the way toward a functional explanation of the phenomenon, in contrast with the theological explanations which preceded. Sarrāj states, however, that external effects are not always indicative of the experience, and thus a purely functional approach is not sufficient.

Ghazālī

As with the other authors being considered, there are numerous examples of the term being used by Ghazālī with little indication of its meaning.

Two examples where functional aspects are highlighted provide some indication of the semantic range. First, in a discussion of the necessity of direct experience to enable true understanding, Ghazālī states that 'the foolish, the frozen, and the hard of heart, who are denied the pleasure of music and poetry, marvel how the listener takes pleasure, and at his ecstasy (*wajd*), disturbance of emotion, and change of colour . . .' (*Iḥyāʾ* II.277.25–26; Mcd. p.230). A second statement is more direct in explaining *wajd* purely as an effect of *samāʿ*: 'Definitive statements concerning *samāʿ* and *wajd* are numerous, and there is no reason to cite many of them, so let us concern ourselves with understanding the meaning for which *wajd* is the expression: we say that it is an expression for a state which *samāʿ* produces; and it is a truthful arrival (*wārid ḥaqq*), following closely from *samāʿ*, and which the listener encounters from his soul' (*Iḥyāʾ* II.290.3–5; Mcd. p.722). This comes close to a functional definition which is not dependent on behavioural symptoms or other external criteria. It is also inclusive in accounting for the whole spectrum of behaviours and psychological states associated with the appearance of *wajd*.

Two other examples of the term being used by Ghazālī illustrate different aspects of its meaning. First, the term is used in association with the verb *wajada*, which is cited in parallel with *ṭariba*, 'be moved by emotion, delight', the sense of one verb following the other, or else used as synonyms. Relating a story of a young boy who threw himself off a mountain in an ecstatic state of marvel at the wonders of God, Ghazālī comments that 'he was so moved by emotion (*ṭariba*), that he fell into an ecstasy (*wajada*), and through the ecstasy cast himself down' (*Iḥyā'* II.279.4; Mcd. p.234).

A related example shows the similarity of the state of *wajd* to that of drunkenness. The author states: 'Of those who fall into ecstasy (*wajd*) there are some overcome by a state similar to drunkenness which confounds their reason' (*Iḥyā'* II.286.21–22; Mcd. p.710).

Hujwīrī

Reference has been made above to Hujwīrī's explanation of *wajd* and *wujūd* which is based on the author's understanding of the root senses of the verb. The explanation centres around *wajd* being taken in the sense of Persian *andūh* ('grief'), and *wujūd* as Persian *yāftan* ('to find'). This distinction leads to a bipolar analysis of the effect of *samāʿ*, as 'grief' at the loss of the beloved, a painful affection of the heart arising from joy or sadness, and 'finding' or attaining the object of desire, removal of grief from the heart, and so on (*Kashf* 538.14ff; Nich. pp.413ff). This scheme is similar to other such bipolar analyses familiar in Sufi literature. Whether the polarity advocated by Hujwīrī is of value remains doubtful in view of the artificiality of his analysis, and his desire to explain a whole range of emotions and states in terms of simple, contrasting elements. The artificiality is also seen in the author's use of the term *wujūd* which is not found elsewhere in discussions of *wajd*, and only appears in later Sufi writings in a different meaning, particularly in connection with Ibn al-ʿArabī's philosophy.[10]

ʿAṭṭār

The hagiographical and non-thematic nature of ʿAṭṭār's writing means that the term *wajd* only arises in a documentary fashion in the context of actual descriptions and recollections of events from the lives of the Sufi masters. Such a non-theoretical approach is valuable, however, in showing the semantic range of the word.

It is related of Sahl Tustarī (d.282/896) that when he heard *samāʿ*, *wajd* would become manifest in him, which included a kind of trance state lasting about three weeks. During this time he would not eat, and though it was winter, he would sweat profusely such that his clothes would be drenched. As well, he declined to speak of his experience during this time, since his words 'would have no benefit' to a listener (*T.A.* I.255.16–20). This is a detailed behavioural description of one of the kinds of state indicated by *wajd*. It shows the profundity of the phenomenon, both in physical terms, and in affecting the thought and speech of the subject.

It is related of Abū Bakr al-Shiblī (d.334/946) on three occasions that he was 'overwhelmed by *wajd*' (*ghalabāt-i wajd*), once with the added description of 'like one who was drunk'. In this state he was summoned before the Caliph's court, and his words in defending himself had such a powerful effect that the Caliph dismissed the charges against Shiblī and sent him home. What is more, the Caliph experienced a mild state of shock himself, confessing that he was afraid of falling from his throne! (*T.A.* II.167.1ff.)

ʿAṭṭār's work also includes a number of short sayings by the Sufi masters on the nature of *wajd*. These are of less value for our purposes, because of their theoretical and theologically influenced character, or else are repetitions of sayings found in the earlier sources already mentioned.

ḥāl

Modern scholars are largely in agreement about the nature of *ḥāl*, usually denoting 'state'. D.B. Macdonald is representative: 'In mysticism a *ḥāl* is a mental condition, given immediately and momentarily by divine grace, not to be gained by application or effort, consisting of joy, sorrow, depression, exaltation etc.'[11] Many writers also contrast *ḥāl* with *maqām* ('stage') by stressing the greater constancy of the latter, and its achievement by human effort rather than as a divine gift.[12] Similarly, Nicholson distinguishes 'stages' as constituting the ascetic and ethical discipline of the Sufi from 'states' which form a psychological chain.[13] In a related way, Massignon defines *ḥāl* as a psychic state, a mystic state, or a state of consciousness.[14]

Lane[15] observes that *ḥāl* may denote 'a fleeting, or quickly transient, quality', and this echoes Ibn Manẓūr's statement that it denotes 'the present moment you are in' (*Lisān* vol.2, p.190). Neither of these sources relates this to mystical usage, but it is clear that Sufi texts often speak of *ḥāl* in this transitory way. This underscores the root verbal meaning of *ḥ-w-l* as 'to change, be transformed, shift'.

Sarrāj

In that part of the *Kitāb al-Lumaʿ* which explains Sufi terminology, Sarrāj offers a definition of *ḥāl* attributed to Junayd, and one attributed to unnamed sources:

> *ḥāl* is what comes upon the servant (of God) at a certain time (or: 'momentarily', *fī 'l-ḥīn*), and it settles in the heart due to the presence of contentment and trust and other qualities. It purifies (the heart) during the occurrence of this state and its momentary presence, then it ceases; this is as Junayd has said. According to others, *ḥāl* is what settles in the inmost heart (*asrār*) due to the purity of one's recollection of God; it does not cease, but if it does cease then this is not *ḥāl*.
>
> (*Lumaʿ* 335.1–4)

These two 'definitions' are quite different, in fact almost contradictory. Junayd's description mentions the transitory nature of *ḥāl*, but the second description stresses its lasting qualities, elsewhere associated with the concept of *maqām*. In line with the modern authorities cited, the divine granting of *ḥāl* is implied in Junayd's phrase, 'what comes upon'. As well, the presence of certain qualities of the heart is mentioned in association with the 'descent' of *ḥāl*.

Junayd's description thus provides a succinct but comprehensive meaning for this widely used term. It may be inferred that, as elsewhere, Sarrāj accepted the view of Junayd, though his actual use of the term will not always coincide with this definition.

As with other writers, Sarrāj uses the term *ḥāl* in several non-mystical senses. First, in the plural meaning 'circumstances': '. . . there is listening to music or verse for various reasons and in diverse circumstances (*liʾaḥwāl shattāʾ*)' (*Lumaʿ* 294.15).

Second, meaning 'condition', 'spiritual constitution' or 'state of being', as at *Lumaʿ* 293.4–5: 'That which you mentioned concerning the weakness of your spiritual constitution (*ḥāluka*), by which you mean your change in composure and your trembling; now what is needed to have a strong state of being (*qūwata 'l-ḥāl*)?' It could be argued that the more usual 'temporary state' applies in both cases here, but the sense of spiritual constitution or condition is more appropriate in the context, given the greater permanence of the state being described.

A third distinct sense is that of an everyday, waking state of consciousness, as at *Luma*ʿ 282.2: 'Then I return to my usual state of consciousness (*aḥwālī*), and to the company of people, and nothing remains of this (warning from the Qur'ān)'; or at *Luma*ʿ 292.15: 'When he returned to his normal state (*ḥāl ṣaḥwihi*), I asked him about what had happened . . .'

The senses of *ḥāl* outlined here are used far less frequently in Sarrāj's work than the usual mystical sense of the term. It is often difficult to give an adequate English translation which covers the mystical sense of *ḥāl*, and the alternatives offered by Massignon, 'psychic state', 'mystic state', or 'state of mystic consciousness' are possible resorts. The term must cover the notions of extraordinary and uncommon states of experience or awareness, including elation, fear, sorrow, perplexity, among a whole range. In Sarrāj's writings, such detailed contextual considerations are not often provided, and thus the qualities of the *ḥāl* being spoken of cannot be specified.

An important distinction here is that Sarrāj uses the term in one of two ways: either in a concrete, phenomenological, experiential sense, or else as an abstract, theoretical term.

The first of these denotes the immediate, experienced psychic state or unusual awareness, often referred to in the course of a narrative about a certain Sufi. Examples include *Luma*ʿ 286.10: 'Meanwhile the young man was saying: "By God, You change me with the Truth when I am in a certain state of awareness (*fī ḥālī*)"'; and *Luma*ʿ 303.2: 'Their momentary experience is disturbed, and their state of awareness (*al-ḥāl*) is altered.'

The second, more abstract sense, sometimes using the plural form *aḥwāl*, describes more didactic or scholarly concepts, such as attainments on the Sufi path portrayed in a schematic or categorical way. For example, at *Luma*ʿ 272.9: '(The second mercy) accords with their knowledge, and they speak only when they have reached the 'states' (*aḥwāl*) of the sincere and the front ranks of the Sufis'; at *Luma*ʿ 290.10: 'This is why some of the Sufi masters superintend the states of awareness (*aḥwāl*) of those lower than their level of attainment.'

ḥāl has a wide range of meanings in the writings of Sarrāj, and it may be assumed that there are further subtleties hidden in his text. Unfortunately the context does not always allow for close identification of the sense intended.

Sulamī

Two occurrences of *ḥāl* are noteworthy in Sulamī's *Ṭabaqāt al-Ṣūfīya.* The first relates to a tradition concerning Abū Ḥafṣ al-Naysābūrī who would not mention the name of God without due reverence. When he mentioned God's name, his *ḥāl* would change so that it was obvious to all those present (*T.S.* 116.6ff). This use of *ḥāl* as 'complexion, countenance, outward aspect' occurs elsewhere in Sufi writings to indicate an inner transformation which shows itself in outward change of appearance. The change usually consists of a brightening or lightening of the countenance, or the appearance of light shining from the face.[16]

The second occurrence of note is the use of *ḥāl* as an equivalent of *wajd*. Abū ʿAbd Allāh al-Ṣubayḥī is reported as saying that when someone experiences *wajd* genuinely, he should be protected against censure or disparaging talk about his *ḥāl* (*T.S.* 330.10–12). It is evident from the text that *ḥāl* is here used interchangeably with wajd.

Qushayrī

Qushayrī's explanation of the term *ḥāl* is similar to that outlined above by Macdonald. The Sufi author understands it as an 'idea' or 'significance' (*maʿnan*) which comes upon the heart unintentionally and without 'acquisition' or conscious striving, such as joy, or sorrow, desire, anxiety, and so on; in other words, a state of consciousness or mind (*Ris.* 57). A *ḥāl* is granted, whereas a *maqām* is acquired and striven for; the former comes from the divine source while the latter results from expending effort; in the latter one is secure, while with a *ḥāl* one advances to the next stage. The transitory aspect, noted in the lexicons, is indicated in Qushayrī's argument that it is just like its name: as it descends (*taḥull*) upon the heart, so it vanishes.[17]

Unfortunately, in the chapter relating to *samāʿ* in the *Risāla*, Qushayrī rarely uses the term *ḥāl* in an illustrative or exemplary sense which might allow for an evaluation of its semantic range.

Ghazālī

The sense of *ḥāl* as equivalent to *wajd* occurs frequently in Ghazālī's writing, the term often referring to phenomena which are the direct effect of *samāʿ*. For instance, at *Iḥyāʾ* II.266.29: 'listening to music or verse yields a state (*ḥāla*) in the heart called *wajd*'. Similarly, at 277.26, Ghazālī states that the person who does not value *samāʿ* 'marvels how the listener takes pleasure, and at his ecstasy (*wajd*), his disturbed state (*iḍṭirāb ḥālihi*), and change of colour'.

The momentary nature of *ḥāl* is emphasised in Ghazālī's comment on the narrative of a young Sufi who fell into an ecstatic state and died after hearing some verses of poetry which he understood as God's word spoken directly to him. Ghazālī states that 'he was immersed in momentary ecstasy (*al-waqt*) in his state (*bi-ḥālihi*) with God' (*Iḥyāʾ* II.286.4; Mcd. p.709).

Later in this same passage, there occurs the notion of *ḥāl* as a pre-existing state of mind, or spiritual constitution, as mentioned in the writings of Sarrāj above. Ghazālī asserts that the youth 'heard what accorded with his *ḥāl*', evidently meaning his already existing state of mind, conscious or not (*Iḥyāʾ* II.286.5; Mcd. ibid). Similarly, the sense of returning to one's usual *ḥāl* (*Iḥyāʾ* II.300.3; Mcd. p.6) has this more permanent sense, though it also carries the meaning of everyday, waking consciousness, as discussed above in relation to Sarrāj.

Finally, as previously indicated in Sarrāj's writings, the theoretical, more abstract sense of *ḥāl* used as a term of academic discussion is also found in Ghazālī's *Iḥyāʾ*. Rather than describing experiential events in a narrative setting, such usage occurs in the more scholarly and didactic sections of the work, as a general theoretical concept (so *Iḥyāʾ* II.288.6; Mcd. p.715; and elsewhere).

Hujwīrī

It was noted above with the concept of *samāʿ* that there was a notable extension of meaning in Hujwīrī's writing. This occurs also with the term *ḥāl*. Hujwīrī uses the term standing alone to indicate specifically 'ecstasy, ecstatic state': 'the novice, in being overwhelmed by *samāʿ*, should have such a state of ecstasy (*ḥāl*) that his *samāʿ* delivers the wicked from their wickedness' (*Kashf* 533.14–15; Nich. p.409; and elsewhere).

ʿAṭṭār

There are several noteworthy additions to the semantic range of *ḥāl* discernible in ʿAṭṭār's writings. First, the meanings of 'condition, spiritual constitution, state of being' noted above with Sarrāj are given a further dimension. In a narrative concerning a disciple of Junayd who used to cry out aloud when the master spoke, ʿAṭṭār relates that the disciple 'kept watch over himself so that his *ḥāl* remained in place' (*T.A.* II.20.16). The evident sense here is 'composure, temperament' or 'state of mind'. A second variation on this sense occurs in ʿAṭṭār's biography of Shiblī where the author recounts that when Shiblī's *ḥāla* was strong, he would go to the mosque in order to preach esoteric teachings (*T.A.* II.166.15). Either the meaning intended here is, as noted with Hujwīrī, 'a state of ecstasy', or else the sense of 'frame of mind, composure', which, on becoming strong, gave Shiblī the courage and zeal to preach publicly the secrets of the Sufis.

Finally, *ḥāl* is used in the sense of 'experience', more specifically 'spiritual experience', or 'experience of the transcendent'. Near the beginning of the biography of Sufyān al-Thawrī (d.161/778), for example, ʿAṭṭār relates an episode of Sufyān's first mystical or transcendent experience, commencing as follows: 'The beginning of his *ḥāl* was that . . .' (*T.A.* I.188.22). Several other examples of this usage occur in ʿAttār's work.

waqt

This term is used quite frequently in many Sufi writings. On occasion it comes close to being a synonym of *ḥāl*. If *waqt* is defined as a very short period of time, distinct from *zamān*,[18] then it can be used to indicate a transitory or quickly passing state. It is thus distinct from *ḥāl* only in its shorter duration.

Massignon, in an article on the concept of time in Islamic thought, argues against this notion of 'state', claiming that atomistic, non-durational 'instants' of time are meant by such terms as *ān* and *waqt*. There are no 'states' or constants in the notion of time, neither in grammar with its verbal aspects, nor in mysticism with its 'instants' of fleeting experience. This outlook is based on the theological construct of God's creative fiat which orders time not as a continuum but as a constellation of instants.[19] In writing of the term in Ḥallāj's experience, Massignon describes *waqt* as 'the dissonance which surprises, the prick that brings one back to consciousness . . . the instant, like the ecstasy, is a transitory thing, a means, not an end, of grace'.[20]

Gerhard Böwering has written more recently that, for the Persian Sufis at least, *waqt* is often interchangeable with *ḥāl* and *ān.* The term is understood as 'the present moment' or the present experience, described imaginatively in Qushayrī's *Risāla* as the sharp edge of a sword, or as bolts of lightning.[21]

Sarrāj underscores the transitory aspect of *waqt* in his 'definition' of the term as: 'what is between the past and the future. Junayd said that *waqt* is precious since what has passed is not attainable, referring to your breath and your *waqt* which is between the breath just past and the one to come; if it passes by while you are negligent in remembering God, then you cannot ever attain it again' (*Luma*ʿ 342.7–10). Defining *waqt* as 'what is between the past and the future' is a round about way of saying it is 'the present instant'. This is reinforced by Junayd's longer explanation concerning the elusiveness of the present moment and its importance and value for remembrance (*dhikr*).

The Arabic lexicons are not very helpful in giving precision to the term *waqt*. If anything, they tend to extend the time indicated by the term to a far lengthier period than the Sufis would claim. Lane speaks of 'A time; or space, or measure, of time, . . . appointed for any affair; a season . . .'[22] There is no indication here of a short period, moment, or instant, as required by the Sufis. There is support, however, for Massignon's philosophical argument about the non-durational and divinely ordained nature of time in the verbal root meaning of 'determined, defined, limited' (as to time). Both Lane and Ibn Manẓūr are clear on this point, the latter defining *waqt* as 'a determined measure of time' (*Lisān*, vol.14, p.107.)

Sarrāj

The transitory aspect of *waqt* is indicated in Sarrāj's discussion of the onset of ecstatic experience where he writes: 'How is it with His chosen ones, those near to Him, with what comes upon them at every moment (*waqt*) and occasion (*zamān*) and in the blinking of an eye, or even less . . . ?' (*Luma*ʿ 314.7–8). The juxtaposition of *ṭarfa ʿayn* (blinking of an eye) indicates the rapid passing of these states.

Sarrāj uses the term in its ordinary non-mystical sense of 'time', 'moment', but it is more common to find the special mystical sense being employed. Here the meaning 'momentary experience or state' is indicated. One example among several is: 'They hear from that something which corresponds to their mystical states and their momentary experiences (*aḥwālahum wa-ʾawqātahum*)' (*Luma*ʿ 278.1). Similarly: 'With regard to their momentary experiences (*awqātihim*) and what overwhelms their hearts . . .' (*Luma*ʿ 296.15). The translation 'experience(s)' seems appropriate on occasion: '(Others) dislike these practices because their states are steadfast, their experience (*wa-ʾawqātahum*) abounds, their recollection of God is pure . . .' (*Lumaʿ* 300.5–6).

Sulamī

There are very few occurrences of the term *waqt* in Sulamī's *Ṭabaqāt al-Ṣūfīya*. One such is in a context which leaves some ambiguity as to whether it is used in a mystical or non-mystical sense. Sulamī records an ecstatic outburst by Junayd, occasioned by a walk through Baghdad alleys in the company of Abū ʾl-ʿAbbās b. Masrūq, where they heard a singer reciting a verse. Junayd was overcome with weeping and began to speak longingly of past times: '. . . I never cease to yearn for the origin of my desire, with a keen path, and terrors as my steed, desirous to attain my goal; but look at me now during days of indolence: I yearn for my past times (*awqātī*)' (*T.S.* 240.12–14). This is the most obvious, perhaps literal, meaning of the key term here, translated as 'times', corresponding to 'days' (*ayyām*) mentioned in the previous phrase. It is likely, given the highly charged and poetic nature of Junayd's utterance, that he is also alluding to these 'times' as 'moments of ecstatic experience' glimpsed in the past. This is more probable when one compares his utterance with the rich, allusive language of Junayd's known writings represented in his letters,[23] as well as the many fragments of utterances recorded in the early Sufi authorities such as Sarrāj and Qushayrī. It is in the style of Junayd's sayings and writings, and congruent with his desire to prevent the divulgence of esoteric Sufi teachings, that such subtlety and allusiveness should be present.[24]

Qushayrī

Qushayrī introduces the notion of divine 'ordering' or foreordainment, perhaps even 'fate', in his explanation of the semantic range of *waqt*. He writes:

> (The Sufis) intend by the term *waqt* what happens to them from that which God disposes toward them, without their choosing it for themselves. They say: 'So and so is under judgement of *waqt*', i.e. that he has submitted to what appeared to him from the transcendent realm (*al-ghayb*) without his choosing.
>
> (*Ris.* 55)

Again there is little use of this term in the *Risāla* apart from this formal discussion of its meaning.

Ghazālī

Ghazālī employs the term *waqt* only rarely in his chapter on *samā*ʿ in the *Iḥyā*ʾ. Two examples are found, the first being a non-mystical usage of *al-awqāt* as 'on occasions' (*Iḥyā*ʾ II.269.3; Mcd. p.209). In any case, this is simply a quotation from a *ḥadīth*, and not Ghazālī's own statement.

In the other occurrence, there is some ambiguity as to whether it is used in a mystical or non-mystical sense. Following a narrative account of a beggar who was overwhelmed and died after hearing some verse recited, Ghazālī comments: 'The purport is that this man considered himself drowning at the time through his state (*mustaghriq al-waqt bi-ḥālihi*) in relation to God . . .' (*Iḥyā*ʾ II.286.4; Mcd. p.709). This is Macdonald's translation; it is possible, however, that Ghazālī meant 'immersed in momentary experience in his state . . .', a rendering that is quite feasible given the frequent juxtaposition of *waqt* and *ḥāl* in Sufi writings. This is more awkward grammatically than Macdonald's translation, however, and there are no other examples of *waqt* used in this mystical sense.

It might be suggested that Ghazālī has avoided the mystical sense of *waqt* for some reason. He had ample opportunity to employ the term, as Sarrāj did frequently, given the similarity of content and genre of the two writers' works.

Hujwīrī

In the two Persian writers being considered, there is a development in the use of *waqt* to mean virtually the equivalent of *ḥāl* or *wajd*, a development which could be said to continue from where Sarrāj left off.

Three examples occur in Hujwīrī's chapters on *samā*ʿ. In the first, there is a clear equivalence with *ḥāl* meaning simply 'state, condition, position' without any reference to mystical concepts. Hujwīrī writes that some people refuse to practise *samā*ʿ because they are neither spiritual adepts, nor superficial or sensual people who indulge in the practice for amusement. The abstainers claim that 'it is preferable for us to be occupied with something suitable to our state (*waqt*)' (*Kashf* 538.2; Nich. p.412). This use of *waqt* appears to be non-mystical, referring to the position of this group of people in relation to other believers. They acknowledge that they are not in the spiritual vanguard, but nor are they intemperate and heedless; they are merely ordinary believers who do not regard the practice of *samāʿ* as suitable for themselves.

In the second occurrence of the term, *waqt* is clearly equivalent to *wajd* meaning 'rapture, intense experience'. In describing the effects of *samāʿ* in causing involuntary movement and agitation, Hujwīrī writes that 'throbbing of the heart becomes manifest, and trembling takes control of the inner self, rapture (*waqt*) becomes intense, (and) a state of trembling becomes evident . . .' (*Kashf* 542.6–7; Nich. p.416). The sense of *waqt* here is either 'rapture', as translated, or perhaps 'moment of intense experience', which reveals the word's etymology.

The third occurrence is somewhat ambiguous as to whether it refers to a mystical 'moment of experience'. Discussing the *ādāb* or etiquette of *samāʿ*, Hujwīri is concerned with the person who is not experiencing any effect, unlike other participants. Such a person should not regard 'in sobriety' those who are 'intoxicated', but they should be 'in quest of their own moment of experience (*waqt*), and establish that moment's dominion, so that they may receive its blessings' (*Kashf* 545.18; Nich. p.419). This appears to be the meaning intended by the author; Nicholson's translation, however, reads: 'but he must keep quiet with his own "time" (*waqt*) and establish its dominion . . .' This is rather equivocal, though Nicholson's translation does highlight the allusiveness of the term.

ʿAṭṭār

The usage of the term *waqt* in ʿAṭṭār's *Tadhkirat* shows clearly that for this Persian writer the meaning of 'state' (=*ḥāl*) in its various senses is dominant.

Sahl Tustarī is reported to have been overcome by *samāʿ* on occasion, whereupon he would go into a kind of trance for some weeks, would not eat, and so on. If he was asked questions during that period, he would reply that what he had to say 'in this state (*waqt*) would be of benefit to no-one' (*T.A.* I.255.19–20). This clearly refers to the 'state' of dissociation or trance brought on by his listening to *samāʿ*.

Three other examples show the meaning of *waqt* to be synonymous with 'mood'. A disciple of Yūsuf b. al-Ḥusayn (d.304/916–7) recited some secular verse to his master, whereupon 'his mood (*waqt*) became cheerful' (*T.A.* I.319.2). Abū Ḥafṣ al-Ḥaddād (d.265/878–9) ventured into the desert with some companions and spoke to them; 'their mood (*waqt*) became cheerful' (*T.A.* I.324.12). Similarly, 'It is related that one day Shiblī's mood (*waqtash*) was cheerful, and he went to the bazaar . . .' (*T.A.* II.166.12). These examples all show a common idiom, not merely 'momentary experience', itself a development from the root idea of *waqt* as 'moment', but a longer lasting, more stable 'state' of experience. Perhaps the best English equivalent in these cases is 'mood', in the sense of disposition, temperament, or frame of mind.

qalb

This word is one of the most difficult in the Sufi vocabulary, both in terms of its meaning, and in finding an adequate translation. It is an important and widely used concept within Sufi psychology.

Traditional lexicography has difficulty in attempting to define the core meaning of the term, since *qalb* is seen by lexicographers to involve 'changeability'. Thus Ibn Manẓūr cites Qur'ān 24.37 where the 'turning about' or 'commotion' (*tataqallabu*) of hearts is mentioned. In this verse, the heart's knowing the promises of the Day of Resurrection is explained as the reason for its disquiet (*Lisān*, vol.10, pp.685–6). Such associations of changeability and commotion are an unlikely derivational basis for the usual description of the heart as the seat of knowledge.

Despite the lexicographical complications, however, the heart has traditionally been viewed as the apprehender of divine knowledge. Nicholson explains: 'Whereas the intellect cannot gain real knowledge of God, the *qalb* is capable of knowing the essences of all things, and when illuminated by faith and knowledge reflects the whole content of the divine mind.'[25] From Qur'ānic usage on, this knowledge has been more than merely intellectual. It involves the conscience, one's actions and obedience of the whole life, as L. Gardet's explanation of the heart suggests: '(It is) the organ of conscience and seat of religious knowledge and of life in the presence of God'.[26]

While 'heart' is the usual English equivalent for *qalb*, it is inadequate as a meaning for the 'organ' which 'sees by the light of unification and love',[27] or apprehends divine knowledge, particularly when there is only a tenuous and mysterious connection with the physical organ.[28] One alternative might be 'soul', provided this term is understood as the apprehender of knowledge. *qalb* is probably much closer to our 'mind' or 'soul', as suggested by Lane's definition:[29] 'The mind, secret thoughts and the soul . . . the mind, meaning the intellect or intelligence.'

Sarrāj

It is perhaps curious to discover that in Sarrāj's writings the notion of *qalb* as the receiver of divine knowledge is found infrequently. There are some examples, however, such as where Dhū 'l-Nūn is reported to have described *samāʿ* as 'the occurrence of Truth which arouses hearts to the Truth' (*Lumaʿ* 271.9). Similarly, Sarrāj quotes Yaḥyā b. Muʿādh (d.258/872) as saying that 'the word of wisdom that arises from the heart has an effect upon the heart' (*Lumaʿ* 295.11).

What is more often found is the notion of *qalb* as being attentive to revelation, or the recital of the Qur'ān or other means of *samāʿ*, and as a spiritual and emotional entity often overwhelmed by revelations. It may be described as 'burning', or as experiencing emotions such as grief or joy. There is one instance which may well provide the key to reconcile these apparently disparate senses of *qalb* involving knowledge and emotion. Sarrāj writes that 'God has made it known concerning hearts that they observe and understand, and that is ecstasy (*wajd*) for them' (*Lumaʿ* 301.6). This suggests that the heart does lay claim to knowledge, gained by observation and understanding, and that this knowledge involves an emotional and ecstatic element rather than a purely intellectual content. This agrees with the widespread Sufi notion that knowledge of God is much more than a rational exercise, and that it involves direct, intuitive and ecstatic apprehension. If this reasoning holds true, it provides an explanation for the frequent use of *qalb* in an emotional and experiential sense. It is the entity which is attentive to, and is sometimes overcome by, divine revelation, or which experiences the heightened emotion of *wajd*.

In its attentiveness to revelation or to *samāʿ*, Sarrāj writes: 'Reliable Traditions regarding listening to the Qur'ān show that presence of heart is required, as well as close consideration, contemplation and recollection. They also describe what the listener's heart encounters during recitation' (*Lumaʿ* 283.2–3). There is also mention elsewhere of the necessity of superintending the heart during prayer, and of praying with 'presence of heart' (*Lumaʿ* 293.12–13; 302.9).

On occasion *qalb* is used in a sense similar to the English 'heart' meaning the seat of sensitivity and feeling. Sarrāj writes that 'one may perhaps complete many recitations of the Qur'ān without finding *riqqa* (sensitivity or feeling) in one's heart from having recited' (*Luma'* 284.2–3). Similarly, 'when he (Isrāfīl, a teacher of Dhū 'l-Nūn) saw me he said: "Would you not do well to recite some verse?" I said: "No". He said: "You have no heart"' (*Luma'* 288.13). This appears much like the English sense of feeling or kindness.

The sense of *qalb* experiencing heightened emotion or states occurs quite frequently in Sarrāj. An illustrative example shows it as the receiver of *wajd* and *ḥāl*: 'If the listener is not experiencing a special state, and there is no disclosure of emotion in the heart, there only reaches him what has been heard from the Qur'ān . . .' (*Luma'* 283.4).

Finally, it must be noted that *qalb* often occurs in juxtaposition with the word *sirr*, these two terms sometimes being indistinguishable in meaning. For example: 'One hears (divine) address with attentive ears, an observant heart and a pure soul (*sirrin*)' (*Luma'* 302.9); '. . . an exhortation or maxim which appealed to him and which stirred up strong emotion in his inner soul (*sirrihi*), or a burning in his heart' (*Luma'* 295.13–14).

Qushayrī

In the *Risāla*, Qushayrī also refers to the term *qalb* as a spiritual organ sensitive to revelations or the recital of *samā'*. Qushayrī writes of *qalb* as the place which *samā'* affects 'in a special state (*ḥāl*), in the purity of its arrival' (*Ris.* 336).

Qushayrī mentions elsewhere the notion of the heart as a 'living' entity, presumably referring to its spiritual life. He quotes his master, Abū 'Alī al-Daqqāq, as saying that *samā'* is a legally recommended action (*mustaḥabb*) for 'our companions' (i.e. Sufis) because their hearts are 'alive' (*Ris.* 340).

Ghazālī

At one point in the *Iḥyā'*, Ghazālī comes close to a definition of *qalb*. He writes: 'I do not mean by the "heart" the flesh and blood, but a subtle secret entity which has a hidden relationship to the visible organ behind which is the secret entity of the spirit deriving from the command of God.'[30]

The emphasis on the non-material and transcendent nature of the heart in this statement is accompanied by a wide range of meanings in Ghazālī's use of the term in his writings.

The *qalb* is sensitive and open to the effects of *samā'*: 'There is no access to hearts except by the anteroom of auditory stimuli; . . . *samā'* is the true touchstone for the heart' (*Iḥyā'* II.266.18–20; Mcd. p.199; and elsewhere). *samā'* rouses 'what is in the heart' by way of hidden spiritual treasures and the remembrance of what God has placed there (*Iḥyā'* ibid., and elsewhere).

There is often reference made to the heart as either being 'on fire' or as causing fire: '*samā'* . . . is what strengthens one's passion and love, and it inflames the kindling of one's heart, bringing forth from it states of revelations . . . ; these states are causes of other actions which burn up the heart with their fires and purify them . . .' (*Iḥyā'* II.277.17–20; Mcd. p.229). Similarly poetry 'acts the part of the fire steel which lights the kindling of one's heart. Its flames blaze up and longing is aroused . . . causing states not usually encountered' (*Iḥyā'* II.285.16–7; Mcd. p.706). There is reference also to hearts being 'inflamed' by love of God or by the fire of His love (*Iḥyā'* II.266.6; Mcd. p.198). The notion of 'light' shining in hearts is also found: 'When they taste *wajd* and its light is spread in their hearts, all doubt and uncertainty falls away' (*Iḥyā'* II.289.17–8; Mcd. p.720).

The effect of *samā'* in causing 'fire' and 'light' in hearts is to purify and to animate them to greater love and nearness to God. *samā'* follows the paths of the heart toward the spiritual world (*Iḥyā'* II.289.32; Mcd. p.721). Furthermore, '*samā'* produces purity of heart which causes revelation . . . and it is strengthened to witness what it was unable to beforehand' (*Iḥyā'* II.290.17–8; Mcd. p.723). The revelation of new 'states' and of witnessing divine realities results from the purifying action of *samā'* and its cleansing 'fires' or 'light'. This is where the heart's real purpose is found: 'The task of the heart is seeking after revelation and beholding the secrets of the Kingdom' (*Iḥyā'* II.290.19; Mcd. p.723). This defines the heart as the apprehender of divine knowledge, not intellectual understanding, but intimately witnessing and experiencing the secrets of the divine realm.

Hujwīrī

In Persian, the word which closely corresponds to Arabic *qalb* is *dil.* This term is nearly always used where we would expect *qalb* if the writing was in Arabic, and there is a similar range of meanings with the Persian word.[31]

Hujwīrī uses the term in a particular sense as the seat of emotion and joy. He recounts that a man accompanying Ibrāhīm Khawwās (d.291/904) on a journey said: 'A thrill of emotion came to my heart' (*Kashf* 534.15; Nich. p.410). Similarly, in describing the effects of *samāʿ*, Hujwīrī writes that 'a feeling of lightness comes upon the heart' (*Kashf* 542.6; Nich. p.416). This relates back to the usage of *qalb* in Sarrāj as a spiritual or emotional entity, sometimes being overwhelmed by revelations or ecstasy.

The heart as the centre of ascetic aspirations and spiritual life is seen in Hujwīrī's use of the term in the context of renunciation and asceticism. He writes of those who are remote from evildoing by means of their 'self mortification and austerities and spiritual renunciation of all created things' (*Kashf* 537.18; Nich. p.412). 'Spiritual renunciation' here is literally 'detachment of the heart' (*inqiṭāʿ-i dil*).

The heart is also used to refer to the centre of spiritual knowledge, or the 'mind', as Nicholson translates: '*Tawājud* is "taking pains to produce *wajd*", by representing to one's mind (*dil*), for example, the bounties and evidences of God . . .' (*Kashf* 541.9–10; Nich. p.415).

ʿAṭṭār

The heart as a place where light shines, noted with Ghazālī's use of *qalb*, is also evident in ʿAṭṭār's use of *dil*. An eminent Sufi related that he passed by an assembly where Aḥmad b. Ḥarb (d.234/849) was engaged in discourse. While the Sufi remained there, his heart became light like the 'sun of forty years' (*T.A.* I.242.4–7). ʿAṭṭār also relates that Sarī al-Saqaṭī performed an act of kindness to an orphan child; immediately Sarī saw a light in his own heart, and his complexion changed colour (*T.A.* I.270.14–22).

Among many other instances of *dil* in familiar senses, ʿAṭṭār uses the term *sukhta-dil*, literally 'burned of heart' in describing a youth who is anxious, troubled in mind, or depressed (*T.A.* II.166.21). It is argued in the chapters on the psychology of *samāʿ* that this description of the youth as 'troubled in heart' is not a mere rhetorical flourish. It is an indication of a pre-existing anxiety state which helps explain the youth's sudden collapse and death when he is spoken to by Shiblī.

Notes

1 William James, *The Varieties of Religious Experience*, Glasgow: Collins, 1960 (1982), p.367.

2 Louis Massignon, *Essai sur les origines du lexique technique de la mystique musulmane*, nouvelle éd., Paris: J. Vrin, 1954; Paul Nwyia, *Exégèse coranique et langage mystique*, second edition, Beirut: Dar el-Machreq, 1991.

3 See Carl W. Ernst, 'Mystical Language and the Teaching Context in the Early Lexicons of Sufism', in Steven T. Katz (ed.), *Mysticism and Language*, New York, NY: Oxford University Press, 1992, pp.181–201; and ʿAbd al-Razzāq al-Qāshānī, *A Glossary of Sufi Technical Terms*, transl. Nabil Safwat, London: Octagon Press, 1991.
4 John A. Haywood, *Arabic Lexicography: Its History, and its Place in the General History of Lexicography*, second edition, Leiden: E.J. Brill, 1965, p.78.
5 E.W. Lane, *An Arabic–English Lexicon*, Cambridge: Islamic Texts Society Trust, repr. 1984; R. Dozy, *Supplément aux dictionnaires arabes*, 2 vols, Leiden: Brill, and Paris: Maisonneuve, 1881.
6 Lane, ibid., p.1429.
7 Muḥammad b. Mukarram Ibn Manẓūr, *Lisān al-ʿArab*, Beirut: Dār Ṣādir, Dār Bayrūt, 15 vols, 1955–6.
8 Jean During, article *samāʿ* in *E.I.*, vol.8, p.1018.
9 Lane, op.cit., 2924.
10 See A.E. Affifi, *The Mystical Philosophy of Muhyid Din Ibnul Arabi*, Lahore: Ashraf, 1979 repr., Chapter 1.
11 *Shorter Encyclopaedia of Islam*, Leiden: E.J. Brill, 1953 (1974), p.127; Similarly, R.A. Nicholson, *The Mystics of Islam*, New York, NY: Schocken Books, 1975 repr., p.29.
12 Ibid.
13 Nicholson, *The Mystics of Islam*, op.cit.
14 Massignon, *Essai*, op.cit., pp.191, 211, 305.
15 Lane, op.cit., p.675.
16 See *Iḥyāʾ* II.277.26; Mcd. p.230; and ʿAṭṭār, *T.A.* II.183.3–8.
17 Ibid.
18 As defined by R. Dozy, *Supplément*, op.cit., vol.2, p.827.
19 Louis Massignon, 'Le temps dans la pensée islamique', in *Opera Minora*, vol.2, Beirut: Dar al-Maaref-Liban, 1963, pp. 606–12.
20 Louis Massignon, *The Passion of al-Hallāj*, transl. H. Mason, Princeton, NJ: Princeton University Press, 1982, vol.2, pp.68–9.
21 Gerhard Böwering, 'Ideas of time in Persian Sufism', in Leonard Lewisohn (ed.), *Classical Persian Sufism: From its Origins to Rumi*, London: Khaniqahi Nimatullahi Publications, 1993, pp.223–4.
22 Lane, op.cit., p.2958.
23 See Ali Hassan Abdel-Kader, *The Life, Personality and Writings of Al-Junayd*, London: Luzac, 1976.
24 Ibid., pp.53–9.
25 Nicholson, *The Mystics of Islam*, op.cit., p.68.
26 L. Gardet, article *ḳalb* in *E.I.*, vol.4, p.487.
27 So Hujwīrī describes the Persian equivalent *dil* in *Kashf* 38.6; Nich. p.33.
28 On this mysterious connection, see Al-Qāshānī, *A Glossary of Sufi Technical Terms*, op.cit., p.97.
29 Lane, op.cit., p.2554.
30 Iḥyāʿ II.288.26–8; Mcd. p.717. Cf. Al-Ghazālī, *Al-Munqidh min al-Ḍalāl*, ed. Jamīl Salība et al., Beirut: Dār al-Andalus, 1996, p.151.
31 See I.A. Vullers, *Lexicon Persico-Latinum etymologicum*, Graz: Akademische Druck-u.Verlagsanstalt, 1962 repr., vol.1, p.889.

4

THE PSYCHOLOGY OF *SAMĀʿ* (PART 1)

Introduction

The source writings studied in this book contain many descriptions of unusual states of mind and behaviours manifested by Sufis both famous and unknown, and by ordinary people overcome with intense religious experiences. In the following two chapters these descriptions are brought together and compared to similar phenomena known to modern psychology.

A previous work which covers part of this area is Gilbert Rouget's *Music and Trance*, first published in the 1970s.[1] Rouget's work deals with the theoretical issues, particularly his distinction between 'ecstasy' and 'trance', and between 'ritualised' and 'non-ritualised' trance resulting from *samāʿ*. His work is extremely valuable and groundbreaking, but its brevity and lack of detail concerning the phenomena recorded in the early sources limit its worth. In the intervening years since publication of this work, much important research has been carried out in this rapidly expanding area of psychology. In Islamic studies, however, there has been little substantial progress made in the psychology of *samāʿ*. The exception to this is Jean During's *Musique et extase*, which is admirable for its handling of the rites, the literature, and the theoretical issues of *samāʿ*.[2] Discussion of the psychological aspects of the topic, and of the specific behavioural phenomena found in the early source writings, is lacking in During's work. The present study does not claim to be comprehensive, but it does attempt to deal with these issues not adequately covered by previous works.

At the outset it is important to acknowledge several limitations on any analysis of the subject in question. The philosophical and methodological issues which must be confronted are daunting. It is generally accepted that the available source writings describe experiences that go beyond the bounds of ordinary consciousness. As Moshe Idel argues, however, there are important implications in this acceptance for the study of these phenomena: 'At its best, the mystic's testimony is a veil covering a psychic process that as such must remain beyond the scope of textual studies'.[3] He goes on to claim that 'The chance of success in reconstructing the nature of a mystical experience from written texts is close to nil.'[4] Researchers from a psychological background may tend to explain in a reductionist way, given the nature of their science. Even if this is not the case, the varying and allusive components involved – the human psyche, external and internal conditions, and 'supernatural' aspects of the experience – make the process of reconstruction a very hazardous undertaking.

In the present case, there can be little escape from this sceptical position argued by Idel. There is very little chance of understanding the nature of a particular experience from the scant details contained in the early Sufi source writings. Most of the descriptions in these sources are at best second-hand accounts, even if their transmission over the intervening millennium is trustworthy. Most provide only the briefest of details, and many are simply descriptions of external behaviours.

It is clear that the modern researcher cannot hope to approach an account of the experiences of these early Sufi mystics. Given the available data, one cannot attempt a representation of their psyche or their states of consciousness. What can be reconstructed, however, are patterns of unusual behaviours and physical signs which allow for identification of the types of altered state behaviours, trance patterns and other dissociative states known more thoroughly from modern psychology. It is not possible to know the precise nature of the altered state involved; the evidence is purely literary, briefly stated, distant by approximately a millennium, and reaches across a vastly different cultural context. Yet the repetition of detail, and hence the emergence of patterns, as well as the evidence of similar phenomena available in the present day, allows for an approximation which is useful for the purposes of modern psychology and Islamic studies.

Methodologically, there are two important limitations on the textual evidence available from the source writings. The first has been mentioned above, namely the brevity of description, and paucity of detail afforded by the sources. This means that the 'behavioural' or functional approach attempted here is limited by the scarcity of detail contained in the primary evidence. This is somewhat compensated for by the frequent number of incidents of altered states attested in the sources. The similarity of details recorded also allows for some confidence in the patterning of behaviour which can be reconstructed.

The second question which arises concerns that of the reliability and authenticity of the accounts contained in the source writings. Many of these are clearly 'traditions' handed down orally, and only later committed to writing. In the later authors, particularly ʿAṭṭār, there is some evidence of accretion to the narratives originally recorded by earlier sources. One example concerns ʿAṭṭār's account of the death of the famed mystic, Nūrī. In Sarrāj's *Luma*ʿ, Nūrī suffered cuts and wounds to his legs from sharp reeds while wandering around in a trance-like state after attending a *samā*ʿ session (*Luma*ʿ 290.11–17). In ʿAṭṭār's version, there is the pious addition that the blood which dropped from his leg wounds formed the word Allāh on the ground (*T.A.* II.55.5–12). ʿAṭṭār also adds other incidental details to the account of Nūrī's death, claiming Sarrāj as his authority, yet these details do not occur in Sarrāj's text at all.

Clearly this process of pious accretion must be acknowledged, and this leads the modern reader to rely more heavily on the earlier texts. Fortunately for our present purposes, the earliest and most authoritative source, Sarrāj's *Luma*ʿ, contains the majority of narrative accounts dealing with altered state behaviours. Most of the later sources repeat these accounts more or less verbatim, but Sarrāj, who was nearer to the actual events, remains the dominant authority. As for this author's reliability, the fact that his work was an apologetic treatise on Sufi practice means that he would not have included bizarre or extreme behaviours in his accounts of the mystics. Any such outlandishness would have brought the Sufis into more disrepute, and would have undermined his purpose. Given the traditional, conservative training of Sarrāj, and his well-known 'sobriety' of outlook, the narratives which he has preserved would, if anything, err on the side of caution. He is more likely to have understated any accounts of unusual behaviours, and to have ascertained the authenticity of his sources beforehand.

Finally, there is the question of terminology for the unusual behaviours and states about which we are speaking. Up to this point in the study, they have been referred to by a variety of terms, such as 'altered states', 'dissociation states', 'states of consciousness', 'ecstatic states', 'trance-like states', and so on. The reason for this is that a general range of behaviours is being alluded to, rather than a specific condition which could justify a scientifically accurate designation. Moreover, it is clear that not just one condition is being referred to, but a number of associated behaviours, and to prefer one term over another without evidential justification would be misleading and would appear to pre-ordain a particular 'correct' designation. What is more, even if there is certainty about the actual condition being referred to by the early sources, there is still no consensus in modern psychology regarding the appropriate terminology. It is thus preferable to refer to these states in a general, non-specific way, even if this results in some vagueness and lack of precision.

Description of the evidence

In this section, evidence is presented for the physical and behavioural effects of *samāʿ* upon which a psychological assessment is based. This evidence consists mostly of reports from eyewitnesses of unusual behaviours or accounts of altered state episodes recorded in the source writings.

In these accounts, there is often mention of more than one physical effect or behaviour arising from *samāʿ*, and for the purposes of this study these different effects are considered separately.

For example, one account recorded by Ghazālī in the *Iḥyāʾ* mentions an unnamed practitioner of *samāʿ* who heard a verse being recited; the melody and words excited him and he went into 'ecstasy' (*wajd*). He began repeating the verse, substituting the letter *nūn* for the letter *tāʾ* of the verbal prefixes, thereby changing the referents of meaning, until he fainted with joy and pleasure (*Iḥyāʾ* II.285.22–26). This account shows evidence of several behavioural effects. The man became excited; he began repeating the verse in what would seem to be an automatic, involuntarily fashion, due to the ecstasy; he eventually fainted; and it is also noted that he was overtaken by joyous feelings. Each of these effects can be considered as separate behavioural entities, although they are of course related. Such terms as 'being overcome by ecstasy (*wajd*)' is not considered as a separate entity since this is an overall description of the state. It does not include specific information about the behaviour of the person, and in any case 'being overcome by *wajd*', or a similar description, is assumed as a preliminary in all these cases.

The following tabular summary presents a brief but comprehensive overview of the range of behaviours and effects found in the source writings. Each discrete effect or behaviour is recorded as a single item, and the groupings range from the most positive and beneficial, such as 'healing effects' and 'joyful feelings', through more neutral effects, to negative, unpleasant and sometimes pathological effects, ending in 'attempt at suicide' and 'sudden death'.

Physical–behavioural effects of *samāʿ*.

A Healing effect:	Known to soothe crying infants (*Lumaʿ*)
	Treatment of melancholia in ancient times (*Lumaʿ*)
	Junayd restores to consciousness person who fainted (*Lumaʿ*; *Ris*; *Iḥyāʾ*)
	Makkī's ill follower restored by recitation (*T.S.*)
B Joyful, pleasurable feelings:	An unnamed *samāʿ* hearer (*Iḥyāʾ*)
	Yūsuf b.al-Ḥusayn at recitation of secular verse (*Lumaʿ*; *Ris*; *Iḥyāʾ*; *T.A.*)
C Unspecified arousal:	An unnamed *samāʿ* hearer (*Iḥyāʾ*)
	Companion of Abū Ḥafṣ during *samāʿ* (*T.S.*)
D Rising in ecstasy:	Companions of Abū Qāsim b.Marwān (*Lumaʿ*; *Iḥyāʾ*)
	Dhū 'l-Nūn and his imitator (*Lumaʿ*; *Iḥyāʾ*; *Ris*)
	Muḥāsibī at a recitation (*T.S.*)
	ʿAbdallāh Ḥanẓala at verse, and can't sit (*Kashf*)
	Nūrī in trance leading to death (*Lumaʿ*; *Iḥyāʾ*)
	Nūrī's companions at recitation (*Lumaʿ*)
	Yūsuf b.al-Ḥusayn at secular verse (*T.A.*)
E Ecstatic utterances:	Nūrī's last trance; repeating verse (*Lumaʿ*; *Iḥyāʾ*)
	Shiblī in mosque; repeating verse (*Lumaʿ*; *Ris*; *Iḥyāʾ*)
	Samnūn cried out and spoke ecstatically (*T.S.*)
	Junayd wept and spoke ecstatically (*T.S.*)
	Shiblī when his *ḥāla* was strong (*T.A.*)
	Sahl Tustarī in a trance (*Lumaʿ*; *T.A.*)
F Making face to glow:	Sarī al-Saqaṭī; 'like moon' (*Lumaʿ*)
	Shiblī in mosque; turned 'red' (*Iḥyāʾ*)
G Loss of colour (in face):	Shiblī in mosque (*Lumaʿ*)
(in hair):	The Prophet at recitation of Qurʾān (*Iḥyāʾ*; *Kashf*)
H Suppression of appetite:	Sahl Tustarī fasted 24–25 days (*Lumaʿ*; *T.A.*)

I Perspiring:	Sahl Tustarī (*Lumaʿ*; *Ris*; *T.A.*) A disciple of Junayd (*Lumaʿ*; *Ris*; *Iḥyāʾ*)
J Tremor, agitation:	Shiblī in mosque (*Lumaʿ*; *Ris*) (shoulder blade acc. to *Iḥyāʾ*) Sahl Tustarī 'to point of falling' (*Lumaʿ*; *Ris*) Unspecific references (*Lumaʿ*; *Iḥyāʾ*; *Kashf*) Shiblī's agitation at not being able to commit suicide (*T.A.*) A youth just prior to his death, at being spoken to by Shiblī (*T.A.*) Caliph who dismissed charges against Shiblī for murder of youth in above story (*T.A.*)
K Sighing, groaning, crying out:	Companions of Prophet (*Lumaʿ*; *Iḥyāʾ*) Shiblī in mosque (*Lumaʿ*; *Ris*; *Iḥyāʾ*) Junayd's disciple (*Lumaʿ*; *Iḥyāʾ*; *T.A.*; *Kashf*) A beggar hearing verse (*Lumaʿ*; *Ris*; *Iḥyāʾ*; *Kashf*) A man questioning Junayd (*Lumaʿ*; *Iḥyāʾ*) ʿUtba al-Ghulām hearing verse (*Iḥyāʾ*) An unnamed Sufi hearing Qurʾān verse (*Iḥyāʾ*) Samnūn cried out and spoke (*T.S.*) Abū Ḥafṣ (*T.A.*) Sound of hissing or boiling in the Prophet's heart when he prayed (*Iḥyāʾ*)
L Weeping:	The Prophet at Qurʾān recital (*Iḥyāʾ*) Companions of the Prophet (*Iḥyāʾ*) Yūsuf b.al-Ḥusayn (*Lumaʿ*; *Ris*; *Iḥyāʾ*) 'variant' account in *T.A.* Companion of Abū Ḥafṣ (*T.S.*) Junayd on hearing a verse (*T.S.*)
M Loss of sensitivity to pain:	Nūrī; cut by sharp canes (*Lumaʿ*; *Iḥyāʾ*; *T.A.*) Junayd and Sarī argue over pain caused by being hit by a sword (*Lumaʿ*) Abū Ḥafṣ touched hot iron from the furnace (*T.A.*)
N Fainting, loss of consciousness:	Sarī's disciple restored by Junayd (*Lumaʿ*; *Ris*; *Iḥyāʾ*) Companions of the Prophet (*Lumaʿ*; *Iḥyāʾ*) The Prophet at Qurʾān verse (*Iḥyāʾ*) Abū Ḥulmān hearing street crier (*Lumaʿ*; *Ris*) Sarī speaking to Junayd (*Lumaʿ*) An unnamed *samāʿ* hearer (*Iḥyāʾ*) Dhū ʾl-Nūn fell to ground (*Lumaʿ*; *Ris*; *Iḥyāʾ*) ʿUtba al-Ghulām hearing verse (*Iḥyāʾ*) Ibrāhīm Khawwāṣ (*Kashf*)
O Restless wandering:	Nūrī in trance leading to death (*Lumaʿ*; *Iḥyāʾ*) Nūrī with a brick (*Lumaʿ*; *Iḥyāʾ*; *T.A.*) Al-Duqqī at night (*Lumaʿ*) (Al-Raqqī in *Ris*) Shiblī's restlessness (*T.A.*)

P	Loss of voluntary control of limbs:	General catalogue of effects (*Lumaʿ*)
Q	Throwing oneself (or being thrown) to the ground:	A disciple of Ḥasan of Baṣra at Qurʾān verse (*T.A.*)
R	Attempt at suicide:	'Israelite' youth on mountain (*Iḥyāʾ*) Shiblī tries by various means (*T.A.*)
S	Sudden death:	Many who heard the prophet David (*Lumaʿ*) Companions of the Prophet (*Lumaʿ*; *Iḥyāʾ*) A disciple of Junayd (*Lumaʿ*; *Iḥyāʾ*; *T.A.*) A beggar hearing verse (*Lumaʿ*; *Ris*; *Iḥyāʾ*) Disciples of two shaykhs (*Lumaʿ*) A man drowned in Euphrates (*Iḥyāʾ*) Junayd's questioner 'departed' (*Lumaʿ*) 'died' (*Iḥyāʾ*) Audiences of Yaḥyā Muʿādh while preaching in Khurāsān (*T.A.*) Audience of Junayd while preaching (*T.A.*) A youth spoken to by Shiblī (*T.A.*) Others mentioned briefly in *Kashf*.

It was noted above that several of the narrative accounts used as the basis for this table include more than one behavioural effect. This means that the listing of these effects makes for a longer table than might otherwise be justified. These discrete effects also tend to be homogenised by such a tabular summary as that given above. Some of these behaviours may have been more significant than others at the time of their occurrence, but given the nature of the evidence, these shortcomings can hardly be avoided. In any case, it is the overall pattern of behaviours which emerges as the important outcome of this evidence, not individual peculiarities.

The behaviours and the narrative accounts from which they derive will shortly be examined in detail, but for the moment it is worth making some initial observations based on the above summary.

First, it must be noted that there are some behavioural effects which occur frequently, and which could be said to be indicative for the condition(s) caused by *samāʿ*. These include D, Rising in ecstasy, E, Ecstatic utterances, J, Tremor and agitation, K, Groaning or crying out, L, Weeping, N, Fainting or loss of consciousness, and S, Sudden death. Not all of these effects can be considered together, however, since not one of the narrative sources includes a case where all, or even the majority, of these effects coincide at the one time. There is one case where three of these effects coincide, the case of Shiblī in the mosque, and one example where two effects are recorded, that of Nūrī's last ecstasy. Yet both of these cases also contain other elements which may suggest different conditions operating. This leads to an initial observation that more than one particular condition or 'outcome state' is in operation here. Indeed, this seems to be part of the argument of the source writers themselves: that there are many facets to the outcome of *samāʿ* and that it is not appropriate to reduce these to a single state.

A second general observation to be made from this table is the infrequency of any specific mention of joyful and pleasurable feelings arising from *samāʿ*. There are only two instances where such feelings are noted, though there are also two specific cases of healing effects, and some other minor references. There are also two cases of unspecified arousal, which may include joyful feelings, though this is not actually stated.

The reason why this is significant is that Sufi writers, ancient and modern, often refer to the beneficial, therapeutic and pleasurable effects of the practice of *samāʿ*.[5] Indeed, the pleasurable and sensual aspect of the practice was part of the reason for its disapproval by conservative scholars and authorities.[6] In this catalogue of effects, however, it is clear that there are far more neutral as well as decidedly unpleasant and pathological outcomes. These latter could hardly be characterised as joyful or beneficial unless one ascribes to a more sadistic philosophy which goes beyond the usual instrumental view of the benefits of suffering.[7] Nor is there any mention of *samāʿ* as a means of suffering in the early Sufi sources. Such ascetic practices and austerities which engendered physical or mental anguish are regarded as distinct from the practice of *samāʿ*. The lack of emphasis on pleasure in the source texts could be because it is less obviously manifested relative to the other behaviours mentioned. It may also be a suspect outcome for theological or other cultural reasons.

Other observations may be made, but these are best left to a more detailed examination of the evidence which will be attempted in the next section.

Analysis of the evidence for physical/behavioural effects

A Healing effect

Under this category, the first two pieces of evidence presented by the earliest source are general statements about the therapeutic effect of music and beautiful sounds. First, Sarrāj in his *Kitāb al-Lumaʿ*

writes that music or sweet sounds can soothe and put to sleep a crying infant (*Lumaʿ* 269.13–14), this general statement being demonstrated by universal experience. It is next stated that the ancients (*al-awāʾil*) treated melancholia with music and sweet sounds (*Lumaʿ* 269.15–16). This is a reference to ancient Greek physicians, for by Sarrāj's time there were translations of the Greek writings of Hippocrates and the Pythagoreans readily available to the scholarly community.[8]

It would appear that a variety of 'music therapy' was practised in the Middle East at that time, as demonstrated by an interesting reference in Hujwīrī's *Kashf al-Maḥjūb*. He writes that: 'In a hospital in Turkey they have invented a wonderful thing called *ingilyūn* [Greek: *evangelion*] . . . it resembles a stringed musical instrument, and on two days of the week they bring the sick to listen to it for a length of time according to their illness' (*Kashf* 531.7–12; Nich. p.407).[9]

The two other examples listed under this category are narrative accounts dealing with actual cases of healing by aural means. First, there is an unusual case of a 'homoeopathic' cure being procured by the very means which produced the condition in the first place. Sarrāj, Qushayrī and Ghazālī[10] relate that Junayd once visited Sarī al-Saqaṭī and found there a man who had fallen unconscious upon the recital of a Qurʾānic verse. Junayd suggested that the same verse be recited again, whereupon the man recovered. On being questioned about this cure, Junayd related that he considered the case of the patriarch Jacob's blindness (Qurʾān, Sūra 12) which was caused by a 'created being', i.e. Joseph, as was his restoration to sight. By analogy, the man's sudden illness was caused by a human voice, albeit reciting the Qurʾān, and not by divine fiat, hence the same human means could be used to restore the man's consciousness. This is a rather ingenious explanation on the part of Junayd which must have appeared necessary in order to counteract the suspicion of magic or occult powers being used to procure the recovery. It would seem more appropriate, however, that Junayd had witnessed or been party to such 'homoeopathic' cures previously, as these are a feature of folk medicine. It is implausible to suggest that he derived this cure solely from the Qurʾānic model, though it certainly legitimised his action.

Junayd's explanation is not central to the case in question, however, which involves lapsing into and recovering from fainting by means of Qurʾānic recitation. There is no indication that the semantic aspect of the recited verse was the cause of the fainting. Semantic considerations are frequently involved elsewhere in the Sufi sources where a dissociative reaction occurs upon hearing a particular recitation.[11] This would thus be the most likely cause in the present case, yet if so, it was not considered significant enough to include in the narrative.

The other causal factor would be the quality of voice or the purely rhetorical element of the reciter's delivery of the verse. It is well known that the resonant and sonorous qualities of a voice can have dramatic emotional effects on listeners, quite apart from any meaning being conveyed. It is partly by such means that the ritual chanting of *dhikr* has such power spiritually and emotionally in Islamic culture.[12]

It is not surprising that the sonorous quality of voice and/or the semantic element of the verse could have brought about the fainting seizure. It also appears from the present case that repetition of the same sequence of sounds brought about the reversal of the condition and allowed consciousness to be regained. One should not discount the possibility of spontaneous revival, as is mostly the case with similar types of dissociative seizures.[13] The narrative clearly states, however, that the recovery was concomitant with the second recital of the verse, this latter being the crucial factor.

There is some evidence from the analysis of similar dissociative states to support the narrative's conjunction of these two events. Studies of shamanic journeying show that the practitioner is able to terminate his altered state at will, and at a particular point in the proceedings, without being dependent on spontaneous revival.[14] Moreover, studies of the phenomenon of glossolalia or 'speaking in tongues' indicate that a common method of recovery is the mention of a short phrase or some catchwords by the leader of the ceremony, much like the hypnotist's command which ends a hypnotic trance.[15] Similar in some ways to the present case under discussion, one means of inducing the glossolalia state is by rhythmic driving using aural stimuli, the repetition of words and phrases causing entry into the state.[16] Thus the means of induction and recovery in glossolalia can be of a similar kind, though the former is usually a lengthier process. The notion of loss of consciousness being restored by the repetition of a verse is thus not unreasonable in the light of these documented methods of recovery from similar dissociative states.

The final narrative under this category of healing effects occurs in Sulamī's *Ṭabaqāt al-Ṣūfīya*. It is related that ʿAmrū b.ʿUthmān al-Makkī came to Isphahan where he gained a young follower. The youth's father prevented this association, whereupon the follower became ill. Makkī and a reciter came to visit him, and at the youth's invitation, the reciter delivered a verse about not being visited when ill. The youth stretched and sat up, imploring the reciter to continue. He again recited a verse, this time about rejection being more vexatious than illness. The youth continued to recover until he arose and departed with them. On being questioned about this event, Makkī explains that he sensed the recovery before the beginning of the recitation, which indicated to him that it was 'from above', i.e. divinely ordained. Had the recovery been due to the recitation, which Makkī calls *samāʿ*, it would have indicated that it was 'from below' i.e. of infernal origin. Since the signs were that it was 'from above', just a little *samāʿ* was needed to cause healing; if it had been 'from below', just a little would have caused destruction (*T.S.* 204.11–205.6).

This narrative has some similarity with the preceding case in that the recital of verse appears to have had a healing effect; however, this similarity is only a superficial one. The story of Makkī's healing is more explicable on a transparent psychological level. It would appear from the sequence of events that the youth's illness in the first place was precipitated by his father's refusal to allow him to associate with his adopted master. A psychosomatic response is indicated, caused by the youth's grief and yearning to be with his master, though this is not specified by the text. The visit of Makkī, a highly respected, perhaps even charismatic figure,[17] is the significant event which by itself could have been sufficient to alter the youth's condition for the better. There is evidence from studies of religious groups associated with charismatic or forceful leaders that signs of the leader's favour and submission to his dominance are sufficient to produce feelings of exhilaration and well-being in followers.[18]

Makkī explained after the event that he sensed the youth was on the way to recovery before the application of his recitation therapy (*samāʿ*); this could indicate that he sensed a change due to his own presence. The next step was to apply *samāʿ*-therapy, which seems to have operated on the semantic as well as the sonorous level. The therapeutic benefit of poetry eloquently recited cannot be denied; Makkī made sure he was accompanied by a *qawwāl* or 'professional reciter'. On the semantic level, the poetry spoke directly to the youth's situation, mentioning a complainant who is ill but is not visited by his 'patron'. This had such a beneficial effect that the youth stretched out and sat up, asking the reciter to continue. The next verse recited may perhaps be translated as:

> More grievous to me than my illness is your rejection;
> the rejection of your servant weighs heavily upon me.

This verse also seemed to meet the youth's need, having an immediate therapeutic effect, and allowing him to depart with his master.

The best explanation of the recovery is the therapeutic effect of the visit of a revered, even charismatic, authority figure, following rejection or frustration at not being allowed to follow the master. That the illness was psychologically caused by imposed absence from the high-status master is shown by the immediacy of the recovery once the master showed compassion on his would-be follower. Makkī virtually admits this in his explanation of the case by indicating that the recovery was already beginning before the therapeutic effect of *samāʿ* took place. The recital of the verses, both by their semantic and euphonic impact, assisted in confirming what was otherwise a psychotherapeutic outcome.

B Joyful, pleasurable feelings

In this second category there are only two examples recorded in the source writings. As was noted above, this lack of mention of the joyful aspects of *samāʿ* is perplexing, as these aspects were acclaimed by advocates as part of the beneficial value of 'listening', and denounced by opponents as sensual and abhorrent.

Ghazālī in the *Iḥyāʾ* records the example of an unnamed *samāʿ* participant who heard an arousing verse and was overcome by ecstasy. He began to repeat the verse, 'The messenger said: "Tomorrow you will visit", and I said: "Do you know what you said?"' The man substituted the letter *nūn* for *tāʾ* as a verbal prefix, thereby altering the meaning of the verse to refer to first person plural instead of second person singular: 'Tomorrow we will visit'. This had the effect of making the verse's meaning more personal, referring directly to the listener. The man was thus overcome by the direct communication he believed he was receiving, and he continued repeating the verse until he fainted with joy and pleasure. On being asked to explain what had occurred, the man replied that he took the verse in the light of a *ḥadīth* which spoke of the inhabitants of paradise visiting their Lord every Friday.[19] This might imply that the man understood the verse as an indication of his imminent death and reception into paradise and the divine presence (*Iḥyāʾ* II.285.22–26; Mcd. p.707).

The sensation of joy and pleasure felt by the man is explicable as part of his overall dissociative experience. Practitioners of dissociative behaviours often report feelings of peace, joy, inner harmony and well-being, and if there is a religious dimension to their activity, these feelings are seen as an assurance of divine love and acceptance.[20] Recent neuropsychological research suggests that repetitive auditory stimuli can drive neuronal rhythms in the brain and produce intensely pleasurable and ineffable experiences. Such repetitive stimuli can bring about simultaneous intense discharge from both the arousal and quiescent systems, only one of which predominates in normal brain functioning, with excitation of one usually inhibiting the other. With prolonged rhythmic stimuli, however, simultaneous strong discharge of both parts of the autonomic nervous system creates feelings of intense pleasure.[21] The report of joy and pleasure in this narrative must also be seen as part of the overall experience of *wajd*, which here included compulsive behaviour, the repetition of the verse, and eventual loss of consciousness. These other behaviours will be dealt with under their respective categories.

The second case which specifies observable feelings of joy and pleasure is recorded in ʿAṭṭār's *Tadhkirat* and has a more doubtful status as to its reliability. The narrative recorded by ʿAṭṭār is a variant on similar accounts given by Sarrāj, Qushayrī and Ghazālī. In the earlier accounts, which are nearly identical, Yūsuf b. al-Ḥusayn of Rayy (d.304/916–7) is visited by Abū ʾl-Ḥusayn al-Darrāj (d.320/932) after a long journey from Baghdad. Darrāj has difficulty locating him, as the people of Rayy all regarded Yūsuf as a freethinker or heretic and would not give directions as to Yūsuf's whereabouts. He eventually finds him in a mosque, and after inquiries about the journey, Yūsuf asks his visitor to recite some verses of secular poetry. Darrāj begins to recite, and after two verses, Yūsuf is overcome and begins to weep bitterly. He explains that the people are right to call him a heretic because he has been reciting the Qurʾān all morning but felt no emotional effect. A mere two verses of poetry, on the other hand, was sufficient to make him weep bitterly.[22]

In ʿAṭṭār's version, it is Ibrahīm Khawwāṣ (d.291/904) who visits Yūsuf after hearing a heavenly voice tell him to go and say to Yūsuf that he is one of the rejected. Ibrahīm is reluctant to do this, but eventually goes and finds him in the mosque. Yūsuf asks his visitor to recite some verse, whereupon he becomes joyful (*waqt khwush shud*), and begins to weep tears mingled with blood. He then proceeds to give the same explanation about reading the Qurʾān all morning, and being rightly called a *zindīq* 'heretic, freethinker' because two verses of poetry have a greater effect on him (*T.A.* I.318.19–319.8). ʿAṭṭār also adds that Ibrahīm was perplexed and went out into the desert. There he met Khiḍr who explained the situation to him, saying that in fact Yūsuf had a very high status in God's eyes.

There is some doubt about the authenticity of ʿAṭṭār's account, not least because of the respective dates of Yūsuf b. al-Ḥusayn and Ibrahīm Khawwāṣ. The latter was of an earlier generation than Yūsuf, though in ʿAṭṭār's narrative he is portrayed as the disciple of the younger man. This might not be of great significance were it not that the earlier authorities, Sarrāj, Qushayrī and Ghazālī, are unanimous in naming Abū ʾl-Ḥusayn al-Darrāj as the disciple in question. Darrāj being a younger contemporary of Yūsuf makes for a more plausible scenario, besides having the weight of authority of the three earlier sources.

This narrative of ʿAṭṭār's records a quite explicable sequence of joyful behaviour resulting in bitter weeping, both of these acting as 'release' mechanisms, the weeping described with a touch of poetic colour as 'tears mingled with blood'. There is nothing extraordinary about this account which should raise questions about the veracity of the events. It would appear, however, that there is a mistaken identification concerning Darrāj and Ibrahīm Khawwāṣ. The additional details which do not appear in the earlier accounts of Sarrāj, Qushayrī and Ghazālī cannot, on balance, be accepted as authentic and reliable.

There is an absence of any other mention of joyful feelings or behaviours in the sources, apart from these examples. This is a very slim basis from which to argue that such feelings and behaviours formed an important part of the dissociative reactions resulting from *samā*ʿ. What is significant in this, however, is that this is an unusual situation in the psychological study of dissociative/altered state reactions. A.M. Ludwig's symptomatology of altered states includes two categories where positive affect is noted.[23] The first results from a perceived change in meaning and the attachment of increased significance to subjective experience or external cues. This can lead to thrilling feelings of insight and revelations of 'truth'. The second is a simple affect category which includes feelings of rejuvenation, renewed hope, rebirth, and so on. Researchers into glossolalia, shamanic journeying, and various types of Eastern meditation also report resulting positive affect, sometimes to the point of 'ineffable bliss'.[24] This is one area in which the dissociation resulting from *samāʿ* differs from these comparable altered states.

C Unspecified arousal

This category includes references in the narrative accounts to arousal of an unspecified type, without a particular behaviour or affect being mentioned. Such unspecific arousal is a noted feature of altered states.[25] Two examples of this are noteworthy in the Sufi source writings.

In what can be seen as a *locus classicus* on the mystical use of poetry in Islam, Ghazālī offers a discussion on the subjective nature of poetry, and the varying understanding which different listeners perceive from the same verse (*Iḥyāʾ* II.285.22–6; Mcd. p.707). The author illustrates his argument with the account of the unnamed *samāʿ* practitioner who was mentioned in the previous section B. The man heard a verse whose melody and words excited him (*istafazzahu*). A typical dissociative reaction ensued and the man began repeating the verse, substituting letters of the verbal prefixes to give a first person reference. Finally, the man was overcome by joy, and fainted.

Though the arousal is not specified, it is stated to have been the effect of the music (or melody) and the words, i.e. resulting from both the sonic and the semantic impact of the verse recital. The arousal produced or accompanied the dissociative reaction which included the compulsive repetition of the verse, and eventual fainting with joy.

Such arousal is a noted outcome of listening to music. Physiological arousal, as measured by such laboratory tests as galvanic skin response, respiration and pulse rates, or muscular activity has been shown to be produced by listening to music, though a simple stimulus–response situation does not seem to occur.[26] There are obvious cultural elements which come into play, such as one's exposure to, or previous learning of music. Certain types of 'stimulative' music seem to have a greater effect, and this is borne out by field studies where it is clear that rhythmic music can have a significant impact on listeners.[27] Neurologically, rapid external rhythms are likely to drive the autonomic arousal system to such intensity that the quiescent system is activated. Breakthrough of the quiescent system may lead to a change in activation of the hippocampus which is correlated with trance or dreamlike states.[28] With Sufi recitals, the response of arousal to the performance of the *qawwāl* or professional reciter has been described by Qureshi as a 'range of spontaneous expressions . . . directly reflecting the devotee's state of mystical arousal'.[29] In this context of formal and ritual performance, as studied by Qureshi, these expressions of arousal take various forms, such as rhythmic swaying, arm and head movements, exclamations, weeping, and so on. It is likely that the arousal mentioned in Ghazālī's narrative was of some observable type such as those witnessed in present-day performances.

These considerations are aptly illustrated by the second example of unspecified arousal which comes from Sulamī's *Ṭabaqāt*. It is related that a companion of Abū Ḥafṣ al-Naysābūrī made a habit of going around *samāʿ* performances. As he listened he would be aroused or agitated (*hāja*), and would weep, and tear his clothes. The context implies that this is unacceptable behaviour, and Abū Ḥafṣ is asked to do something about this man's conduct (*T.S.* 119.3–5).

D Rising in ecstasy

This category refers to a particular dissociative behaviour which occurs as a result of *samāʿ*. The action of rising or standing up from one's reclining or seated position is a characteristic element of ecstasy associated with ritual listening sessions. In fact its characteristic nature is illustrated by an account in Qushayrī's *Risāla* that Shiblī once went into ecstasy while seated. That this was unusual is indicated by his being questioned as to what the matter was, and why he remained seated (*Ris.* 349). The behaviour is always indicated in Arabic by use of the simple first form of the verbal root *qūm* ('stand, rise'). This verb takes a special idiomatic meaning of 'to rise to one's feet under the influence of ecstasy'.[30]

In the psychological literature relating to altered states, there are very few references to this behaviour of 'rising' indicated in other forms of dissociation. In the literature on glossolalia, among the various forms of kinetic or motor behaviours associated with this practice, the activity of jumping, while kneeling, from kneeling to standing, and while standing, are the nearest which are documented.[31] Several types of dissociation, including non-epileptic seizures and glossolalia, record behaviours of slumping downwards, or falling to the ground, which suggest a loss of conscious or voluntary muscle control.[32] The activity of 'rising' appears more indicative of a trance-like state, with directed behaviour resulting from a substitution of automatic for voluntary control.[33]

Qureshi's description of this 'rising' behaviour in contemporary *samā*ʿ performance shows that this action precedes ecstatic dancing or other directed movements: 'Occasionally the emotion [generated by music] is not to be overcome and culminates in complete ecstatic abandonment – the third stage of arousal. This condition is normally indicated by the devotee's rising to his feet in order to be able to move more freely. Once he moves on his feet, he is considered to be in the state of ecstatic dancing (*raqṣ*).'[34] Such is the ritual expression of this dissociative state. Qureshi describes elsewhere a further ritual elaboration on this 'rising': 'In recognition of the divine gift of this ecstatic state, the leader of the assembly rises and with him all other listeners, until the state subsides'.[35]

The accounts recorded in the Sufi source writings present a variety of situations, formal and otherwise, where this behaviour occurred. There is no mention in these sources of any imperative development from 'rising' to movement and dance, except in one account where a trance-like state ensued which compelled the subject to wander distractedly all night. These early accounts may have failed to mention the ritual elaborations following the 'rising' behaviour for various reasons, but it is more likely that these features are a later addition. This is so since the source accounts are historically at an early stage of ritual development, and show signs of formative processes at work.

There are many recorded examples of this 'rising' behaviour, which indicates that it is characteristic of the dissociation resulting from *samā*ʿ. The first example is narrated by both Sarrāj and Ghazālī, with the later author slightly abbreviating the account. Abū Qāsim b. Marwān (mid to late third/ninth century) was noted as one who did not attend *samā*ʿ for many years. Once, at the invitation of companions, he attended and heard a verse recited which made all except him 'rise' in ecstasy. He asked his fellows about the meaning of the verse, but was not satisfied with the answers any of them gave. He then offered his own explanation of the verse.[36]

It is not stated whether Abū Qāsim's explanation was considered superior to the others, but this can be assumed by the way in which it is recorded in the two accounts, and by Ghazālī's additional comments on its meaning. There is a further implication in this narrative that Abū Qāsim's habit of not participating in *samā*ʿ is commendable and beneficial. His failure to 'rise' in ecstasy shows his independence, against the others with their collective behaviour. Unless this is simply an example of group conformism, this mass behaviour appears to be a ritual elaboration much like that witnessed by Qureshi.[37] Abū Qāsim's independent stance and objectivity also shows itself in his ability to 'understand' the intrinsic meaning of the verse which had such an overwhelming effect on his fellow listeners. Despite this effect on them, their 'explanations' about the verse and its significance were evidently inferior to his.

The second example of this behaviour also illustrates the hierarchies in these early Sufi communities and their tendency to conformism and imitative behaviour. Sarrāj, Qushayrī and Ghazālī report an account concerning the highly respected and influential Dhū ʾl-Nūn al-Miṣrī (d.245/860). On arriving in Baghdad he attended a *samā*ᶜ session, and on hearing some particular verses 'he rose up and then fell down on his face'. Immediately another man rose up also, but Dhū ʾl-Nūn quoted to him a verse from the Qurʾān: 'He who sees you when you arise', whereupon the man sat down again.[38]

Sarrāj and Ghazālī both offer a similar explanation of this episode, that the other man was attempting to imitate or perhaps rival the master by his pretence to 'rise' in ecstasy. The quotation from the Qurʾān informs the man that it is none other than God who is the adversary in his claim to ecstasy, the authors' use of legal terminology emphasising the seriousness of the case. Both authors also point out that if the man had been genuine, he would not have sat down again immediately he had been rebuked. This acknowledges the involuntary nature of the dissociative state which provides a means of distinguishing genuine from feigned, and, in this case, imitative behaviour.

The third example in this category is also recorded by Sarrāj and Ghazālī: Abū ʾl-Ḥusayn al-Nūrī's last trance which led to his death. Again it appears that Ghazālī has followed Sarrāj's account closely. Nūrī was at a *samā*ᶜ session when, on hearing a particular verse, he arose and went into ecstasy (*wa-tawājada*). He began to wander around, trance-like, coming upon a thicket of newly shorn reeds which cut his feet and legs, making them bleed. Oblivious to the pain, he continued in this fashion all night, repeating the verse over and over. His legs swelled and suppurated, leading to his death some days later.[39]

Nūrī's 'rising' behaviour cannot really be considered as an isolated event in this account of a classic dissociative reaction. It is part of a larger set of trance-like actions of which his 'rising up' may be simply a narrative device of continuity with the subsequent account. If the use of this term actually indicates part of the dissociative process, it points to the initial behavioural reaction which was followed by the automatisms of trance-like wandering, compulsive verbalisation, and loss of sensitivity to pain.

In the fourth example considered here, Nūrī is also a chief player. In a chapter concerning the difference between genuine and imitative, or affected, ecstasy, Sarrāj recounts a narrative in which Nūrī was present at a disputation on an academic question. Nūrī began to recite several verses of love poetry, whereupon the whole assembly 'arose' and went into affected ecstasy (*wa-tawājada*) (*Lumaʿ* 304.18–305.7).

This narrative has some similarity with the first example mentioned above, namely the mass display of dissociation which can partly be explained by the ritual setting and by group conformist behaviour. What is remarkable in the present case is that the subjects were not impressionable *samāʿ* participants who would readily go into ecstasies, but sober, learned scholars gathered for the purpose of academic disputation. The only mitigating circumstance here is the use of the term 'affected ecstasy' (or pretended, attempted ecstasy), which suggests that imitative and conformist behaviour was indeed operating. That these scholars who were engaged in theoretical arguments abruptly responded in such an ecstatic way suggests a ritualised reaction, at least partly resulting from the strict socialisation inherent in religious life.

A similar mass response, which is a feature of the 'rising' phenomenon, occurs in an account related in Sulamī's *Ṭabaqāt*. The famed and respected Sufi, Ḥārith al-Muḥāsibī, was present at an assembly where some love poetry was recited; 'He arose in near ecstasy, and wept, so that all those present were moved for him' (*T.S.* 60.7–12).

The difference in this episode is that the mass reaction was one of sympathy and emotional involvement, rather than actual dissociation, whether genuine or feigned. The high status of Muḥāsibī partly accounts for his being shown obeisance and respectful treatment by the others present. It is likely, however, that the sincerity of his actions, including his weeping, was truly felt by those present, and as such provided a genuine stimulus to their sympathetic response.

Hujwīrī relates a number of short narratives dealing with the psychological effects of *samāʿ*, one of which is important for the present category. On hearing the recital of a Qur'ān verse mentioning the torments of hell, ʿAbdallāh b. Ḥanẓala (d.?) began weeping to excess, and rose to his feet. He was told by his companions to sit down, but he replied: 'Fear of this verse prevents me from sitting down!' (*Kashf* 512.9–12; Nich. p.394).

There is some evidence here for a dissociative reaction, including excessive weeping. His 'rising up' appears to be an automatic behaviour, though he is conscious enough to be able to converse, and to realise that he has no voluntary control over his standing or sitting. Such a reaction is not as severe as the type experienced by Nūrī (above); with Ibn Ḥanẓala there is only partial dissociation.

The final example in this category has largely been dealt with already, in the narrative of Yūsuf b. al-Ḥusayn mentioned in category B above. It is only in the account presented by 'Aṭṭār that Yūsuf 'rises up' at the recital of the secular poetry, though all three versions mention his weeping to excess.[40] Given the problems inherent in ʿAṭṭār's account, this small detail may not be noteworthy, and could be a simple narrative device of conjunction. If it is of importance, however, it is a further example of the concurrence of secular poetry recitation and the 'rising' behaviour. All but one of these cases were caused by the recitation of secular or love poetry, and the Qurʾān verse which brought about the other case was characterised by its emotive content.

In conclusion, there emerge several important features of this classic reaction to *samāʿ*. The involuntary nature of the behaviour and its automatism, which appears in all the examples recorded, means that it can be considered as a genuine dissociation or altered state.

There are also important social dimensions coinciding with this 'rising' behaviour. It is nearly always associated with large assemblies, such as *samāʿ* concerts. In only one instance was the behaviour witnessed in a private setting, where there were two persons present.

The corollary to this observation is that 'rising' is often a group behaviour. There may be several reasons for this, and in the examples mentioned above ritual behaviour may account for some of the occurrences. Another factor is the issue of conformist and imitative tendencies arising from the hierarchical structure and socialisation practices of Sufi groupings. There is also the probability of a genuine sympathetic reaction displayed by a whole group toward a respected elder, as in the case of Muḥāsibī.

A further observation here is that the particular behaviour is nearly always provoked by the recitation of sensual or emotive verse. All but one of the cases above involved a reaction to secular, particularly love, poetry. The other example involved a reaction to an emotive, if not fear-inspiring, verse from the Qurʾān. It is clear that the emotionally charged content of the verses or poetry had an important role in provoking dissociative reactions.

E Ecstatic utterances

This category deals with speech and other utterances evoked as dissociative reactions to *samaʿ*. Strictly speaking, these phenomena should not really be termed 'ecstatic utterances', nor described as *shaṭḥiyāt* in the technical sense of inspired mystical expressions. Carl Ernst makes clear in his study of *shaṭḥiyāt* that such inspired expressions have an important doctrinal and theological role to play, as well as having legal implications in questions of heresy and infidelity.[41] This view is also the position of the early Sufi writers on *shaṭḥiyāt*, notably Sarrāj and the Persian author and mystic Rūzbihān Baqlī Shīrāzī (d.606/1209).[42]

The phenomenon arising from *samāʿ*, however, appears notably different from the classic forms of ecstatic sayings uttered by mystics such as Abū Yazīd al-Bisṭāmī and Ḥallāj. In the early sources dealing with *samāʿ*, the 'utterances' linked to dissociative reactions are much more mundane and circumscribed. There are no profound, theologically challenging and audacious sayings or expressions of unitary experience. There is no question of an esoteric doctrine being formulated, of secret teachings for the initiated, with the need for detailed commentary and refutation of charges of blasphemy. Such were required for the classic 'ecstatic' sayings of Sufism. For example, Junayd wrote a commentary on the audacious sayings of Abū Yazīd al-Bisṭāmī, parts of which are preserved in Sarrāj's *Lumaʿ* (380.10ff). Rūzbihān Baqlī wrote an extensive commentary on the sayings of various early Sufis in his *Sharḥ-i Shaṭḥiyāt* (*Explanation of Ecstatic Sayings*). Junayd also reprimanded his more outspoken contemporaries for divulging the 'secrets' of Sufi teachings.[43]

Some of the utterances resulting from *samāʿ* do indeed come close to being 'ecstatic' in the sense of emotionally expressed, sincere outpourings of the mystic's spirit. These are the exception, however, for mostly they are closer to automatisms of dissociation, or to glossolalia utterances. It is worth considering that although the external forms are rather different, the source of both ecstatic utterances and those evoked by *samāʿ* may well be similar.

Ernst did not include a discussion of psychological aetiology in his work on ecstatic utterances. This is a lack which can only partially be filled by the present study, since here we are dealing only with the specific question of *samāʿ* and its effects. There may be some overlap, however, as the more general area of *shaṭḥiyāt* is placed in focus by examining the emotive responses to *samāʿ*.

It would seem that for an early Sufi author such as Sarrāj, the source of 'ecstatic utterances' is the same as for the dissociative phenomena resulting from *samāʿ*. Sarrāj could as well be describing the source of the latter in his definition of *shaṭḥ* as 'an ecstasy that overflows because of its power, and that creates commotion by the strength of its ebullience and overpowering quality.'[44] These notions of 'overflowing' and 'commotion' are underscored by the author's etymological treatment of the word *shaṭḥ*. He claims that the ideas of water overflowing and of agitation and movement are contained in the verbal root of the word. Such ideas well describe the dissociative phenomena of ecstatic utterances where there is a sense of the overflowing of a powerful experience often not wholly under voluntary control.

The source writings describe two basic categories of ecstatic utterances. The first category is that of an apparent automatism, the compulsive repetition of a phrase or verse carried out in a seemingly involuntary fashion. There are several references in the sources to such behaviours which are clearly dissociative reactions.

In the discussion above concerning the 'rising' behaviour, the narrative about Nūrī's last trance was related. Part of his dissociative reaction was the continuous repetition of the verse which had evoked his trance. This is a model case for the psychological study of *samāʿ* as many of the typical reactions are exemplified in Nūrī's episode. The involuntary nature of the repetition as an apparent automatism is clear, with the narrators (both Sarrāj and Ghazālī) stating that this behaviour continued all night.

A similar classic episode concerning Shiblī is recounted by Sarrāj, Qushayrī and Ghazālī.[45] Shiblī was praying in a mosque during the month of Ramadan. A verse recited by his Imam caused him to cry out, change colour (turn green according to Sarrāj, red according to Ghazālī), and begin to tremble. He then began repeating continually the phrase: 'With such words do lovers converse!' Again the automatism of this verbal behaviour is evident in association with the other physical signs. It is of interest to note that this episode occurred during the fasting month of Ramadan when it was not unusual for extra austerities to be carried out by Sufis.[46] It is acknowledged that physical deprivations, involving food, sleep, light, and so on, can have a conditioning effect on the activation of dissociative states.[47]

A similar case has also been referred to above in category C dealing with unspecified arousal. An unnamed practitioner of *samāʿ* was excited by a particular melody and verse. He went into ecstasies and began repeating the verse, substituting letters in certain words to give first person references, until he fainted with pleasure. There may be less evidence here of an automatism; it could be that the man consciously altered the letters of the verse, being in voluntary control of his speech. However, there is a likely dissociative reaction alluded to by his other behaviours. This would suggest that the substitution of letters was an involuntary action occasioned by the subject's self-absorption in his altered state.

The second main category of ecstatic utterance found in the source narratives concerns short, emotional speeches which are reactions to *samāʿ*. As mentioned above, these may appear similar to the classic *shaṭḥiyāt* statements of Islamic mystics, but on closer scrutiny there are some differences. Unlike *shaṭḥiyāt* utterances there is no doctrinal or theological import, and they are more spontaneous and transitory outbursts. There appears more of an emotive quality to these utterances, responding to the needs and temperament of the moment. There is a lack of 'studied' expression, of mature reflection and memorability noticeable in the classic *shaṭḥiyāt* of Abū Yazīd or Ḥallāj. However, it is difficult not to consider that both these types of utterances spring from the same source. Their characteristics are similar in many ways, apart from their mystical import or their theological significance. Both types of utterance are highly charged in emotion, and both erupt as outpourings of sensitive spirits.

Sulamī records two similar instances of ecstatic speeches, the first related of Samnūn b. ʿAbd Allāh. Samnūn was called 'the lover' because of his discourses and poems on the theme of mystical love;[48] hence it is not surprising that his ecstatic utterances were recorded. It is noted in Sulamī's account that he 'cried aloud', indicating an emotional or dissociative reaction, and then was heard to say: 'Would that mankind cried out due to the force of His ecstasy in His love, to fill what is between the horizons with cries!' (*T.S.* 195.6–8.)

The second example recorded by Sulamī concerns Junayd who was walking in Baghdad with Abū ʾl-ʿAbbās b. Masrūq. On hearing a singer recite a verse about past glories, Junayd began weeping bitterly, and then spoke ecstatically to his companion: 'Abū ʾl-ʿAbbās! How good are the stages of concord and familiarity, and how lonely are the states of antipathy! I never cease to yearn for the origin of my desire, with a keen path, and terrors as my steed, desirous to attain my goal! But look at me now during times of indolence: I yearn for past times!' (*T.S.* 240.8–13). This utterance is a very personal and emotional outpouring, prompted not only by the singer's verse, but by Junayd's temperament and inner concerns of the moment. This ecstatic speech is reminiscent of Junayd's intense, lyrical *saj*ʿ (rhymed prose) style in his *Kitāb al-Fanā*ʾ (*Book of Annihilation*).[49]

A final example in this category comes from ʿAṭṭār's account of Shiblī. It is related that when Shiblī's 'state' (*ḥāla*) was strong, he would go to the 'assembly' (probably the mosque) and divulge mysteries (*sirr*) to the common people. Junayd upbraided him for doing so, accusing him of divulging in the streets what the Sufis heard in grottos or cellars. Shiblī replied ecstatically: 'I speak what I hear; in both worlds, what is there apart from me? Nay, for self is a word which goes from God to God, and Shiblī is not in the midst!' Junayd then accepted what he had to say (*T.A.* II.166.14–19). This last statement of Shiblī's appears very like a classic *shaṭḥ* utterance, with its profound, audacious and teasing quality, characteristic of this roguish, unconventional mystic. It is important to note in this account, however, that Shiblī was under the influence of an altered state (literally 'his state was strong') when he ventured to speak such mysteries. Moreover, Shiblī claims to have spoken 'what I hear'; his 'hearing' made him speak aloud, and he was merely a conduit between the Source of his words and the world at large.

One example of ecstatic utterance falls into neither of the two categories described above. Both Sarrāj and ʿAṭṭār present similar accounts of the trance-like state witnessed of Sahl b.ʿAbdallāh Tustarī. As a result of *samā*ʿ, Sahl would go into a trance lasting some twenty-four or twenty-five days; he would not eat, and he would sweat profusely even during the winter. If he was questioned in this state, he would reply: 'Do not ask anything of me, for my words would be of no benefit to you at this time' (*Luma*ʿ 307.4–8; *T.A.* I.255.16–20). It would seem that Sahl's utterances during this trance-like condition were caused by his altered state, but there is no further indication as to their characteristics. It may be that they were inarticulate ravings, or even fully articulate but likely to be misunderstood as blasphemous or heretical. This was often the case with the ecstatic utterances of mystics, that in a different context they would be misconstrued as heretical.[50] It is possible that Sahl was fearful of such an outcome in this situation.

Qureshi has noted the occurrence of verbal manifestations of dissociation in contemporary *samā*ʿ settings among Sufi groups. Often these take the form of exclamations or shouts, or short verbal expressions, and these depend on the stage of arousal achieved.[51] The automatism of repeating verses noted in the early Sufi sources is a further form of such manifestations. It could be argued that the longer, more 'studied' and conscious utterances known as *shaṭḥiyāt* are the other end of a continuum which begins with simple shouts and exclamations. The evidence could also point to a basic distinction, however, between automatisms on the one hand, and conscious, voluntary utterances on the other. The source writings show the non-creative, involuntary nature of the former type of utterance which is clearly an outcome of dissociation.[52] The writings also demonstrate the phenomenon of fully conscious, articulate and crafted expressions which are in strong contrast to these automatisms. Yet these may also result from a dissociative state, albeit of a milder, perhaps qualitatively different form. These ecstatic utterances are driven by a highly charged but creative mind, the emotional state of the speaker flowing over with articulate expression.

If this distinction between the phenomena of automatism and conscious utterance holds, the aetiologies of these two behaviours may also be separate. In the case of the former, the definition offered by Felicitas Goodman for glossolalia utterances is equally valid here. Goodman argues that glossolalia should be seen as 'a vocalization pattern, a speech automatism, that is produced on the substratum of hyperarousal dissociation, reflecting directly . . . neurophysiologic processes present in this mental state'.[53] If cortical control is switched off, a connection between the speech centre and some subcortical structure may be established, with the latter in control. Vocalisation then becomes an audible manifestation of rhythmic discharges of the subcortical structure.[54] This could account for inarticulate utterances which have no semantic content, and, by extension, the compulsive repetition of phrases as noted in the source writings.

With conscious, articulate utterances at the other end of the spectrum, different causal factors may be operating. The explanation may possibly be found in higher arousal levels and the stimulus these provide for more urgent and emotive vocalisation. The evidence from the Sufi source writings is abundant that a type of 'hyperarousal' dissociation is operating in these behavioural outcomes. There are obvious somatic agitations and arousals which are the opposite of those witnessed in the somatic calming or 'hypoarousal' of classic meditation disciplines.[55] These higher arousal levels can be associated with heightened vocalisation behaviours, in terms of excitational level, and with urgency, speed and volubility of speech. This is readily demonstrated in everyday life when a person is observed in an elated or excited mood. It is also demonstrated in certain types of psychopathologies, such as in the manic phase of bi-polar mood disorder (manic-depressive illness).

The positing of heightened arousal levels as part of the dissociative reaction to *samā*ʿ may explain this second type of ecstatic utterance where conscious control and creativity are amply demonstrated.

F Making face to glow, and *G Loss of colour*

These two categories should be considered together, since they are both concerned with changes in facial aspect. When viewed closely, the evidence for this apparent physiological effect of *samā*ʿ is rather sparse. Only one undisputed instance of a person's face glowing is recorded in the narratives, and a further instance has conflicting testimony (one source mentions glowing, another mentions pallor). This is not a sufficient base of evidence to support the view that the effect is an important physiological reaction, and thus it can only be considered a marginal characteristic.

In the first example, Sarrāj records that Sarī al-Saqaṭī and Junayd were discussing the theme of love. Sarī grabbed the skin of his own forearm and let it go again, saying: 'If I had said that this (hand) has withered the other (forearm) from love, it would have been so!' Sarī lost consciousness and his face began to glow red (*tawarrada*) until it became 'like the halo of the moon, and we were not able to look upon it because of its beauty, so that his face covered us (with light)' (*Luma*ʿ 307.10–14). This is a rather enigmatic story, and is only connected with *samā*ʿ because of the effects of Sarī's near-ecstatic, cryptic statement. Nevertheless, the change of aspect is recorded as a principal feature of the dissociation, along with the loss of consciousness. Some allowance for hyperbole must also be made in the description of the face, though similar accounts of faces glowing with light are given in other sources.[56]

The second instance comes from the narrative of Shiblī in the mosque, where, on hearing a Qur'ānic verse, he cries out and begins to tremble.[57] Sarrāj's account has him 'turn green' (*ikhḍarra*), i.e. he loses colour in the face or turns pallid. Ghazālī's account, on the other hand, has Shiblī 'turn red' (*iḥmarra*). The difference between these two accounts may be due purely to faulty textual transmission. The two verbs in question are distinguished only by the middle root letter, and a change from *mīm* to *ḍād* or vice versa is easily made. There is also a minor orthographic difference of two diacritical points. Given the lack of any other examples of a person's face 'turning pallid', it may well be that Ghazālī's text is the more original, and that Sarrāj's text has suffered in transmission.

The only other example of a related phenomenon is the Tradition that the Prophet's hair turned white at the recitation of some Sūras from the Qur'ān.[58]

The observation of these overt physical signs of reaction are common in cases of altered state behaviours. Both pallor and flushing are noted among several other indicators of underlying physiological changes, and are often associated with fear or anxiety symptoms, as may be expected from fear-inspiring verses of the Qur'ān.[59]

H Suppression of appetite

There is one instance recorded in the source writings of an evident dissociative state causing loss of appetite in the subject. Sahl Tustarī experienced apparent trance-like states, as recorded in two sources mentioned above (*Lumaʿ* 307.4–8; *T.A.* I.255.16–20). The main symptoms of this state were Sahl's loss of appetite for over three weeks at a time, and excessive perspiration, even in winter. During this time, he would either become inarticulate, or what he had to say 'would be of no benefit' to listeners.

It is difficult to classify this dissociative state into a more specific category than to say that it has trance-like features. The sources indicate that this was not a once-only event; it happened on various occasions, though no specific frequency is given.

There is general agreement that fasting prior to the onset of an altered state facilitates its induction, and is a widespread practice.[60] The reason for this is probably that the lowering of blood sugar levels is an aid to the altering of consciousness. Normal brain function requires a constant supply of enriched blood; a fast of over three weeks could produce serious effects, and would almost certainly result in altered consciousness. In Sahl's case, there is no mention that he fasted before the onset of the state. It appears that his fasting was either the result of the state, or else a voluntary action on his part to enhance the altered state.

I Perspiring

The case of Sahl Tustarī mentioned in the last category includes the phenomenon of excessive perspiration as one of the symptoms of his reaction. The sources state that his perspiration was so great that his clothes would become drenched, and this occurred even in the season of winter. This last statement serves to underscore that the perspiration was due to internal somatic factors rather than environmental conditions such as hot or humid weather.

Another curious instance of this phenomenon is contained in a narrative reported by Sarrāj, Qushayrī and Ghazālī. A disciple of Junayd would go into dissociation on hearing any recollection (*dhikr*) of God. The disciple would cry out so much that Junayd ordered him to be quiet on pain of dismissal. The man tried so hard to control himself from crying out that 'every hair of his body would exude a drop of water'. Eventually this effort became too much for him, and one day he lost control, cried out and 'burst his soul', meaning euphemistically that he died.[61]

An interesting elaboration of this narrative is contained in ʿAṭṭār's *Tadhkirat* where no mention is made of the man perspiring under the effort of self-control. Yet ʿAṭṭār adds the curious detail that when he died, all that was left under his cloak was a heap of ashes. This allusion to the dubious phenomenon of spontaneous human combustion possibly accounts for the omission of any mention of perspiring![62]

Both of these examples point to an underlying anxiety condition or internal crisis in each subject. In Sahl's case, this condition involved a trance-like state which lasted over three weeks. His excessive perspiration was one of the symptoms of such a crisis situation, other aspects of which were discussed in the previous section. For the disciple of Junayd, his perspiring was the main symptom of an attempt at 'self-control'. He endeavoured to prevent the outward display of an automatism, or what was a dissociative phenomenon, involuntary crying out or shouting. As with a sufferer of Tourette's syndrome, this attempt proved very difficult, and in this case was ultimately unsuccessful. The underlying anxiety of the attempt, particularly since it was instigated by a revered Sufi master, would seem to be the cause of the excessive perspiration.

J Tremor, agitation

This category is one of major importance in the psychology of *samāʿ*. The phenomena of tremor and agitation are characteristic of the dissociation being studied, as evidenced by numerous references in the source writings. Initial investigation again points to anxiety-like states as being contributory.

The episode of Shiblī in the mosque has been mentioned above. In this classic case of dissociation, Shiblī's face changed colour, and he began to tremble, according to Sarrāj, though in Ghazālī's account his shoulder muscles quivered. He then began repeating automatically the verse which had caused this reaction.

Sarrāj and Qushayrī relate that Sahl Tustarī's servant of sixty years reported witnessing his master tremble to the point of falling down. This occurred only once in all that time, as mostly he was unaffected by *samā*ʿ. Another witness reported a similar instance concerning Sahl on another occasion, suggesting that this was not such an uncommon occurrence (*Luma*ʿ 292.11–293.2: *Ris.* 347). It is noteworthy also that the two Qurʾānic verses which induced the reaction were verses of threatened punishment on the day of judgement.[63]

The Qurʾān is also mentioned by Sarrāj and other writers as contributing to various cases of trembling and agitation. In particular, a verse which speaks of 'the skins of those who fear their Lord tremble; then their skins and their hearts soften at the remembrance of God . . .' (Qur.38.23) is mentioned by Sarrāj as causing a similar reaction (*Luma*ʿ 302.12–3).

Apart from some other brief references to this phenomenon in several of the source writings, two more substantial cases revolve around the controversial figure of Shiblī.

First, ʿAṭṭār's *Tadhkirat* contains a disturbing account of a period of insanity in Shiblī's life which ended in his being committed to an asylum. The main features of this insanity include his restless wandering, caused by the hearing of a voice, his increasing agitation, and his desire and attempts to commit suicide. The cause of this episode was Shiblī's hearing a sudden 'voice' or 'prompting' which said: 'How long will you go about seeking the "Name"; if you are a true seeker, set about finding the Namer!' This had such an effect on him, continues the text, that he lost his composure, 'love's power took hold', and he became distracted and overwhelmed. He tried various means of suicide, throwing himself into the Tigris, self-immolation, seeking out hungry lions, and throwing himself off a mountain. Each of these proved unsuccessful, and his agitation (*bī-qarārī*) increased a 'thousand fold', ending in his being shackled and confined in an asylum (*T.A.* II.162.18–163.3).

This is a description of a complex case, which in modern terms would be considered a psychotic episode. The main symptom outlined in the source, apart from the suicidal behaviour, is his being overwhelmed by an unspecified anxiety and agitation. The terms used to describe this condition are quite general and non-specific in ʿAṭṭār's text, and even the term *bī-qarārī* has a wide range, including 'instability, restlessness, disturbance' and so on. The general picture is clear, however, that Shiblī suffered a derangement in which his previous composure gave way to severe disturbance and agitation of mind and body. The complete and generalised way in which such psychosis overtakes its subject leaves little room for isolating particular, noteworthy symptoms. This may account for the transmitter of the narrative conveying a generalised picture by his use of non-specific description.

The cause of the episode is given as Shiblī hearing a 'voice' which urged him to seek 'the Namer'.[64] There is no mention of the source of this voice, though in ʿAṭṭār's work there is a frequent occurrence of similar auditions specified as having a divine origin. The only reason to suspect that the present case was meant to be seen any differently is the decidedly negative outcome of this audition. While ʿAṭṭār leaves some ambiguity in the question of the voice's origin, in modern medical terms there would be no doubt about the psychotic quality of the voice, particularly in view of the suicidal behaviour which ensued.

Whatever the origins of the voice, the text clearly describes the overwhelming agitation as both a manifest symptom and part of the disease which caused Shiblī's restlessness and suicidal behaviour. His agitation was compounded 'a thousandfold', as the text overstates, by his inability to carry out suicide. This inability came about by a divinely ordained 'conspiracy' of natural forces to thwart his attempts: the river cast him back upon the shore, the fire did not burn him, the hungry lions ignored him, and so on. This benign conspiracy only enraged and frustrated Shiblī further, compounding the distress of his failure to relieve his torment by self-inflicted death.

ʿAṭṭār records that at a later stage in Shiblī's career, his words were able to produce in others the same agitation which the 'voice' in this earlier episode had produced in him. He was once heard repeating the word 'Allāh!' over and over. A youth with a 'burned heart', or laden with anxiety, questioned him as to why he did not repeat the *shahāda* formula 'There is no god but God.' Shiblī sighed and replied that he feared uttering the negative 'There is no god', lest he was unable to reach the affirmative 'but God'. These words had such an effect on the youth that he was struck by a seizure and died. The youth's companions hauled Shiblī before the Caliph's court and accused him of murder. Shiblī, however, was in a state of ecstasy, and spoke eloquently of the youth's readiness for death, his being overwhelmed with love, his purity of heart, his soul being like a bird ready for flight, having severed all earthly connections. The Caliph accepted Shiblī's plea of innocence, and was so 'agitated' by his words that he feared toppling from his throne! (*T.A.* II.166.20–167.9.) Shiblī's ecstatic utterance about the *shahāda* and his eloquent speech about the youth's inner state produced reactions of ecstatic agitation in his listeners, such was the power of his oratory.

Anxiety-type states are again seen as contributory to most of the various episodes of tremor and agitation recorded in the source writings. Shiblī's 'psychotic' episode has clear signs of being anxiety-driven, with the initial agent a disturbing voice (whatever its origin), and subsequent reinforcing factors compounding the original anxiety to intolerable levels. In this case, the symptoms and their aetiology largely coincide, the initial anxiety and the later compounded agitation being difficult to isolate.

The earlier episodes of Shiblī and Sahl Tustarī experiencing agitation on hearing awe-inspiring verses from the Qurʾān again appear anxiety-driven. These well-documented accounts are reinforced by other references to similar reactions recorded of lesser known or unknown people, to the point where their existence is a 'type' or paradigm occurring in certain situations.

The later episode concerning Shiblī with the youth has an anxiety component, but this and the account of his audience with the Caliph are also notable as examples of the entrancing effect of (Shiblī's) oratory, the penetration and power of both its semantic and euphonic qualities. Such effects were noted earlier in this analysis, with the powerful influence of oratory causing fainting and other reactions.

K Sighing, groaning, crying out

This category includes a variety of inarticulate sounds produced as a reaction to *samā*ʿ. The assumption in much of the psychological literature dealing with altered states is that such utterances are largely non-voluntary.[65] This assumption holds well with the evidence from Sufi writings as collated in this analysis, and from contemporary Sufi practice as witnessed by Qureshi. The sounds covered by this category can be seen as symptomatic of dissociative states in which there is a greater or lesser relinquishing of conscious control over utterances and audible respirations. This category has probably the largest number of instances cited in the sources, and can thus be regarded as characteristic of the dissociation resulting from *samāʿ*.

A variety of terms is used in the sources to refer to these audible respirations or inarticulate utterances, most notably Arabic *shahaqa* ('utter a cry'), *ṣāḥa* ('cry out loudly'), *zaʿaqa* ('call out'), and in Persian mostly *naʿra zadan* ('raise a cry').[66] It is uncertain whether any variation in behaviour is indicated by the three distinct verbs used in the Arabic texts. No appreciable difference in semantic range is indicated by these verbs, and the alternative forms could simply reflect literary concerns.

The characteristic reaction of Shiblī in the mosque, as noted in the earlier categories, included his 'crying out' as the first sign of an altered state. Indeed this sign was so spectacular that the witness, Abū Ṭayyib al-ʿAkkī (d.?), relates that he thought that Shiblī had uttered a death cry (*Lumaʿ* 282.20). Al-ʿAkkī then noticed the other signs of Shiblī's reaction.

In category I there was reference made to the disciple of Junayd who could not control himself from shouting out at the recollection of God. His efforts to restrain himself from performing an obviously non-voluntary behaviour, and the accompanying anxiety, led to his ultimate collapse and death.

A narrative which is given considerable space by Sarrāj, Qushayrī, Ghazālī and Hujwīrī also has the subject cry out as a prelude to sudden death. A young servant man or beggar dressed in rags overheard a slave girl singing to her wealthy master on the balcony of a mansion beside the Tigris river. The youth was overcome with the verse, and called for the girl to repeat it. When she did, he spoke cryptically of hearing a divine message through the verse, whereupon he cried out and died suddenly. The people of Basra came to bury the man, and the wealthy owner dismissed the girl, gave away his property and took flight, never to be seen again.[67]

This is the most colourful of several examples of a 'death cry' reaction to hearing verse or speech regarded by the listener as especially significant. In one of these narratives, a Khurāsānian questioned Junayd on a point of Sufi teaching. When Junayd answered, the man 'cried out' and 'departed' (*kharaja*), according to Sarrāj, but in Ghazālī's text, he 'died' (*māta*).[68]

A meal among friends was left in disarray when a reciter intoned a verse upsetting ʿUtba al-Ghulām (second/eighth century), who cried out and fell down in a faint (*Iḥyāʾ* II.290.28–33; Mcd. pp.724–5). This episode, like several others in this category, is comparable to an epileptic-like seizure.

In category E above, reference was made to Sulamī's narrative about Samnūn crying out and speaking ecstatically. This is clearly a different case from crying out as an indicator of seizure or sudden death. In this example, Samnūn's cry indicates the sudden onset of a dissociative state which features ecstatic utterance (*T.S.* 195.7–8).

ʿAṭṭār relates the conversion of Abū Ḥafṣ al-Naysābūrī. Working as a blacksmith in his shop, he once heard a blind man reciting from the Qur'ān. Distracted by this, Abū Ḥafṣ touched the iron in the furnace, brought it out and began working on it until it was pure. When his apprentices shouted to him, Abū Ḥafṣ returned to his normal state, cried out and threw the iron away. He immediately abandoned his trade and became a Sufi.[69] This is an example of a different type of inarticulate utterance. Abū Ḥafṣ' dissociative state was one in which he lost the faculty of pain sensitivity. His return to normality meant that he suddenly felt the heat of the iron in his hand, whereupon he cried out in pain and flung the iron away.

A final example is of a different type yet again, and perhaps stands alone as a case of inarticulate respiration. Ghazālī quotes a *ḥadīth* among a list of references to the Prophet's reactions to *samāʿ* attesting that when he prayed, there was a hissing or boiling sound (*azīz*) in his chest like that of a cooking pot (*Iḥyā'* II.294.6; Mcd. p.734). The exact nature of this phenomenon is unclear, but the text suggests that this unusual respiration was heard as a concomitant to his praying, indicating the fervour and intensity of his action. A related phenomenon may be that witnessed of Sufis involved in intense *dhikr* chanting which produces 'excitational trance', as termed by Gilbert Rouget.[70] Some types of *dhikr* involve vocal chord vibrations during inhalation and exhalation with very guttural sounds. A raucous panting recalling back-and-forth saw movements is produced, such breathing being likely to cause hyperventilation and subsequent physiological effects.[71]

Apart from the last two examples above which have their own particular explanation, two broad types of inarticulate utterance are indicated by the source writings. The first is the groan or cry which heralds a dissociative reaction, and is occasionally the only noted behavioural change. More often, there are other signs of the altered state, such as pallor or fainting, which follow the utterance. Shouting or crying out is a recognised dissociative response to *samāʿ* witnessed in contemporary settings, as noted by Qureshi.[72] In the psychological literature, it is documented that patients suffering from convulsive non-epileptic seizures often demonstrate vocalisation such as groaning, moaning, crying, gagging and gasping at the commencement of their episode.[73]

The second type may be simply an extension of the first, but may also be seen as a distinct phenomenon, notably the utterance of a 'death cry'. This is dissociation of a radical kind, a seizure overwhelming the subject to such an extent that sudden death is the outcome. It should be kept in mind, however, that this 'cry' may simply be a conventional, narrative feature of the source accounts. Arabic has the stock expression 'he cried out and died',[74] much as in English one says 'the person collapsed and died', whether or not actual falling down takes place.

L Weeping

Weeping can be seen as another feature of dissociative states, as recognised in the psychological literature.[75]

An episode given some detail and contained in four of the source writings concerns the narrative of Yūsuf b.al-Ḥusayn of Rayy and his visitor, Abū ʾl-Ḥusayn al-Darrāj. After a long journey from Baghdad, Darrāj has difficulty tracing Yūsuf in Rayy because the local people regard the latter as a freethinker or heretic (*zindīq*). Eventually Darrāj finds Yūsuf in a mosque where he has been reading the Qur'ān all morning without any obvious effect. Al-Darrāj's recital of two verses of secular poetry sets Yūsuf weeping bitterly. He immediately confesses his 'guilt' of heresy, as claimed by the local people, because of his insensitivity to the Qur'ān, and the dramatic effect of secular poetry.[76] The texts are ambiguous as to the cause of Yūsuf's weeping. In the context of a discussion about *samāʿ* and its effects, it could be seen as an emotional reaction following from the recital. Given Yūsuf's explanation and confession of 'heresy', on the other hand, his weeping could simply be caused by sorrow and feelings of guilt, though this presents something of a cause-and-effect conundrum. Without the weeping, or some other obvious emotional sign, Yūsuf has no cause for expressing regret or confessing his guilt. Is his weeping the result of his guilty feelings, or is it the cause, given that he feels such emotion on hearing secular verse recited, but not on hearing the Qur'ān recited? Unfortunately, there is no guidance offered by the source texts through this convoluted cause and effect situation.

A classic case of weeping as an emotional reaction to *samāʿ* is recorded by Sulamī concerning a companion of Abū Ḥafṣ al-Naysābūrī. The companion had a habit of attending *samāʿ* sessions, and would become aroused, and begin to weep and tear his clothes. Such behaviour was regarded as quite suspect by those who complained to Abū Ḥafṣ and asked for some reprimand for the man (*T.S.* 119.3–5). The text's mention of arousal (*hāja*) is most adequately interpreted as a reaction of dissociation, the weeping and other behaviours being caused by emotional responses to the beauty and rapture of the music or poetry.

Sulamī also refers to an incident involving Junayd, who, on hearing a verse recited in a Baghdad street, began to weep bitterly and speak ecstatically, embellishing the verse he had heard. This episode has been referred to above in the category E dealing with ecstatic utterances. Junayd's weeping appears to be a reaction to hearing the verse, as the utterance he makes is a personal and emotional outpouring prompted by his inner preoccupations at the time.

The behaviour of weeping as a typical reaction is documented in the psychological literature dealing with altered states.[77] Despite this connection, however, most of the cases recorded in the Sufi sources can be adequately explained as simple emotional reactions to varying personal and psychological circumstances. The sudden incursion into the psyche of particular music or verse significant to the listener can have a dramatic and overwhelming effect which may not necessarily be due to a special altered state. Some of the categories of reactions dealt with so far indicate the operation of altered states or of dissociation, but with the present instance ambiguity remains as to whether such factors need to be invoked. In the Sufi sources, however, such behaviours as weeping in these circumstances do indicate special reactions which can be regarded as dissociative.

M Loss of sensitivity to pain

The loss of sensitivity to pain is one of the most interesting of the psychological reactions to *samāʿ*, particularly in its similarity to trance states and other altered state phenomena.

One of the defining characteristics of a trance state is that the person is conscious but seemingly unaware or unresponsive to usual external or internal stimuli.[78] Roger Walsh's analysis of the criteria for mapping various altered states includes reduction of awareness to the environment as the first among a list of characteristic dimensions.[79]

This reduction of environmental awareness or reduced responsiveness to external and internal stimuli may include an increase in the pain threshold. A complicating factor in the analysis of *samāʿ* reactions is that most of the responses encountered are due to an aroused or ergotropic state where sensitivities are heightened, rather than reduced. Hyperarousal conditions do not lead to an expectation of reduced sensitivity to pain; this would more usually be expected of hypoarousal or desensitisation.[80]

The Sufi sources offer two examples of the phenomenon of reduced sensitivity, and an account of a discussion about the possibility of this reduction.

The classic trance-like state reported of Nūrī in the final days of his life has been referred to above in category D. Responding to recited verse, Nūrī rose up and began wandering around distractedly, stumbling upon newly cut reeds whose sharp canes injured his feet and legs. Though there was severe bleeding, Nūrī did not seem to notice, and in a few days the wounds suppurated and caused his death, possibly due to septicaemia. Nūrī's loss of sensitivity to pain appears clearly as a trance-like feature consistent with his other behaviours at this time. Being overwhelmed by what he perceived and understood of the *samāʿ*, he became distracted and preoccupied, repeating the verse over and over, wandering around in a daze, and hence oblivious when sharp canes cut his feet.

The narrative of Abū Ḥafṣ al-Naysābūrī and his conversion, as recorded by ʿAṭṭār, has been referred to above in category K. Being distracted by a blind man's recital of the Qur'ān, Abū Ḥafṣ unknowingly placed his hand in the furnace, and drew out a piece of hot iron which he beat until it was pure. Returning to his normal state, Abū Ḥafṣ cried out and flung the iron away, though he was apparently uninjured. Until he cried out, we may assume he felt no pain from the hot iron, his distraction with the recital causing him to become oblivious to the heat which his hand must have sensed.

One feature of this and similar accounts in ʿAṭṭār's *Tadhkirat* is that no evident injury is ever received.[81] In the narrative of Nūrī's trance recorded by the older and more reliable works of Sarrāj and Ghazālī, mortal injury is inflicted, though the pain of the cut reeds was not felt at the time. With ʿAṭṭār's account, more of a miraculous element seems to be operating, where any evident injury is unaccountably avoided. ʿAṭṭār also relates his own version of Nūrī's trance, with additional, more fantastic elements, such as his bleeding legs trickling the word 'Allāh' onto the ground (*T.A.* II.55.5–10). These considerations make ʿAṭṭār's account less trustworthy than the earlier sources.

In the *Kitāb al-Lumaʿ*, Sarrāj records a discussion between Sarī al-Saqaṭī and Junayd concerning the possibility of loss of sensitivity to pain (*Lumaʿ* 306.5–12). Sarī maintained that a person experiencing *wajd* could be hit on the face with a sword and not feel the impact. Junayd is more sceptical about such an event occurring without the subject feeling any pain. Sarī maintains his position, but no anecdotal or theoretical arguments are advanced by either party, and the reported discussion ends there.

Situations where loss of sensitivity is reported as an outcome of *samāʿ* show all the features of being trance-like states. A similar process would appear to be operating with trance states recorded in other cultural settings.[82] Consciousness is retained, but the subject is unaware of vital external stimuli, distraction being one of several related experiences congruous with such a state.

N Fainting, loss of consciousness

This behaviour is typical of the psychological reaction to *samāʿ*, being one of the largest categories of responses recorded in the sources. Loss of control, either of consciousness, or of general postural and muscle co-ordination, is one of the features of altered states in A.M. Ludwig's system of classification.[83]

In category A above, reference was made to the disciple of Sarī al-Saqaṭī whom Junayd restored to consciousness after he fell in a faint at the recital of a Qurʾānic verse. It was suggested in relation to this case that the rhetorical and semantic elements of the verse and its recital might be suspected as contributing to the fainting seizure. The text clearly states that the recovery was associated with a repetition of the verse which caused the seizure in the first place. It was suggested that induction into and recovery from the altered state associated with glossolalia might be seen as a parallel phenomenon. The use of verbal signals, a short phrase or sentence to both induce and recover from the state might have similarities with the case of Sarī's disciple. Whatever the mechanisms involved, the text is unambiguous about the behaviour being both a direct reaction to *samāʿ*, and that the same means was used to allow the subject to recover.

Sarrāj records a narrative concerning Abū Ḥulmān al-Ṣūfī (d.?) which represents a situation of 'double entendre', or rather, a classic case of 'mishearing' which sends the subject into an ecstatic state. Encountering a street vendor who was crying out: *yā saʿtarā barrī*

('Wild thyme!'), Abū Ḥulmān fell down in a faint. Explaining his reaction later, he said that he thought the vendor had said: *isʿa tarā birrī* ('Strive to see My righteousness!', said by God). Sarrāj comments that what a person hears depends on what is in their heart at the time, subject to their immediate concerns and state of mind (*Lumaʿ* 289.7–14).

The text is clear that Abū Ḥulmān's reaction is that of being overwhelmed by his perception of being addressed by God through the medium of the street vendor. Sarrāj also adds that the preparedness of the listener's mind is a necessary prerequisite, indeed the author intimates that the preoccupations of the mind govern what is perceived.

There is the sense in this and certain other cases where a sudden overwhelming occurs that the subject is on the borderline between everyday consciousness and an altered state. It can be assumed that because almost all the subjects mentioned are Sufis, they would often be in a state of preparedness for altered consciousness, by means of constant fasting, meditations and other austerities. There is ample evidence to show from modern psychological studies that such preparedness acts as a strong initiator into altered states.[84] This evidence and the relative ease of occurrence of altered state behaviours suggests that many of these subjects experience a 'twilight' consciousness, living daily in a borderline situation where only a slight stimulus is required to induce a change of state. Abū Ḥulmān's situation illustrates this proposition: because of his mind's preoccupation, a slight mishearing of a street vendor leads him to imagine that God is speaking to him through this human agency. The import of the 'message' is such that, because of his ascetic preparedness, he readily undergoes a change in consciousness, in this case leading him to fall in a temporary faint.

In category F above, reference was made to the encounter between Junayd and Sarī al-Saqaṭī, where there was a discussion about love (*Lumaʿ* 307.10–4). Sarī grabbed the skin of his own forearm and said: 'If I had said that this (hand) has withered the other (forearm) from love, it would have been so!' Sarī lost consciousness and his face glowed red, covering those around him with light. These two reactions are seen in the text as resulting from his enigmatic and powerful statement, an almost ecstatic utterance attesting to the vast power of love. The force of what he had to say is partly demonstrated immediately by Sarī's loss of consciousness and the reddening of his face. This is how the situation is portrayed by the text, and in psychological terms it is readily understood. In light of the 'borderline' consciousness outlined with the previous case, Sarī's own statement initiated a crossover into an altered state manifested by his temporary loss of consciousness.

A similar case has been outlined previously in category B, with the unnamed *samāʿ* practitioner referred to by Ghazālī (*Iḥyāʾ* II.285.22–6; Mcd. p.707). Hearing a verse which excited him, the man began repeating it, using first person referents to apply to himself, and he eventually fainted in pleasure.

A different type of reaction is involved in Dhū ʾl-Nūn's encounter with an imitator mentioned in category D above. When Dhū ʾl-Nūn 'arose in ecstasy' at a *samāʿ* session, he immediately 'fell on his face', i.e. fell to the floor, possibly in a gesture of adoration or prayer. Another man present also rose up, but Dhū ʾl-Nūn addressed him with a verse from the Qurʾān, warning of God's watching over him, whereupon the man immediately sat down (*Lumaʿ* 289.20–290.9; *Iḥyāʾ* II.291.19–25; Mcd. p.727).

Both Ghazālī and Sarrāj who record this encounter focus their interpretative attention onto the imitative and posturing behaviour of the man. Dhū ʾl-Nūn's falling to the ground, following so closely upon his 'rising' in ecstasy, is probably a dissociative reaction from the ecstasy he experienced. According to the events related in the text, there was no loss of consciousness involved with this falling, as Dhū ʾl-Nūn was able to speak immediately to the man who attempted to imitate his behaviour. It is possible that the falling was a direct result of his sudden 'rising' to his feet, being caused, for example, by a sudden lowering of blood pressure which led Dhū ʾl-Nūn to faint momentarily. It is also possible, as mentioned earlier, that he arose in an altered state but quickly fell to the ground in adoration or a similar gesture appropriate to the elation and ecstasy he experienced.

Reference was made earlier in categories K and L to Ghazālī's narrative about the meal at which ʿUtba al-Ghulām was a guest. When a reciter intoned some verse, ʿUtba cried out and fell in a faint, while his companions left the meal untouched (*Iḥyāʾ* II.290.28–33; Mcd. pp.724–5).

A final example will suffice from Hujwīrī's *Kashf al-Maḥjūb* (534.14–535.4; Nich. p.410). Ibrāhīm Khawwāṣ (d.291/904) was walking with a companion when the latter began to sing some love poetry. Ibrāhīm was so enthralled that he danced a few steps and his feet seemed to penetrate the rocks as if the latter were wax. He then fell down *bī-hūsh*, literally 'out of his senses', or unconscious. On recovering, he said: 'I was in the garden of paradise and you did not see (i.e. you were unaware).' It is worth noting that the frequent expression found in the Persian texts, *bī-hūsh*, covers both the senses of 'unconscious' and 'in ecstasy', illustrating the close relationship in semantics as well as in reality between unconsciousness and altered states.

An hypothesis was offered earlier in this discussion suggesting that 'borderline' consciousness among the Sufis may be a factor in allowing an altered state to occur so readily. There is support for such an idea in psychological studies of altered states which examine factors assisting changes of consciousness. It has been shown that fasting, by reducing blood sugar levels, readily affects consciousness in dramatic ways.[85] It was mentioned above that austerities and ascetic practices among the Sufis were common, and it is quite probable that these would have been a contributing factor in some of the cases of fainting dealt with here. Clearly there is no reference in the narratives to the condition of any of their subjects, but the likelihood of ascetic practices playing a part should be kept in mind. Such factors as hyperventilation and rhythmic sensory stimulation or 'driving', as carried out in *samāʿ* sessions, are also known contributors to altered states.[86] Given that several of the above cases of fainting occurred in *samāʿ* sessions, it is likely that these physiological factors also played a role.

The cumulative effect of these factors tends to mitigate the unexpectedness and the abnormality of altered state reactions such as fainting. When a physiological explanation is able to account for some of these reactions in non-pathological terms, there is a greater sense that such events are quite expected and characteristic.

In terms of the Sufi source writings themselves, all these reactions are seen as 'overwhelming' crises resulting from perceived auditions. It is not what is actually heard that is the cause, but what is perceived by the subject, given his/her particular state of mind at the time. The subject's predisposition and preparedness for what is perceived is all-important, but unfortunately for the modern reader, few background details on the subjects are ever given. Indeed, for the source writers, it sometimes appears not to matter much whether fainting, crying out, weeping, or any other reaction occurs, as any and all of these are expected outcomes. The psychology of the source writers will be dealt with in more detail in Chapter 6 of this book.

O Restless wandering

This is one of the less frequently recorded behaviours associated with *samāʿ*, some four examples occurring in the source writings. This behaviour is clearly part of an altered state reaction, and classic notions of trance seem to be indicated. In wandering distractedly, the subject often performs highly stereotyped and patterned behaviours, seemingly acting without personal volition or conscious control.[87] It is typical that the person experiencing this state has decreased sensitivity to environmental stimuli, and apparent increased preoccupation with inner events and promptings.

These characteristics are amply illustrated by the episode of Nūrī's final trance, discussed in categories D, E and M above. When Nūrī heard the verses which so affected him, he arose and began wandering about distractedly, oblivious to his stumbling upon sharp reeds. The stereotyped behaviour displayed here was his continuous audible repetition of the verse, and his wandering about in a trance-like manner, showing a lack of conscious control. His obliviousness to pain caused by walking over the sharp reeds shows reduced sensitivity to external stimuli and increased preoccupation with internal events.

Nūrī also figures in a narrative recounted only by ʿAṭṭār and, in an abbreviated form, by the Sufi author Abū Bakr al-Kalābādhī in his *Kitāb al-Taʿarruf* (*Book of Knowledge*).[88] In ʿAṭṭār's version, Nūrī is reported to have been seen wandering about for some days with a brick in his hand, not eating or drinking, but performing all the rites of prayer at the proper times. Junayd is reported to be in disagreement with his companions over whether this is a true altered state. Junayd argues that it is, since God 'preserves' those in ecstasy to observe the rituals of worship. This episode of Nūrī's has many classic trance-like features, with a genuine diminution of awareness, and stereotyped behaviour in his wandering about distractedly. It appears, however, that he retained a channel of consciousness open to the external world whereby he knew the times for ritual prayer. This notion of a channel is also apparent in that Junayd drew Nūrī out of his trance-like state by speaking words of good counsel to him. Apparently his reasoning faculties were not completely closed off to external stimuli, as Junayd's words were able to have a healing effect.

A short narrative is related by Sarrāj concerning Abū Bakr Muḥammad al-Duqqī (d.366/977) who arose in the middle of the night and wandered or stumbled around (*yatakhabbaṭa*), falling over, and rising up again. The people around him wept, and his behaviour was remembered in verse (*Lumaʿ* 292.4–6). This appears much like a case of somnambulism, where some purposeful or preoccupied state is assumed, with clumsy behaviour ensuing.[89] However, the text presupposes some auditory causation for this episode, though none is actually stated. It must be assumed, then, that a trance-like reaction is indicated, an altered waking state rather than a situation where the subject is asleep. In this respect, there are some similarities with the first case of Nūrī outlined above, namely the lack of apparent conscious control, and heedlessness toward the external environment as well as to pain stimuli.

The fourth example which is related to this category is the 'psychotic' episode recorded of Shiblī, as mentioned above in section J (*T.A.* II.162.18–163.3). When Shiblī heard a divine voice, he became agitated to the point of wanting to commit suicide, and travelled afar seeking various means of deliverance. His wandering distractedly in this way could be classified under the present category, though it should probably be seen as part of his more general, overwhelming agitation and obsessive directedness of behaviour. Some of the qualities associated with a trance-like state of restless wandering are applicable, namely his inner orientation and directedness, an apparent decrease in voluntary control, and lack of regard for consequences.

The four cases cited here have several features in common which suggest a similar typology. These features include a decrease in environmental awareness, trance-like or stereotyped qualities, such as obsessively directed behaviour and preoccupation of mind, and a decrease in voluntary control. There are some obvious overlaps here with behaviours from other categories previously mentioned, but this particular reaction has its own features which warrant their own discussion.

P Loss of voluntary control of limbs

There is little mention of this aspect of the reaction to *samā*ʿ, apart from some general, vaguely worded references which occur in 'catalogues' of effects. At one point in Sarrāj's *Luma*ʿ there is a lengthy discussion about the preference of showing no external signs of reaction over showing signs such as agitation and involuntary motion of limbs (*Luma*ʿ 308.3ff). This discussion of Sarrāj's is purely theoretical and didactic, with no additional information about the phenomenology of the behaviour.

Mention of this reaction, however vaguely given, is important for the description of the altered states associated with *samā*ʿ. It is an expected addition to the portrayal of these states, given the existence of the other behaviours referred to more frequently. Where trance-like states are encountered in various forms, with loss of voluntary control over certain behaviours, the loss of motor co-ordination can also be expected. Studies of non-epileptic seizures show that this loss of control or of co-ordination is a characteristic feature, whether the seizure is convulsive or otherwise.[90] Many seizures can closely resemble epileptic fits in their display of these obvious symptoms, though such seizures appear to have a psychogenic rather than neurological basis.

Such epileptiform reactions come very near to some of the behaviours following the practice of *samāʿ*. In modern Sufi settings, however, there is little mention of this reaction, though Qureshi does refer to ecstatic activities where more ordered and controlled motor responses are expressed.[91]

Q Throwing oneself (or being thrown) to the ground

A reaction such as being thrown to the ground is clearly an epileptiform behaviour, and it would appear that similar causative processes as with the previous category are operating. A psychogenic basis for this activity would seem appropriate, yet the resultant form resembles behaviour stemming from abnormal neurological causes.

ʿAṭṭār relates a narrative concerning Ḥasan of Basra (d.110/728), one of the earliest Sufis, revered for his piety and outspokenness. Ḥasan had a disciple who would be thrown to the ground every time he heard a verse from the Qurʾān. Ḥasan spoke to the man about his affliction, telling him that if this was a voluntary action, he was kindling the fire (of hell) for all his actions in life. If it was not voluntary, warned Ḥasan, it was an affliction from Satan which must be overcome (*T.A.* I.28.17–24). In either situation, as Ḥasan saw it, the man was on dangerous ground with this undesirable, perhaps demonic condition. It also shows clearly that for the pious of this early period in Islamic history, such activity was seen no differently from that of seven centuries earlier. In Palestine during the time of Jesus, or at least of the gospel writers, epileptiform behaviour was viewed as stemming from demonic possession, the only recourse being miraculous intervention.[92] Ḥasan does not go as far as suggesting actual possession, but unfortunately the text is unclear as to the precise nature of what action should be taken if there is a demonic cause.

This narrative is suggestive of the account discussed earlier of Junayd's disciple who cried out upon hearing *dhikr*. In both these cases the sound of the reciting provoked a dissociative response with epileptiform characteristics. Both crying out and falling to the ground can be viewed as stemming from similar causative factors, either neurological or, more likely, psychogenic.[93]

R Attempt at suicide

This is one of the more extreme reactions to *samāʿ*, suggesting a highly emotional response of psychotic proportions. It is possible that in a subject suffering extreme stress, there is temporary derangement of the mind, aided by the emotive stimulus of *samāʿ*, which could cause an attempt at suicide. This is the scenario in one of the recorded accounts, while in the other, there is a longer lasting psychotic derangement where suicide is attempted several times.

This latter case is that of Shiblī's insanity referred to on various occasions above (categories J and O). Driven to distraction by a 'voice' which instructed him to seek 'the Namer' (or 'the Named'), Shiblī became highly agitated and sought death on a number of occasions by various means, including drowning, jumping off a mountain, and self-immolation. Being frustrated by his unsuccessful attempts, his anxiety increased so much that he needed restraining and placing in an asylum (*T.A.* II.162.18–163.3). The pathological nature of this episode is clear, as it has many of the signs of a paranoid psychosis. One of the unfortunate effects of psychotic illness is that the auditory hallucinations often become so intense that the sufferer seeks relief through extreme and dangerous means. This was the case with Shiblī, who was driven to distraction by the 'voice' he heard, and by the accompanying agitation. It is also shown by the narrative that this was no momentary derangement; his varied attempts at suicide indicate a lengthy process, as does his confinement in an asylum, where he remained for some time. The narrative continues from the account of his insanity to describe his activity while he stayed in the asylum, giving teaching to visitors and followers, and his evident recovery.

The other narrative in this category has a rather more tragic outcome, with the subject succeeding in his attempt at suicide. The description of Shiblī's psychosis is disturbing enough, but the account of the Israelite youth who threw himself from a mountain has a darker and more perplexing aspect. This strange account is recorded only by Ghazālī, and is claimed as a Tradition reaching back to the Prophet. The youth, who was unnamed, was reported to have asked his mother some profound questions about the identity of the Creator of the heavens and the earth, the mountains and the clouds. The mother replied in traditional fashion 'God Most High' in answer to each question. The youth then proclaimed 'Indeed I hear something from God!' whereupon he threw himself from the mountain and was killed (*Iḥyāʾ* II.278.35–279.3; Mcd. p.234).

Ghazālī explains that it seemed that the youth 'heard' something which indicated God's power and majesty and which sent him into an ecstasy, causing his suicide. Several questions remain unanswered, however, by this account. First, there is real ambiguity over the source of what the youth heard. It may have been contained in his mother's answers, or he may have suddenly heard a 'divine' or hallucinatory voice speaking to him. If he heard an imagined voice, stemming from his own deranged mind, the suicide is rather more explicable. Yet there is no indication of what the 'voice' said to him.

Various other possibilities present themselves. For example, the youth's claim to have heard 'something' from God may have precipitated delusions of grandeur. Imagining he was being spoken to by God may have led him to believe he had special powers of self-protection. There are other scenarios which could be followed up; indeed this is fertile ground for a psychiatric investigation. The youth's asking 'ultimate' questions indicates a clarity of mind and depth of perception which sometimes precedes certain psychotic episodes, and which may later develop into more bizarre feelings of persecution, hallucinations or severe mood swings.

These various possibilities all point to a disturbed, if not psychotic, mind. The only explanation which does not lead to such a conclusion is if the lad actually heard a divine voice, and that the ecstasy he experienced led to an accidental fall due to a state of physical disorientation. This is close to the explanation offered by Ghazālī, except for the mention of an accidental fall. Both Ghazālī's explanation, and the Tradition he quotes, have the verb *ramā*, 'he threw', as active, with object 'himself'. This can only indicate voluntary, premeditated action, and so the idea of an accidental death must be ruled out. Moreover, the text is replete with indications of mental, not physical, disorientation. Though this derangement may have only been temporary, the stimulus of the situation, and his apparent audition of a 'divine' voice, was sufficient to cause an ecstatic reaction which precipitated his fall. This is part of Ghazālī's argument, though in psychological terms the episode would more likely be seen as psychotic in character.

This leads to the observation that ancient Sufi analyses of such reactions tend to normalise, assimilate and situate them in the context of both everyday life and the prevailing theology. Modern psychological analyses, on the other hand, tend to view such behaviours as 'pathological' and disordered, emphasising their disruption and failure to comply with social or personal contexts. This explanatory difference is rather curious, given the far greater understanding of psychology in today's science, but a reduced ability to allow altered states to be seen as part of everyday consciousness and behaviour.[94]

S Sudden death

This final category deals, of course, with the most serious outcome of all and, for the early Sufi sources, it is one of the most frequently mentioned reactions. Most of the cases referred to here describe death as coming suddenly, with suggestions of a precipitate seizure or collapse of some type. In only one case is the dying process more prolonged: Nūrī died of probable septicaemia some days after being injured while in a trance state.

An ingenious suggestion is to propose that the usual terms, such as Arabic *māta* ('he died') or Persian *jān bi-dād* ('he gave up his soul/life'), indicate not actual death but a type of cataleptic trance. Catalepsy can often mimic death to a very great extent, including lack of pulse, lack of apparent breathing, rigidity and loss of body warmth.[95] These symptoms have occasionally been mistaken for death, and it is not improbable that this occurred more frequently in ancient times. It is possible that *samā'* may have produced a trance-like state of catalepsy, but there is really no evidence for this in the present texts. There is no indication that the usual terms for death mean anything other than their accepted signification.

In discussing sudden death as a result of *samā'*, modern research in related fields suggests that a high proportion of people experiencing altered state behaviours or seizures have pre-existing stress factors in their lives. This may merely be restating some obvious findings such as stress being related to sudden cardiac arrest, yet it may well be significant for the present discussion.

Research into glossolalia has found that more than 85 per cent of 'tongue-speakers' had experienced a clearly defined anxiety crisis just prior to their initiation into speaking.[96] Studies of sudden death in the general population suggest that stressful or critical precipitating conditions were usually present. These included the death or illness of someone close, mourning, grief, personal danger or relief from danger, triumph, loss of status, and others. The precipitating event was impossible to ignore, it was abrupt or dramatic, and produced excitation in a situation over which there was no control.[97] Such studies suggest that predisposing conditions of stress in the individual may help explain the onset of an abrupt seizure. In the psychological literature, sudden death, perhaps due to cardiac arrhythmia, is reported as a possible outcome of what is termed Dissociative Trance Disorder.[98]

In our study of *samāʿ* and its effects, such predisposing conditions are rarely known from the textual evidence. In one case, however, the author does mention the subject having a pre-existing anxiety: ʿAṭṭār refers to a youth as *sukhta-dil*, literally 'burned of heart', i.e. 'anxious, troubled'. It can be shown that this narrative hint is important in explaining the sudden crisis experienced by the youth which caused his death. Unfortunately, such significant indicators are rarely given, and the reader is mostly left uninformed about similar background factors which could assist explanation.

The quite large number of sudden death cases mentioned in the sources may perhaps be reduced when it is considered that several of ʿAṭṭār's examples appear to be literary hyperbole. This is occasioned by the author's desire to characterise some of the Sufi masters as 'saints' by recording their deeds as imitative of the actions of David, the Israelite prophet. A pious tradition has it that David's voice was so beautiful that it entranced those who listened to his recitals of the Psalms, and on one occasion some four hundred listeners were carried out dead from the assembled crowd! (*Lumaʿ* 268.3–6.)

This tradition may well be the basis of ʿAṭṭār's accounts of the preaching sessions of the illustrious Junayd and Yaḥyā b. Muʿādh (d.258/871). The embellishment of the Sufi masters' reputations with accounts of their miracles and their marvellous acts is a well-known feature of ʿAṭṭār's writings. The author is most likely relying on hyperbole in recording that Junayd once preached to 40 people, 18 of whom died, with the remainder left unconscious by the power of his oratory (*T.A.* II.11.10–12). Similarly, Yaḥyā b. Muʿādh began a preaching tour of Khurāsān, and each day more and more people 'died' from among those who listened to him (*T.A.* I.312.2–4). These narratives may be regarded as hyperbole occasioned by a hagiographic desire to sanctify the reputation of these Sufi masters.

This limits to some extent the number of references to sudden death in the source writings. Notwithstanding these mitigating factors, however, there still remain several accounts whose authenticity is less questionable.

The case of Junayd's disciple, who tried to keep himself from shouting out at the recollection of God's name, has been referred to above in sections I and K. This narrative is securely grounded, with its inclusion in four of the sources.[99] The above-mentioned correlation between existing stress factors and sudden seizure is certainly clear in this case. The man's attempt to restrain himself under pain of dismissal from the master's presence showed in symptoms of excessive perspiration. He was obviously suffering extreme anxiety, and a crisis condition ensued during this period. It is plausible that his attempt to control an automatism eventually failed, and that he suddenly collapsed and died.

Another narrative also recorded by three sources is that of the servant/beggar who overheard the slave girl singing to her master (category K). There is less evidence here of the cause and conditions accompanying the man's sudden death. All that can be surmised is that the man experienced a dissociative reaction, evidenced by his almost ecstatic exclamation on hearing the verse. He believed that a divine voice had spoken to him, and that 'God was transforming him by His Truth'. The man then uttered a death cry and died, seemingly as a result of this overwhelming experience.

Sarrāj records a rather strange account whose purpose seems to be an illustration of the power of Qurʾānic recital. A shaykh and his disciples visited a fellow shaykh, and when one of the first shaykh's entourage began reciting from the Qurʾān, one of the other's companions cried out and died. The following morning, the same person began to read, but the second shaykh cried out and caused the reader to die! (*Lumaʿ* 287.5–10.) Though nothing else is known about the background of the two unnamed masters, it would appear from the narrative that a sort of feud or vendetta was being waged between them. There is an almost farcical element in this narrative, and some retributive actions being played out. The text gives a hint of foul play such as a vendetta by stating that the two masters afterwards said to each other that the first action was the more unjust. This narrative is probably a bad illustration of the power of Qurʾānic recital, if this was Sarrāj's purpose, for it merely illustrates the base motives of rivalry and revenge.

There are several other short references to sudden death resulting from *samāʿ* which have little value for this discussion due to the briefness of the accounts. One of these, however, is a short narrative concerning a man who was bathing in the Euphrates when a passer-by recited a Qurʾānic verse of judgement. The man began to tremble or shiver with agitation, and soon sank and was drowned (*Iḥyāʾ*

II.295.5–6, Mcd. p.737). This is a quite straightforward account of death by drowning. There is, however, the secondary cause of hearing the recited verse, which provoked the man's agitation and led to his unsteadiness in the water.

Mention was made in category K concerning the man who questioned Junayd on a dogmatic point, and when Junayd answered, the man cried out and 'died', according to Ghazālī, but only 'departed', according to Sarrāj. A likely explanation of this difference is that Ghazālī mistook Sarrāj's earlier text which read *kharaja*, 'he departed', as a euphemism for death, perhaps on the basis of the man's dissociative reaction to Junayd's speech. In any event, this difference illustrates the questionable reliability of some of these accounts, particularly where sudden death is referred to in a casual, matter-of-fact way. It may also show the reluctance of some authors, particularly the trustworthy Sarrāj, to overplay the frequency of situations where sudden death was reported. Perhaps Sarrāj's use of euphemism, if this can be shown, was due to his natural caution and tendency for understatement.

Finally, there is the case of Shiblī and the youth referred to in 'Aṭṭār's *Tadhkirat*. Shiblī was repeating the name of God when a youth 'burned of heart', meaning troubled or anxious, asked him why he did not recite the profession of faith. Shiblī replied that he feared saying the negative 'There is no god . . .' lest he did not reach the positive '. . . but God'! The youth trembled and died on the spot, and his companions accused Shiblī of murder (*T.A.* II.166.20–167.9). Despite the suddenness of the youth's seizure, an explanatory hint is given in the text's mention of his pre-existing anxiety state which evidently had some role to play in his death. This is significant in light of the modern correlation found between pre-existing stress conditions and sudden death.

Apart from some very brief references which have no value for phenomenological discussion, at the end of this survey there are some four or five instances of sudden death which remain noteworthy. In two of these cases, the youth spoken to by Shiblī, and the disciple of Junayd who could not help crying out, there is a clear condition of underlying anxiety or stress which provides convincing evidence of being a causal factor. Some doubt remains over the narrative of the two shaykhs and the deaths of their followers. This account may be nothing more than an exaggerated record of rivalry and feuding between the two parties, perhaps with some display of 'magic' powers added to the situation. Its reliability remains suspect, and it cannot be regarded in a completely serious vein. The man drowned in the Euphrates is a death by misadventure, probably caused by anxiety at hearing the sacred text proclaiming God's judgement, which was taken literally and personally. The man who questioned Junayd certainly experienced dissociation, but there is some doubt in the texts as to whether or not he died. This leaves the one remaining instance of the beggar who died unexpectedly upon hearing poetry recited, which he understood as God speaking directly to him. Again, he clearly experienced dissociation, but there is no straightforward explanation for his sudden collapse and death.

This is rather inadequate evidence for the direct effect of *samāʿ* in causing death. The question of textual reliability is raised in this present discussion more than in most previous categories. Whether it is ʿAṭṭār's zealousness to sanctify the memory of the Sufi masters by an exaggerated account of the power of their oratory, or the dubious account of the two feuding shaykhs, or Sarrāj and Ghazālī's failure to agree on whether a man 'died' or merely 'departed', this category has attracted more than its share of narrative and textual doubts. This is of particular concern in the case of such a dramatic outcome for *samāʿ* as sudden death. One must concede that the evidence is inconclusive, and it would be hasty to claim that this reaction is a characteristic feature of the altered states associated with *samāʿ*. Equally, like the narratives of the man who drowned, and the anxious youth addressed by Shiblī, there may be other mitigating circumstances and contributory factors which are unknown in those cases which appear to be directly caused by *samāʿ*.

Notes

1 Gilbert Rouget, *Music and Trance: A Theory of the Relations between Music and Possession*, Chicago, IL and London: University of Chicago Press, 1985.

2 Jean During, *Musique et extase: L'audition mystique dans la tradition soufie*, Paris: Albin Michel, 1988.

3 Moshe Idel, *Kabbalah: New Perspectives*, New Haven, CT: Yale University Press, 1988, p.35.

4 Ibid., pp.35–6.

5 For example, *Lumaʿ* 271.7ff; and Regula B. Qureshi, 'Qawwālī: Making the Music Happen in the Sufi Assembly', in *Asian Music*, xviii, 2, 1987, pp.118–157.

6 For example, Ibn Abī ʾl-Dunyā's *Dhamm al-Malāhī*, in James Robson (ed.), *Tracts on Listening to Music*, London: Royal Asiatic Society, 1938.

7 See John Bowker, *Problems of Suffering in Religions of the World*, Cambridge: Cambridge University Press, 1970, pp.128ff.

8 See Amnon Shiloah, *Music in the World of Islam: A Socio-Cultural Study*, Aldershot: Scolar Press, 1995, pp.51ff.
9 References to practical music therapy are found in several Arabic writers such as Ibn Hindū, Ibn ʿAdb al-Rabbih and al-Kindī. See Shiloah, ibid., pp.15; 55ff.
10 *Lumaʿ* 282.9–14; *Iḥyāʾ* II.294.17–20; Mcd. pp.735–6; *Ris.* 345.
11 Cf. the story of Shiblī in the mosque, *Lumaʿ* 282.17ff; Abū Ḥulmān in the street, *Lumaʿ* 289.7ff; and others.
12 See Rouget, op.cit., pp.296–301.
13 As in non-epileptic seizures. See A. James Rowan and John R. Gates (eds), *Non-Epileptic Seizures*, Boston, MA: Butterworth-Heinemann, 1993, pp.5,147.
14 See Roger Walsh, 'Phenomenological Mapping: A Method for Describing and Comparing States of Consciousness' in *Journal of Transpersonal Psychology*, 27, 1995, p.35.
15 See Felicitas D. Goodman, *Speaking in Tongues: A Cross-Cultural Study of Glossolalia*, Chicago, IL and London: University of Chicago Press, 1972, Chapter 6.
16 Ibid., pp.76–9.
17 Al-Makkī was an associate of Junayd and Abū Saʿīd al-Kharrāz (*T.S.* 200.4–5).
18 See John P. Kildahl, *The Psychology of Speaking in Tongues*, New York, NY: Harper and Row, 1972, p.51.
19 See article '*Djanna*', in *E.I.* vol.2, p.449.
20 See Kildahl, op.cit., pp.4,46.
21 See Eugene D'Aquili, and Andrew B. Newberg, *The Mystical Mind: Probing the Biology of Religious Experience*, Minneapolis, MN: Fortress Press, 1999, pp.89–90.
22 *Lumaʿ* 291.2ff; *Ris.* 345–6; *Iḥyāʾ* II.297.28ff; Mcd. pp.746–7.
23 See Wolfgang G. Jilek, 'Therapeutic Use of Altered States of Consciousness in Contemporary North American Indian Ceremonials', in C.A. Ward (ed.), *Altered States of Consciousness and Mental Health: A Cross-Cultural Perspective*, Newbury Park, CA, London and New Delhi: Sage Publications, 1989, p.178.
24 See Kildahl, op.cit.; and Walsh, op.cit., p.42.
25 See Walsh, op.cit., pp.42–3; and Roland Fischer, 'Toward a Neuroscience of Self-Experience and States of Self-Awareness and Interpreting Interpretations', in Benjamin B. Wolman and Montague Ullman (eds), *Handbook of States of Consciousness*, New York, NY: Van Nostrand Reinhold, 1986, pp.16–17.
26 See Donald A. Hodges (ed.), *Handbook of Music Psychology*, Dubuque: Kendall Hunt, 1980, pp.113–19, 141–2, 393–5.
27 See Hodges, op.cit., pp.113–19; and Jeff Pressing, 'Musical Experience, Altered States of Consciousness, and psi', in A. Gabay (ed.), *Proceedings of the Psychic Orientation Conference*, Melbourne: La Trobe University, 1980, pp.43–7.
28 D'Aquili and Newberg, op.cit., pp.99–100.
29 Qureshi, 'Qawwālī', op.cit., p.122.
30 See *Lumaʿ*, English section, p.148.
31 See Goodman, op.cit., p.127.

32 See Rowan and Gates, op.cit., Chapters 1 and 2; Goodman, op.cit., Chapter 5.
33 See H. Newton Malony and A. Adams Lovekin, *Glossolalia: Behavioral Science Perspectives on Speaking in Tongues*, New York, NY: Oxford University Press, 1985, p.99; and E. Mansell Pattison et al., 'Trance and Possession States', in Wolman and Ullman, op.cit., pp.286–310.
34 Regula B. Qureshi, 'The Maḥfil-e-sama: Ṣufi Practice in the Indian Context', in *Islam and the Modern Age*, xvii, 1986, p.154.
35 Qureshi, 'Qawwālī', op.cit., p.123.
36 *Lumaʿ* 288.16–289.7; *Iḥyāʾ* II.287.9–14; Mcd. p.713.
37 Qureshi, op.cit.
38 *Lumaʿ* 289.20–290.9; *Iḥyāʾ* II.291.19–25; Mcd. p.727; See also Qushayrī's shortened version in *Ris.* 344.
39 *Lumaʿ* 290.11–7; *Iḥyāʾ* II.288.16–20; Mcd. pp.716–17.
40 See references in note 22 above.
41 Carl W. Ernst, *Words of Ecstasy in Sufism*, Albany, NY: State University of New York Press, 1985.
42 Ibid., pp.9–20.
43 See ʿAṭṭār, *T.A.* II.166.14–9; and Ali Hassan Abdel-Kader, *The Life, Personality and Writings of Al-Junayd*, London: Luzac, 1976, pp.35ff.
44 *Lumaʿ* 375.5 (Ernst's translation, op.cit., p.12).
45 *Lumaʿ* 282.17ff; *Ris.* 344–5 ; *Iḥyāʾ* II.294.14–7; Mcd. p.735.
46 See, for example, ʿAṭṭār, *T.A.* II.182.23–183.3.
47 See Ralph G. Locke and Edward F. Kelly, 'A Preliminary Model for the Cross-Cultural Analysis of Altered States of Consciousness', in *Ethos*, 13, 1985, pp.35–6.
48 See Farīdu 'ddīn ʿAṭṭār, *Muslim Saints and Mystics: Episodes from the Tadhkirat al-Auliya'*, transl. A.J. Arberry, London: Routledge and Kegan Paul, 1966 (1979) (hereafter: MSM), p.239.
49 See Michael A. Sells (ed.), *Early Islamic Mysticism: Sufi, Qurʾan, Miʿraj, Poetic and Theological Writings*, New York, NY, Mahwah: Paulist Press, 1996, pp.259–60.
50 As was the fate of Ḥallāj and ʿAyn al-Quḍāt al-Hamadhānī, among others. See Ernst, op.cit.
51 Qureshi, 'The Maḥfil-e-sama', op.cit., pp.153–5.
52 The similarity with glossolalia utterances is obvious.
53 Goodman, op.cit., p.124.
54 Ibid. A similar situation may underlie Tourette's syndrome; see Oliver Sacks, *An Anthropologist on Mars*, Sydney: Pan Macmillan, 1995, p.79.
55 Goodman, op.cit., pp.58–60; Fischer, op.cit., pp.16–17; Walsh, op.cit., p.42.
56 For example, with regard to Nūrī (the 'radiant' one), see *T.A.* II.49.25–50.1 (MSM p.226).
57 See references in Note 45 above.
58 *Iḥyāʾ* II.293.28ff; Mcd. p.733; *Kashf* 515.6–7; Nich. p.396.
59 See Locke and Kelly, op.cit., p.38; and article 'Anxiety', in *The Oxford Companion to the Mind*, ed. by Richard L. Gregory, Oxford: Oxford University Press, 1987, p.30.
60 See Goodman, op.cit., p.77; Locke and Kelly, op.cit., p.35.

61 *Lumaʿ* 285.12–8; *Ris.* 345; *Iḥyāʾ* II.299.16–9; Mcd. p.4.
62 *T.A.* II.20.14–7. In Hujwīrī's version (*Kashf* 532.8–15; Nich. p.408) the man did not die, but remained in a trance for a day.
63 Qur. 57.15; 25.26. In the case of Shiblī, the verse spoke of God's ability to remove inspiration from humankind (Qur. 17.86).
64 Or 'the Named', if the text is vocalised differently.
65 See Don W. King et al., 'Convulsive Non-Epileptic Seizures', in Rowan and Gates, op.cit., p.34.
66 See E.W. Lane, *An Arabic–English Lexicon*, Cambridge: Islamic Texts Society Trust, 1984 repr., s.v.; and F. Steingass, *Persian–English Dictionary*, London: Routledge and Kegan Paul, 1892 (1977), s.v.
67 *Lumaʿ* 285.20–286.18; *Ris.* 346; *Iḥyāʾ* II.285.27–286.7; Mcd. pp.707–9; *Kashf* 533.1–13; Nich. pp.408–9.
68 *Lumaʿ* 295.4–9; *Iḥyāʾ* II.295.11–4; Mcd. pp.737–8. Did Ghazālī interpret the earlier version loosely, taking the verb as a euphemism?
69 *T.A.* I.323.18–324.5. Arberry's translation (MSM pp.193–4) omits mention of his crying out.
70 Gilbert Rouget, *Music and Trance: A Theory of the Relations between Music and Possession*, Chicago, IL and London: University of Chicago Press, 1985, pp.300–1.
71 Ibid.
72 Qureshi, 'Qawwālī', op.cit., p.123.
73 See King et al., op.cit.
74 Lane, *Lexicon*, op.cit., p.1613, s.v. *shahaqa*.
75 See Qureshi, 'Qawwālī', op.cit.; Rowan and Gates, op.cit., p.5; and Goodman, op.cit., p.58.
76 *Lumaʿ* 291.2–292.1; *Ris.* 345–6; *Iḥyāʾ* II.297.28–298.9; Mcd. pp.746–7. See section B above for discussion of ʿAṭṭār's version of the narrative.
77 See Qureshi, 'Qawwālī', op.cit.; Rowan and Gates, op.cit., p.5; and Goodman, op.cit., p.58.
78 See Pattison et al., op.cit., p.286.
79 See Walsh, op.cit., especially p.33.
80 See Fischer, op.cit., especially pp.16ff.
81 Cf. the account of ʿAṭṭār's biography of Sarrāj, where the latter was uninjured when he placed his face in a fire during a trance (*T.A.* II.183.3–10).
82 For example, Goodman, op.cit., p.159.
83 See Jilek, op.cit., p.178.
84 See Jilek, op.cit., pp.180–1; and Goodman, op.cit., pp.77–9, 83, 153.
85 See Goodman, op.cit., p.77.
86 See Jilek, op.cit., pp.180–1.
87 See Pattison, op.cit., pp.286ff; and Jilek, op.cit., pp.178ff.
88 Abū Bakr al-Kalābādhī, *The Doctrine of the Ṣūfīs*, transl. A.J. Arberry, Lahore: Ashraf, 1966 repr., pp.143–4; and T.A. II.50.10–20.
89 See article 'Somnambulism', in *The Oxford Companion to the Mind*, op.cit., p.723.
90 See Rowan and Gates, op.cit., p.2.
91 See Qureshi, 'The Maḥfil-e-sama', op.cit., pp.150–5; and idem, 'Qawwālī', op.cit., pp.122–3.

92 New Testament, Mark 1.21–28; 5.1–20; etc. Such views persisted for many centuries into recent times. See Owsei Temkin, *The Falling Sickness*, Baltimore, MD: Johns Hopkins University Press, 1994.

93 See Alec Roy and Madeleine Barris, 'Psychiatric Concepts in Psychogenic Non-Epileptic Seizures', in Rowan and Gates, op.cit., pp.143–51.

94 For a more integrating approach, see David Lukoff, 'The Diagnosis of Mystical Experiences with Psychotic Features', in *Journal of Transpersonal Psychology*, 17, 1985, pp.155–81.

95 See Edward Shorter, *From Paralysis to Fatigue: A History of Psychosomatic Illness in the Modern Era*, New York, NY: Free Press, 1992, pp.130–3.

96 See Kildahl, op.cit., p.57.

97 See Wallace B. Pickworth et al., 'Stress, Arrhythmias, and Seizures', in Claire M. Lathers and Paul L. Schraeder (eds), *Epilepsy and Sudden Death*, New York, NY and Basel: Marcel Dekker, 1990, pp.417ff.

98 *Diagnostic and Statistical Manual of Mental Disorders*, fourth edition, Washington, DC: American Psychiatric Association, 1994, p.728.

99 Though in Hujwīrī's *Kashf* (532.8–15; Nich. p.408) the man only lost consciousness for a day.

5

THE PSYCHOLOGY OF *SAMĀʿ* (PART 2)

The discussion from the previous chapter may best be summarised in the following way:

SUMMARY OF BEHAVIOURS: CONTRIBUTORY FACTORS

A	Healing effect 1 Junayd's 'homoeopathic' cure: 'sonic' cause and recovery 2 Psychosomatic illness: cured by master's presence and by recitation
B	Joyful, pleasurable feelings 1 Evoked by *samāʿ*: dissociation evident 2 Joy followed by weeping: emotional release
C	Unspecified arousal Two cases evoked by *samāʿ*: dissociation evident
D	Rising in ecstasy Two cases of mass rising: ritual? Or socialised behaviour? Nūrī's trance: dissociation evident Al-Muḥāsibī, Dhū 'l-Nūn, Ibn Ḥanẓala and Yūsuf b. al-Ḥusayn: partial dissociation All cases evoked by emotive/sensual verse recitation
E	Ecstatic utterances Two types: 1 Automatism, mindless repetition: appears dissociative 2 Short, emotional outbursts, highly creative and crafted: strong, overwhelming emotion, high arousal
F, G	Glowing face or loss of colour Three varying cases: fear or anxiety reactions?
H	Suppression of appetite Sahl's trance: caused by altered state? Or voluntary, enhancing his state?

I Perspiring
1 Sahl Tustarī
2 Junayd's disciple: underlying anxiety or crisis in both

J Tremor, agitation
Two cases evoked by Qur'ān recitation: dissociation, or fear inspired?
Shiblī's psychosis: anxiety-driven psychosis
Youth spoken to by Shiblī: pre-existing anxiety state
Caliph: Shiblī's words

K Sighing, groaning, crying out
Two main types:
1 Groan/cry of dissociation
2 'Death cry' of seizure before death
Exceptions
– Abū Ḥafṣ: cry of pain on returning to usual consciousness
– Prophet's hissing sound while praying: panting or hyperventilation?

L Weeping
Various cases, emotional reactions to personal/psychological situations: dissociation not needed as explanation

M Loss of sensitivity to pain
Nūrī's trance and Abū Ḥafṣ: trance-like state in both

N Fainting, loss of consciousness
Seven varying situations, all with sudden overwhelming, but by what?: Borderline/twilight consciousness? Fasting and ascetic practices? Other physiological causes?

O Restless wandering
Four trance-like situations: all with altered state symptoms
– less environmental awareness
– directed, obsessive behaviour
– less voluntary control, etc.

P Loss of voluntary control of limbs
Few specific references, though an 'expected' behaviour

Q Throwing oneself (or being thrown) to the ground
Two similar cases concerning disciples of famous masters: dissociation evoked by Qur'ān or *dhikr* recitation: neurological or psychogenic?

R Attempted suicide
Shiblī's psychosis and the Israelite youth: psychosis in both cases

S Sudden death
1 Youth spoken to by Shiblī: underlying anxiety factor
2 Disciple of Junayd: underlying anxiety and stress factors
3 Drowned man: probably caused by anxiety at Qurʾān verse
4 Beggar: overwhelmed by *samā*ʿ; other causes?
5 Man who questioned Junayd: 'departed' (Sarrāj) or 'died' (Ghazālī)

It would appear that with the variety of symptoms and behaviours, there are a variety of possible conditions indicated, as well as a number of contributory factors. There seems to be no one specific condition or state which can be seen as a particular result of *samā*ʿ. Conversely, it appears that the effects of music, recitation and other aural stimuli are multifarious, and dependent on a number of factors, physiological, psychological, cultural, and otherwise.

This is perhaps only a modern way of restating what the early Sufi writers already knew, that *samā*ʿ is a multifaceted and diverse phenomenon. It may also point to the rudimentary nature of modern knowledge about the states and behaviours witnessed in these early texts. One could argue, for instance, that closer analysis of these behaviours might well reveal a single underlying condition. It may also be possible to give a unified explanation, based on greater understanding of the contributory factors. However, the present state of knowledge in the psychology of altered states means that such an explanation is not possible at the moment.

The contributory factors

In the above discussions, it has always been assumed that *samā*ʿ was the primary or initial cause of the observed behaviours. Music, words and other sounds were seen as the principal contributory factors. The significant part played by aural stimuli in heightening emotions, altering moods and changing physiological states cannot be overemphasised. Many of the proposed contributory factors on the right hand side of the above table are a manifestation of this basic assumption.

There is adequate demonstration of this effect in the research literature on altered states, music psychology and from other sources. Gilbert Rouget, in his classic work on trance, argues that in *samā*ʿ the 'culturally conditioned' emotive impact of music has an entrancing effect. The overwhelming, transcendent force of *samā*ʿ produces a crisis which may result in a total invasion and occupation of consciousness, an illumination, a collapse, and unusual behavioural manifestations. Moreover, argues Rouget, music has the power of inducing trance only because it is a vehicle for words charged with meaning.[1] Rouget also asserts that trance can be stimulated by physiological means, as with *dhikr*, by the repetition of words and phrases accompanied by body movements and rhythms. Certain types of breathing can produce hyperventilation, and the combined effect of rhythmic movement or dance is likely to change physiological equilibrium, and even produce convulsive effects.[2]

The preceding analysis tends to question some of these assertions of Rouget. It has been shown, for example, that music has the power to transform without it being merely a vehicle for the semantic impact of words. The 'music' of secular, sensual verse is one case in point where there is minimal semantic content likely to evoke an ecstatic reaction among religious mystics. The episode of the scholars' assembly where Nūrī recited love poetry is an example of this. Nor can it be allowed that the sublimation, in Freudian terms, of such verse with mystical or spiritual meaning legitimates this argument. It is the non-semantic aspect of poetry in Islamic culture which has always given it such evocative power.

As for the physiological effects of *dhikr*, rhythmic chanting and movement, it is notable that these effects frequently occur outside the formal and ritual settings assumed by Rouget's argument. There is no denying that they may occur in formal settings, but many of the episodes recorded by the source writings are in everyday places where there is no possibility of ritual or formal *samā*ʿ. This seems to suggest that these effects or reactions are accessible in a range of situations. It may also be the case that the change from everyday consciousness to an altered state is not such a difficult or unusual process.

With these modifications, however, the essence of Rouget's argument stands. The overwhelming nature of the force or crisis produced by *samā*ʿ is obvious in nearly all the situations described in the sources. This basic fact is clearly present in the minds of the source writers, however much the modern reader may wish to qualify the force of *samā*ʿ by pointing to contributory social or psychological factors.

It is clear from contemporary research in music psychology that physiological responses to aural stimuli can be both significant and detectable, even in sterile laboratory settings. There is some doubt, however, whether consistent reactions can be found over a range of people without variations due to individual differences, cultural habituation to music, or other predisposing factors.[3]

If *samāʿ* can be seen as the primary or initial cause of the reactions recorded in the source texts, the factors on the right hand side of the above table may be seen as secondary or contributory.

Types of secondary factors

Dissociation

The analysis summarised in the above table does not always require a recourse to dissociation or altered states as a means of description or explanation. In other words, many of the behaviours resulting from *samāʿ* can be seen in terms familiar from everyday experience, though at an exaggerated or intensified level. The assumption of abnormal states of behaviour or consciousness is not required for many of the observed phenomena.

It needs to be questioned whether we should assume an underlying dissociative state in cases where 'everyday' explanations can readily be found. Methodologically, it is preferable to assume the more obvious and least complicated explanation than to resort at once to abnormal or pathological aetiologies. This is another aspect of the point mentioned in category R of Chapter 4 about the readiness of modern psychology, at least until very recently, to emphasise the pathological view. The early Sufi writers, in dealing with the same phenomena, saw the integration and relative normality of these behaviours within their particular cultural and religious context.[4]

Yet if an assumption of dissociation is not often required, the examples where it is operative clearly show similar, commonly occurring features. Most of these cases provide evidence of trance-like or epileptiform characteristics, where there are directed behaviours, automatisms, involuntary actions, and the like. These appear symptomatic of a basic disturbance of mental and physiological state, the origins of which cannot be adequately explained from the available textual evidence. It seems likely, in the absence of other significant explanatory factors, that altered states are involved in these situations, even if this provides merely a descriptive mechanism.

Stress and anxiety factors

This class of contributory factors was seen as significant in the above discussion and analysis. While these factors may be more vaguely defined and perhaps less amenable to precise analysis, they are nevertheless present in a number of the episodes recorded in the sources.

In fact, explanations relating to stress and anxiety are as common as any relating to altered states.

The frequency and wide representation of these contributory factors might suggest that psychogenic explanations underlie many of the reactions to *samāʿ*. The 'release' mechanism of Yūsuf b. al-Ḥusayn's joy followed by weeping, or the several examples of anxiety induced by Qur'ān recitation, or Sarī's glowing face and Shiblī's pallor, examples of perspiring, tremor and agitation, weeping, and so on, attest to the variety and characteristic nature of this explanation. Such widely occurring behaviours are attributable to stress or anxiety factors, and many are typical of the reactions to *samāʿ*. This may indicate that psychological, rather than neurological or purely physiological explanations underlie many of these typical reactions.

Physiological factors

The physiological factors which can be seen as contributory fall into two broad categories. First, there are self-induced effects, the results of ascetic practices such as fasting, meditation, the practice of *dhikr* resulting in hyperventilation, and so on. The second category of factors are largely involuntary, and include changes in physiological functioning and psychological states caused by internal bodily and mental processes. The first category tends to affect the second, ascetic practices being mainly designed to induce different states of body or mind. Equally, there is a reciprocal relationship between changes in physiological functioning and the body–mind's influence on ascetic practices and behaviours.

In the discussion and analysis in Chapter 4 there were some clear examples of the effects of ascetic practices. Shiblī's seizure in the mosque during the month of Ramadan is a good example where the practice of fasting is almost certainly contributory. The case of Sahl Tustarī's trance where he would fast for over three weeks is an example of one of the two types of effects just outlined. Either Sahl's fasting was voluntary, which explains the altered state he experienced, or else his internal 'state' itself affected him to the extent that he was unable to eat for a lengthy period.

The scarcity of references in the sources to such physiological effects cannot be due to a lack of knowledge of the direct relationship between ascetic practices and the body–mind's functioning. There can be no question that a sophisticated understanding of these relationships was widespread during this period of Islamic society. Ascetic practices among Sufi groupings depended on this basic knowledge.[5]

This leads to the consideration that such effects are a largely unknown quantity when it comes to analysing the phenomena found in the source writings. It may well be that these widespread practices were simply assumed as operative among participants of *samāʿ*. The reactions recorded were perhaps seen as resulting from such practices already assumed, which were not even worth mentioning. If this was the case, then these physiological factors would be more influential than was previously acknowledged here. It may well be that many of the behaviours which are aetiologically ambiguous to the modern reader were readily explicable in their original setting. However this may be, it is not really possible to go beyond the available textual evidence. It was noted earlier that many possibilities may be extrapolated from the texts, but these cannot be seriously considered without other corroborating evidence.

'Everyday' explanations

This class of factors could perhaps be more aptly named, but the term 'everyday' seeks to include several types of explanation which are familiar from ordinary experience. No special state of mind or behaviour is assumed or required, but rather the heightening or intensification of ordinary emotions, experiences and behavioural responses.

One example of this is the heightened arousal and emotion which may contribute to ecstatic utterances of the non-compulsive type. It is not really necessary to assume that some form of altered state is operating when the type of utterance recorded here is explicable on the basis of strong, overwhelming emotion. High levels of arousal and emotion, with the full operation of consciousness and human creative faculties, are adequate in explaining such utterances, as witnessed in ordinary experience. Similarly, the emotion of strong empathy, for example, explains the reaction of the assembly in Muḥāsibī's presence, when he arose and wept.

Other familiar reactions include the fear aroused by Qur'ānic recital, where the reading of the sacred and revered text evokes a strong emotion or physical response of varying proportions. Some of these responses may appear dramatic, particularly to the modern reader who may have been desensitised by the ready availability of highly charged, evocative music and mass media, and also desensitised to the powerful influence of religious ritual and sacred recitation. Yet these reactions are not out of the ordinary or abnormal, requiring the assumption of altered states. They are simply strong, emotional effects, the heightening of everyday reactions which are probably less familiar in a technological and secular society than in earlier times.

Social and cultural factors

The phenomena being discussed are firmly located within a very specific cultural and religious context. The Islamic societies of the Middle East from the second/eighth to the sixth/twelfth centuries are the historical and cultural setting for the texts and their narratives. Beyond these more obvious settings, however, lie rather more subtle influences on behaviour which are not just outward manifestations of a particular religious system. It has been proposed in the analysis, for example, that some of the group dynamics or social behaviour mechanisms operating within Sufi communities may account for some of the mass behaviours apparent in *samāʿ* rituals. The socialisation processes operating in closed or restricted religious communities where there is a dominant master and a group of inexperienced novices may well account for some of the reactions noted in the texts.

The conflict and tension between Junayd and his aberrant disciple who could not control spontaneous crying out while listening to certain religious texts produced a very onerous burden on the youth. It is not surprising that the anxiety caused by this conflict eventually overwhelmed the disciple.

Though the ritual of *samāʿ* has developed and formalised since the time of these early texts, there is some evidence of ritualised behaviour already in the mass risings recorded in the texts. This is above and beyond the stated rules of etiquette outlined by authors such as Ghazālī in his *Iḥyāʾ*, or his brother Majd al-Dīn in his short work devoted to *samāʿ*, the *Bawāriq al-Ilmāʿ*. The mass risings suggest a ritualised response to the proceedings deriving from a shared, or affected, psychological reaction not mentioned in the relevant texts. They contain the elements of highly structured and socialised behaviour patterns instilled in the community of Sufis.

It is perhaps not unusual that this aspect of behaviour was not commented upon by contemporary authors. Many of these authors were themselves members of similar communities, and critical observations on social psychology could not be expected in their writings. An outsider in time and culture often sees more clearly those things which the insider ignores or assumes. It is unfortunate that many other aspects of the practice of *samāʿ* were not thought of sufficient value for those first authors to document for future inquirers. There are several points in the texts where further elaboration on the social setting of the events taking place would have proved invaluable for understanding the dynamics of these situations more fully. One example is the episode related of al-Duqqī who 'wandered around' at night, falling down and getting up again in a sort of trance state. It is noted cryptically that people would weep at his behaviour, and that his actions became proverbial. Does this mean that a sort of communal or ritual activity was taking place, or do 'the people' refer to members of his immediate family who witnessed his nightly trance? It is unfortunate that we lack the details which would have helped in understanding the social context of such episodes.

Mention was made above about the importance of the relationship between master and disciple in Sufi communities. The episode centring around the dynamic between Makkī and his ill disciple (in category A) is a case in point. Without analysing the social–psychological dynamic between these two unequal persons, the episode of the youth's illness and his dramatic cure becomes less explicable. As a narrative solely concerning the impact of recitation, there is a lack of plausibility, and some element of magic or occultism might even be proposed, given Makkī's statements. The dynamic between the charismatic master and his would-be follower explains more fully what then becomes a more realistic situation.

If more was known about the degree of ritual behaviour, and the social processes operating behind the texts, a great deal of light might be shed on the nature of the reactions to *samāʿ*. What is known from specific writings such as Majd al-Dīn's *Bawāriq*, and from the discussions above, suggests that social psychological factors were indeed very influential. Some of the behavioural reactions can be seen to be significantly influenced by social factors. This aspect will be further developed in Chapter 8 when considering the practice of formal *samāʿ* rituals.

Rouget's analysis of trance and its applicability

Rouget's discussion of *samāʿ* in his important work, *Music and Trance*, provides the only comprehensive psychological treatment of this subject to date. Based mainly on Ghazālī's chapter in the *Iḥyāʾ*, Rouget argues for a fundamental distinction between 'ritualised' and 'non-ritualised' crisis or trance.[6] This distinction is based on whether an ecstatic reaction occurs inside or outside the context of *samāʿ* concerts as formalised or approved within Islam. Non-ritual trance can be dangerous, perhaps leading to madness or even death, and can occur even within *samāʿ* when the resulting reaction fails to conform to the ritual. *samāʿ* can trigger an ecstatic reaction which may be 'expected' in ritual, such as dance, or 'unexpected', leading to a crisis or fit which can be dangerous for the subject.

In essence, Rouget argues for a culturally sanctioned definition of trance or ecstatic reaction, that those reactions occurring within culturally approved conditions are acceptable, and those outside are somehow a 'crisis' condition. This appears little more than a circular definition, simply accepting mainstream religious prescriptions for those activities deemed acceptable or not, in this case relying mostly on Ghazālī's arguments. Such an approach simply codifies the mainstream position, and adds little further insight to the analysis. Moreover, there is no actual psychological explanation offered, rather a cultural or sociological one based on religious criteria.

What is lacking, however, is the inability of such a theory to account for the phenomenological evidence. The textual material detailed in Chapter 4 cannot be neatly divided into 'ritual' settings with acceptable or benign outcomes, and 'non-ritual' situations with crisis outcomes. Rouget does admit that some ritual trances can lead to unexpected crises, an admission which tends to undermine his basic position. All the indications are that trance is often more than just a cultural phenomenon. If all the 'correct', culturally sanctioned conditions can cause unexpected crisis outcomes, this suggests that trance is more complex, more powerful and more unpredictable than a ritually conformable activity.

One example among many is Shiblī's episode in the mosque during the month of Ramadan. The cultic and ritual setting could not be more obvious, yet the experience of Shiblī was so overwhelming to himself and those around him that the narrator thought Shiblī must have died. There is certainly more in question here than simply the performance of a ritual activity. A much larger phenomenon is taking place which only sometimes conforms to cultic requirements.

The source writings which have been considered suggest that as well as ritual situations where 'crisis' outcomes are witnessed, there are many non-ritual settings for *samāʿ* where benign outcomes occur. It would seem that the distinction between these two sorts of outcomes is not based on their ritual or non-ritual setting.

It is the argument of the present study that reactions to *samāʿ* are multifaceted, and do not conform to single, overall explanations. The view of Rouget, dividing *samāʿ* into either ritual or non-ritual, cannot be said to provide an adequate description or explanation of the phenomena.

Notes

1 Gilbert Rouget, *Music and Trance: A Theory of the Relations between Music and Possession*, Chicago, IL and London: University of Chicago Press, 1985, pp.299–300.
2 Ibid., pp.300–1.
3 See Donald A. Hodges (ed.), *Handbook of Music Psychology*, Dubuque: Kendall Hunt, 1980, pp.113–19, 141–2.
4 See Michael W. Dols, *Majnūn: The Madman in Medieval Islamic Society*, Oxford: Clarendon Press, 1992, p.4, and Chapter 13.
5 See article '*zuhd*' by Louis Massignon in *Shorter Encyclopaedia of Islam*, Leiden: E.J. Brill, 1953 (1974), p.661.
6 Rouget, op.cit., pp.261ff.

6

THE PSYCHOLOGY OF *SAMĀʿ* ACCORDING TO THE SUFI WRITERS

Up to this point, the psychological investigations of this study have been concerned with dissecting and abstracting material from the Sufi sources to be viewed in the light of modern findings. There have been only occasional attempts to enquire into the understanding shown by the source writers themselves.

One should always be mindful that these texts were written for contemporary communities of scholars and students, not for the twenty-first century reader. The writings made sense within their own situation, and they do not need later generations to supply adequate interpretations.

It is thus important to ask how these early writers viewed the nature and psychology of *samāʿ*. How was this phenomenon integrated into the Islamic world-view of the time, and does their psychological understanding hold its value today?

The view of Sarrāj

As all later writers depend on the foundational work of Sarrāj, It is best to detail his views at the outset, and use this as a basis for approaching his successors.

There is no one chapter of Sarrāj's work which deals specifically with the nature of *samāʿ* in its psychological dimension. There are, however, several isolated sections of the work which, when taken together, form a cohesive view on the subject.

The second chapter of the *Kitāb al-Samāʿ* details the opinions of various Sufis on *samāʿ*. Sarrāj here mentions the famous statement of Dhū ʾl-Nūn that *samāʿ* involves *warīd*, the 'visitation' or 'arrival' of Truth which arouses hearts toward the Truth (*Lumaʿ* 271.8–10). This statement is quoted by all the later authorities, which attests to its importance. It indicates the revelatory or inspirational nature of *samāʿ*; it is a gift or grace from above, from the realm of divine truths, which arouses human hearts to respond to that divine truth. These two aspects are present in Dhū ʾl-Nūn's statement: the divine gift which 'arrives', and the human response this inspires. The statement continues by asserting that differing responses produce opposing outcomes: 'One who listens to it in truth is confirmed (in that truth), while one who listens to it sensually becomes an unbeliever.'

Sarrāj further emphasises the subtlety and sensitivity of *samāʿ* as a mystical grace or gift. He mentions the view of some unnamed Sufis who believe *samāʿ* to be 'a sweet nourishment for the spirits of those who are aware (*ahl al-maʿrifa*)', being finer and more subtle than all other actions of the psyche. 'It is perceived by one who has a sensitive nature, because of its sensitivity, and by the pure of heart among those who appreciate it, because of its purity and grace' (*Lumaʿ* 271.14–6). This characterisation refers to more than the aesthetic or poetic qualities of *samāʿ*; it relates rather to the subtlety of its nature as a divine gift. As such it is easily ignored or unappreciated by the interference of grosser human qualities in the psyche, or by failure to listen deeply and quietly enough.

This theme is continued in a quotation from Abū ʿl-Ḥusayn al-Darrāj, where the aesthetic beauty of *samāʿ* and its subtlety as a gift of grace is mentioned. Darrāj expresses this in metaphorical language: 'Attentive listening occupied my mind in a beautiful open field, and it made me discover the existence of the Truth as a gift. Then it gave me drink from the cup of purity, and by its means I understood the abodes of contentment, and it brought me into pleasant and spacious meadows' (*Lumaʿ* 271.17–9). The fields and meadows here are surely expressions of the expansion (*basṭ*) of his state of mind, such being common metaphors among mystics for their enhanced and expanded perception of reality.[1] Despite questions of the extent of metaphor in Darrāj's language, it is clear that for him *samāʿ* was a divine gift revealing knowledge, truth and the experience of grace and well-being. The notion of *samāʿ* as an inspiration of subtle character is again emphasised in a later chapter of Sarrāj's work, this time as the view of the author himself. He states plainly that 'all people of a spiritual disposition (*dhī rūḥ*) find a beautiful voice pleasing because it has qualities of the divine spirit, and it heralds the recollection of this spirit' (*Lumaʿ* 278.9–10). Furthermore, 'one who listens in a state of awareness reflects deeply while listening in order that spiritual significance might accrue from recollection' (ibid. 10–1). The author then lists a lengthy series of themes for such recollection, at the end of which he introduces a new metaphor of a firelighter striking flames in the heart. The pure state of recollection or listening causes an action in the heart comparable to a firelighter, the flames or sparks of which result in transformation, agitation and movement in the limbs and body. Depending on the force of this action, conscious control over bodily actions is relinquished, and were it not for divine mercy, all reason and sanity would be lost (*Lumaʿ* 278.19–279.5).

In this short description, Sarrāj provides a summary analysis of the nature and effect of *samāʿ*. It is a subtle and spiritual phenomenon attained only in certain moments of pure recollection or heightened awareness, and then only as a grace. Yet its action as a spiritual enlightener may be quite overwhelming and result in the profound physical and psychological effects detailed elsewhere. This is the nearest the author comes to outlining a description of how *samāʿ* operates.

There is also a correlation here with notions advanced by the fourth/tenth century philosophical group, the Brethren of Purity (*Ikhwān al-Ṣafāʾ*), in their encyclopaedic *Rasāʾil* (*Treatise*). In the chapter dealing with 'The Aphorisms of Philosophers on Music', the authors of the *Rasāʾil* write: 'Music has an eminent quality that language is incapable of rendering manifest or of expressing by the intermediacy of articulate words; it is for this reason that the soul expresses itself in the form of harmonious melodies. Now, when our human nature hears these melodies, it is inspired with delight, rejoicing and happiness. Listen then to the discourse of the soul and its confidential conversations, repulse nature, do not regard its splendours and do not let yourself be seduced by it.'[2]

A further element in Sarrāj's view of what constitutes *samāʿ* is introduced in a later chapter of his work (*Lumaʿ* 295ff). This element might be termed a 'sympathetic resonance' between the perceptions associated with *samāʿ* and the pre-existing state of the listener's heart. When the latter is receptive, in a state of pure recollection, there is a correspondence or resonance with the perceptions encountered in *samāʿ*: 'The object in all their listening is that their hearts encounter something similar to what is (already) in them by way of strong emotions and recollections. The emotion (*wajd*) is strong when it encounters its like' (*Lumaʿ* 296.9–11). Thus the arrival of the spiritual sense of *samāʿ* is anchored in the degree of reception and preparedness of a person's psyche. There develops a sympathetic resonance whereby the effect is amplified if there is a similarity between the two, or else nullified if there is not. Sarrāj also emphasises that 'listening' is not practised for aesthetic reasons, as the previous discussion on its aesthetic qualities may have indicated. Rather it is practised for its spiritual benefits, notably the reflection and magnification of its transcendent meanings in the hearts of adepts: 'So when they hear something that corresponds to their momentary experience (*waqt*), it intensifies the hidden aspects of their inmost hearts (*mukmanāt sarā'irihim*)' (*Luma*ʿ 296.15–6).

These passages from Sarrāj's work form the basis for understanding his view of *samā*ʿ, its nature, function and psychological mechanism.

By nature it is transcendent, inspirational, a gift or grace which reveals divine truths. It is a subtle and sensitive phenomenon, not simply in an aesthetic way, but in its spiritual qualities disclosed during recollection and attentive listening.

Functionally, the metaphor of the firelighter in the heart is used to describe its action. This can lead to 'sparks' or 'flames' which enlighten spiritually; these 'sparks' may also have physical–psychological effects, causing the unusual behaviours and reactions detailed elsewhere in Sarrāj's work.

One of the main mechanisms involved in this is a 'sympathetic resonance' between the revelations of *samā*ʿ and the receptive state of the listener's heart. The spiritual benefits, and the unusual behaviours evoked, depend on the resonance of transcendent meanings in the hearts of listeners.

It hardly needs stating that this notion of *samā*ʿ is only understandable within the theological and intellectual context of an Islamic world-view. The discussion in terms of grace, revelation, divine gift, seeking the Truth, and so on, can only be given meaning within an overall theology of Sufism. Similarly, the concept of the 'heart' and its preparedness, recollection, responsiveness, and so on, only make sense as part of a Sufi psychology.

What is of note in this context is the degree of assimilation and accommodation of these notions within an overall Islamic, and specifically Sufi world-view. There is a remarkable integration of these diverse and unfamiliar concepts, with the unusual behaviours they attempt to explain, within the prevailing intellectual and social conditions of the time. This is one way at least where there is a better understanding of these notions within Islamic society of the medieval period, compared to the medical and pathological preoccupation of contemporary Western society. It was noted in Chapter 4 that the Sufi approach tended to normalise and assimilate these diverse elements into everyday life and current theological frameworks. The modern Western medical view, despite its sophistication, has difficulty coming to terms with these phenomena. Though there are some recent signs of change, the designations 'abnormal' and 'pathological' are still often applied.

Part of this unfortunate contrast lies in the emphasis on the particular type of rationality characteristic of Western science and psychology generally.[3] This rationality considers everyday, waking consciousness to be an objective normality, with all other types of consciousness deemed inferior, abnormal or non-rational. Part of the importance of Sufism within Islam is that it allows so-called 'altered states' to be seen not only as possible in ordinary, everyday life, but as a valued type of experience. The ability to understand directly, intimately and experientially (the term for this being *dhauq*, literally 'taste') is valued more highly in religious understanding than the more familiar 'rational' approach to knowledge.

The view of Ghazālī

Neither Qushayrī nor Sulamī make a contribution to this topic; in Qushayrī's case there is no special mention of the subject, and his adoption of much of his material from Sarrāj means that he probably shared similar views to the earlier author. With Sulamī, his genre of *ḥadīth*-style biographies leaves little opportunity for conceptual discussions. With Ghazālī, on the other hand, there is every opportunity for discussion of this topic and a genuine development of the concept of *samāʿ*.

At the beginning of the chapter on *samāʿ*, Ghazālī presents a rather poetic summary of his conception of the subject: 'Hearts and their inner chambers are treasuries of secrets and mines of jewels. Jewels are contained in them like fire is contained in iron and stone, concealed like water beneath earth and soil. There is no way to extract their secrets except by the firelighter of listening to music and verse, and there is no entrance to hearts except by the anteroom of the ears. Music which is measured and pleasing brings out what is in them (i.e. hearts), and makes evident their beauties and faults. When the heart is moved, there is made evident only what it contains, just as a vessel drips only what is in it. Thus listening to music and verse is for the heart a true touchstone and an eloquent standard. When the soul of music and verse reaches the heart, it stirs only what predominates in the heart' (*Iḥyāʾ* II.266.16–21).

There are some similarities here with the view of Sarrāj outlined above. First, the metaphor of fire in the heart, and the firelighter, is reminiscent of Sarrāj's description. Ghazālī extends this metaphor, based on metallurgy or mineralogy, to the notion of the heart's 'secrets' being precious jewels hidden deep beneath the earth's surface. These precious gems may be struck with the 'flint' of *samāʿ* to produce sparks and disclose their hidden treasure.

Second, the notion of 'resonance' outlined by Sarrāj and elsewhere adopted by Ghazālī is transformed somewhat. Continuing with the metaphor of the heart as a hidden treasure, it is only what is already contained or hidden within the heart that is brought to light or educed by *samāʿ*. As described by the author, this 'bringing out' is seen as a one-way process, evoked by the action of music and verse. It must be assumed, however, that the action is more sympathetic than Ghazālī allows, that the similarity between the heart's treasures and the spiritual nature of the music and verse provides a powerful evocative factor.

R.A. Nicholson writes of one permutation of this concept: 'Those whose hearts He has opened and endowed with spiritual perception hear His voice everywhere, and ecstasy overcomes them as they listen to the rhythmic chant of the muezzin, or the street cry of the saqqāʿ.[4] Nicholson also mentions a further aspect of this: 'Pythagoras and Plato are responsible for another theory, to which the Sūfī poets frequently allude, that music awakens in the soul a memory of celestial harmonies heard in a state of pre-existence, before the soul was separated from God'.[5] This elaboration of the soul and celestial harmonies is probably more at home in the Persian Sufi tradition and in the theosophy of Ibn al-ʿArabī than in the more sober writings of Ghazālī. Yet the basis for such an interpretation is present in our author's statement above. Ghazālī certainly believes that the heart contains 'jewels' evoked by listening to music, and these jewels could only have been implanted there by divine fiat during pre-existence. There is also a sense in which the notion of resonance, or the memory of spiritual harmonies is operative here. This idea is given explicit statement in Qushayrī's *Risāla* in a quote from Junayd that in the covenant of Alast, 'the sweetness of listening to spiritual words was poured forth so that when (humankind) heard *samāʿ*, the remembrance of this was moved in them' (*Ris.* 340).

In contrast to Sarrāj, then, Ghazālī minimises the importance of revelation in *samāʿ*; there is less of a sense of direct intervention from the divine realm. It is rather only what the heart contains that is educed by listening, and presumably the heart has contained these spiritual treasures from the time of its pre-existence.

The notions expressed in the first quote from Nicholson above also apply to a further discussion of the action of *samāʿ* by Ghazālī.

The author at one point speaks of the 'lover' of God who is so enthralled that he sees Him in all things, and hears all things from Him and in Him. The passion of love is described as acting like 'an inflamer of the tinder box of the heart', another use of the metaphor of fire. This igniting causes states (*aḥwāl*) of rapture and ecstasy (*wajd*), burning and purifying the heart and allowing 'visions and revelations' (*mushāhadāt wa-mukāshafāt*) to follow. Ghazālī declares that such states are the ultimate goal of all lovers of God, their cause being a mystery (*sirr*) of God, and among the subtlest of the sciences of revelation (*Iḥyāʾ* II.277.16–25; Mcd. pp.229–30).

The author goes on to discuss the love of beautiful things, but unfortunately does not elaborate on the nature of *samāʿ* in relation to what he has just outlined. He rather blocks off this discussion by declaring the mechanism and effect of listening to music as one of God's mysteries, and thus not open to human explanation. From what he does state, however, it seems that a similar mechanism to that envisaged by Sarrāj is assumed. Thus we may suppose that the flames or sparks which produce the 'states' mentioned above may also cause the physical–psychological effects with which we are concerned.

This is stated more explicitly, though briefly, in a later section of the chapter: 'Know that the first stage in *samāʿ* is understanding what is heard and its application to a meaning which occurs to the hearer; then this understanding results in ecstasy (*wajd*), and this results in movements of the limbs' (*Iḥyāʾ* II.285.1–2; Mcd. p.705).

As for the mechanism of *samāʿ*, there is very little specifically stated by the author, but on occasion there is some reference to the 'sympathetic resonance' concept found earlier in Sarrāj's writings. One example occurs in Ghazālī's comment on the narrative of the beggar who heard the slave girl singing in her master's house beside the Tigris river. The author explains the action of the singing as reinforcing or coinciding with his mental state. He heard the girl's song as if it were a message from God because of his preoccupation with an internal spiritual struggle. This is one way in which there is 'resonance' between the content of what is heard and the listener's heart.

The main difference between the views of Sarrāj and Ghazālī seems to lie in the differing emphasis on the nature and qualities of the heart. For Ghazālī, the heart is described as a 'mine of jewels', presumably deposited in its pre-existence, with its treasures brought to light by 'listening'. With Sarrāj, there is more emphasis on the action of *samāʿ* as a divine grace or revelation, arousing the heart only as much as the latter is prepared and capable of reflecting or resonating. For Ghazālī, there is revelation from within, from the treasure already contained in the heart, rather than directly from above.

The later Persian authors considered in this study do not add further to this understanding of the psychology of *samāʿ*. Hujwīrī does not address the issue in his writing, while ʿAṭṭār with his adoption of a biographical genre leaves no opportunity for conceptual discussion of this type.

The value of these psychological views

The first means by which these ideas have value is in their integrating the unusual phenomena associated with *samāʿ* into the prevailing culture and world-view of the time. It has been noted above that this integration is one of the more remarkable features of this aspect of Sufi thought. Despite the witnessing of bizarre and dramatic behaviours, there is a sense of their 'expectedness' and explicability within Sufi theology and current intellectual terms. This is an example of the inclusiveness of the culture of Islam in these centuries, so that almost no aspect of behaviour was considered outside its realm simply because of some unusual features. This contrasts with certain streams of contemporary Western psychology where there is a tendency for 'classifying more and more of human behaviour as a disorder which needs treatment'.[6]

Related to this, and again in contrast to Western thought, is the notion that different states of consciousness are legitimate and quite natural. Everyday waking consciousness is not seen as necessarily prescriptive, with all other modes somehow abnormal. This legitimisation of differing states allows for the experiences gained in dreams or a range of altered states to be valuable when compared with those of 'rational' states. This is a further way in which the approach of early Sufi psychology is instructive for Western sciences.

As for the explanations of the Sufi writers discussed here, it is true that their psychology forms part of a more inclusive science of mystical theology. It is difficult to accept the explanations offered without also accepting the assumptions underlying Sufi theology. Their psychology does not stand alone but is part of a larger framework of doctrines and beliefs. This is understandable from any objective view of the subject, yet it means that the applicability of the various insights arising from their psychology of *samāʿ* remains limited.

Given this caveat, the explanations of Sarrāj and Ghazālī are sufficiently inclusive to provide a fairly thorough contemporary description of the Sufi psychology relating to *samāʿ*. There is some lack of detail as to the mechanism causing the unusual behaviours, but the overall description is clear and succinct, and is a valuable contribution to the field of Sufi psychology.

Notes

1 See, for example, al-Bisṭāmī's use of such metaphor in his mystical 'journey' recorded in *Lumaʿ* 384.12ff; and Michael A. Sells (ed.), *Early Islamic Mysticism: Sufi, Qur'an, Miʿraj, Poetic and Theological Writings*, New York, NY, Mahwah: Paulist Press, 1996, pp.242ff.

2 Transl. Amnon Shiloah, 'The Epistle on Music of the Ikhwān al-Ṣafā' in idem., *The Dimension of Music in Islamic and Jewish Culture*, Aldershot: Variorum, 1993, p.65.

3 See Kathleen V. Wilkes, '____, yìshì, duh, um, and consciousness', in A.J. Marcel and E. Bisiach (eds), *Consciousness in Contemporary Science*, Oxford: Oxford University Press, 1988, pp.16–41.

4 R.A. Nicholson, *The Mystics of Islam*, New York, NY: Schocken Books, 1975 repr., p.64.

5 Ibid.

6 James Thompson in *The Age, News Extra*, Melbourne, 24 January 1998, p.8. See also Michael W. Dols, *Majnūn: The Madman in Medieval Islamic Society*, Oxford: Clarendon Press, 1992, Chapter 13.

7

THE SUFIS' EXPLANATIONS OF THEIR ALTERED STATE EXPERIENCES

Having considered the psychology of *samāʿ* – the unusual behaviours encountered under its influence – there are further aspects of its effects which deserve attention. Observable behavioural reactions do not exhaust the possibilities which the source materials offer. The question remains: is it possible to approach more closely the experiences recorded by the Sufi authors, or to understand more fully the nature of the special awareness and altered states which their subjects encountered?

One of the few means by which the texts allow us to approach more closely to such an understanding is through the words uttered by the Sufis under the influence of *samāʿ* or after its occurrence. The concern here is not so much with the 'ecstatic' expressions which they may have uttered, as these have been analysed in Chapter 4. Rather it is the ordinary sayings and expressions by which they sought to explain their behaviour or describe the experiences they encountered, as far as words would allow them.

In the introductions to the chapters on psychology and semantics it was argued that mystical experiences are largely ineffable, and that it was clearly difficult to understand their nature. It is not necessary, however, to go to the point of agnosticism, as Gerald Brenan does in his study of the writings of St John of the Cross. St John's poems were written to express his mystical experiences; it follows, argues Brenan, 'since we cannot form for ourselves any notion of these, that they are obscure. We shall not be able to go so far as to meet them with our own experience as we can in the case of most other poetry.'[1] It does not follow simply because mystical experiences are being spoken or written about per se that others can have no understanding of them. This understanding may not be complete or adequate, but some partial knowledge of them is available to those prepared to search and empathise with mystical experience.

Indeed, the failure of those interested in mysticism ever to grasp the ideas of the mystics would mean that the voluminous writings of the latter would all have been in vain. It is surely paradoxical that despite the ineffability of mystical experiences, mystics have always been the most vocal of religious authors, always ready to attempt an explanation of their personal encounters. In Islam there is confirmation of this general rule, as the examples of Ibn al-ʿArabī and Rūmī illustrate. With Rūmī it is ironic that in his lyric poetry he is always enjoining the reader to 'silence!'. This comes strangely from the author of the famed *Mathnawī*, a work of some 25,700 couplets, as well as a collection of lyric poetry which runs to nine volumes!

If mystics have never been reluctant to broadcast their opinions or to describe their experiences, it is surely worth the effort to consider what they have to say. The understanding of the non-mystic may be only partial and limited, but some appreciation is surely achievable and desirable.

With these observations in mind, the following attempt is made to glean from the texts what the Sufis had to say for themselves about their experiences. In the early documents studied here, there are no extensive speeches, lengthy arguments or accounts. There are simply a number of short and scattered statements recorded along with the descriptions of unusual behaviours. In these short statements, the Sufis who encountered *samāʿ* attempted to describe or explain their encounters briefly, either directly, or by more cryptic utterances.

As with the psychological material, the richest source work is Sarrāj's *Kitāb al-Lumaʿ*. Sarrāj's style of including numerous narratives with editorial comment means that there are many colourful, personal and idiosyncratic vignettes of great value to the modern reader. The character of the other sources, for example the philosophical tone of Ghazālī, or the *ḥadīth*-style of Sulamī, makes their works less likely to contain suitable material.

It is convenient to divide these sayings into four distinct categories, though a few sayings are not easily classifiable, and may fit into more than one category.

Plain description

This first category contains sayings that are plainly descriptive. They are usually fairly straightforward accounts of feelings, moods or states, in simple language, and without the use of poetry, metaphor or deliberately cryptic speech. The purpose of these statements is to inform precisely and in a matter of fact way about the experience encountered, without any attempt at embellishment or lyric expression.

The first example in this category involves Shiblī being questioned by Abū ʿAlī al-Maghāzalī (d.?) about the effect of hearing the Qur'ān. He is concerned that this listening 'warns me to abandon material things and to shun the world; then I return to my usual state of consciousness, and to people's company, and nothing remains of this (warning), and I am propelled back to my earlier state.' Shiblī replies by reassuring Maghāzalī that being attracted to God by what he hears from the Qur'ān is good, and an act of grace; similarly his being propelled back to his normal state is also an act of grace, because of the intensity and force (*al-ḥaul wa-'l-qūwa*) required to face that altered state. This episode is recorded in three of the sources, *Lumaʿ*, *Risāla*, and *Iḥyā'*, with a few minor textual differences in the later works.[2]

The narrative describes in plain terms Maghāzalī's experience of being turned away from ordinary, worldly concerns toward the divine and transcendent, by means of hearing the Qur'ān recited. This involves an altered state of some kind, since he describes the difference in affect toward everyday concerns, and his being 'propelled back' to ordinary consciousness. This is also a description of a religious or transcendent experience similar to a typical 'conversion' encounter. Though Maghāzalī's account is only short, it is in essence reminiscent of the similar crisis described by Ghazālī in his autobiographical work, *al-Munqidh min al-Ḍalāl* (*The Deliverer from Error*). Ghazālī writes in detail about being tossed back and forward between the impulse to abandon his career and family in Baghdad to become an ascetic searching for truth, and the impulse to remain with his career and try to ignore his intellectual doubts and insincerities. This struggle is portrayed as a spiritual conflict of real importance, between the urgings of wealth, position and comforts of this world, and the promptings of the need for salvation in the world to come.[3]

It seems that similar conflicts and urgings are apparent in Maghāzalī's situation as with Ghazālī's, though perhaps not to the same degree. Maghāzalī is concerned about his wavering states of mind, the strength of the prompting to abandon worldly concerns, and the ease with which his mind returns to its ordinary state. This concern is addressed by Shiblī's encouraging remarks by which he attempts to reassure Maghāzalī that both his altered state and his return are acts of divine grace.

The second example in this category presents some similarities with the foregoing. Sarrāj relates of Abū Sulayman al-Dārānī (d.215/830) that he complained of becoming transfixed on a particular verse of the Qur'ān during his reading of it. This could last up to five nights, he states; unless he stops contemplating the verse he is unable to continue reading. Moreover, sometimes when reading the Qur'ān he says that his reasoning faculty (*ʿaql*) 'flies away' and it requires a 'restrainer' (*sajjān*) to return it (*Lumaʿ* 282.5–8).

This is a straightforward description of his situation, though some metaphor is used in the reference to his reason 'flying away', and the 'restrainer', or literally, 'warder, gaoler'. His description of being unable to proceed in his reading, of being transfixed to a particular verse, suggests almost an automatism similar to those discussed in Chapter 4. There it was seen that the continuous repetition of a phrase or other involuntary repetitive actions could be the result of an altered state or dissociative reaction. It appears that a similar process is operating in this present case, where the reader becomes quite 'hypnotised' by the verse being read and is immovable from it. The operation of an altered state is also apparent in his description of the perceived loss of his reasoning faculty, characterised dramatically as its 'flight'. This expression is Dārānī's way of describing its sudden departure, with the sudden arrival of the altered state.

The reference to the 'restrainer' may allude to a higher intellectual faculty within his own mind, or even some transcendent faculty of reason. The mention of the need for a 'restrainer' to return the reasoning faculty to its normal state suggests that Dārānī is aware of the possibility of its long-term loss. The arrival of the altered state may herald danger as far as he is concerned, with the possibility of his mind not returning to normal.

The third example in this category has already been mentioned in Chapter 4. Both Sarrāj and ʿAṭṭār present similar accounts of the trance-like state witnessed of Sahl b. ʿAbdallāh Tustarī. As a result of *samāʿ*, Sahl would go into a trance lasting more than three weeks; he would not eat, and would sweat profusely, even during winter. If he was questioned in this state, he would reply: 'Do not ask anything of me, for my words would be of no benefit to you at this time' (*Lumaʿ* 307.4–8; *T.A.* I.255.16–20).

This is a plain description of the situation as seen by Sahl; he is indicating that his 'state' prevents him from speaking in a proper and profitable way. It was suggested in the discussion of this episode in Chapter 4 that two broad possibilities exist as to why he considered his words unsuitable. First, they may have been inarticulate or nonsensical for various reasons associated with his trance-like state. The second possibility is that his words may have been fully articulate but likely to be misunderstood or misconstrued as heretical or blasphemous. It is possible that Sahl was fearful of this outcome which was the fate of several famous Sufi figures such as Ḥallāj and ʿAyn al-Quḍāt, both of whom were executed for alleged blasphemy. The uncertainty surrounding Sahl's statement means that it could also be considered under the heading of 'enigmatic utterances', the third of the four categories dealt with in the present chapter.

Response to hearing verse recited

This second category of utterance involves a spontaneous response to hearing a verse of poetry or the Qur'ān being recited. The response is usually a short statement or sometimes an ecstatic exclamation prompted by the occasion of the verse, and responding to the meaning it conveys. In all the cases found in the source texts, the response indicates that the hearer is experiencing an altered state, and in two cases the subject suddenly collapses and dies.

The first example was discussed above in Chapter 4 in the section dealing with audible cries. Attested in four of the sources, it is the narrative of the young beggar who happens upon a slave girl singing to her wealthy master in his mansion beside the Tigris river. The girl recited: 'Every day you change; other conduct than this would be better for you; dedicated to God is the love freely given from me to you.' This is according to the earliest source, Sarrāj; Qushayrī and Hujwīrī reverse the line order, while Ghazālī omits the second line. This confusion over the lines recited is also reflected in the reported response of the young beggar. According to Sarrāj and Ghazālī he asks the girl to repeat the verse, whereupon he responds: 'By God, you change me with the Truth when I am in a special state!' Qushayrī omits the words following: 'Truth', whereas Hujwīrī has the youth ask the girl: 'For God's sake chant that verse again, for I have only a moment to live; let me hear it and die!' All the source texts relate that the youth uttered a cry and died on the spot.[4]

Hujwīrī's report of the youth's reply should probably be discounted, since it shows a somewhat obvious prescience. The earlier accounts of Sarrāj and Ghazālī appear more credible.

If this is the case, we are left with a very brief account of the youth's altered state in which he believed he was being addressed by a divine source. This is not a situation of auditory hallucinations or some similar psychotic delusion. It is rather that the youth believed the verse he heard contained a divinely inspired message which spoke to his own situation, and that the female reciter was unwittingly the agent of a higher purpose. Thus the youth responded by paraphrasing or reinterpreting the verse to apply to his own situation. He asked the girl to repeat the verse, so as to confirm what he had heard, and then he replied, addressing God: 'By God, you change me with the Truth when I am in a special state! (*ḥāl*)' The implication is that God acted upon him to 'change' him, presumably to alter his conduct for the better, or strengthen his belief, or the like, when he entered an altered state. The utterance may also indicate that he was at that moment aware of being transported by an altered state. Whether he was aware of this or not, the 'state' soon enveloped him and caused him to cry out, collapse and die.

Ghazālī interprets this episode to mean that the youth was already immersed in his altered state, and was concerned at his heart's inconstancy and changeability. His hearing the verse was thus a confirmation and a warning from God as to the inconstancy of his heart.

A somewhat similar case presents itself as the second example in this category. Ghazālī cites a short account of an unnamed Sufi who heard a Qur'ān verse recited: 'O soul at peace, return to your Lord, well-pleased, well-pleasing' (Qur.89.27). He asked the reciter to repeat the verse, and then said: 'How often do I say to it, "Return!" but it does not return!' The man then experienced a crisis state, cried out and died (*Iḥyā'* II.294.27–295.2; Mcd. p.736). In line with Ghazālī's argument in the preceding example, the man was obviously aware of his shortcomings, and was concerned that his soul did not obey his longing to 'return' to God. This indicates that he was already in an altered state when he heard the verse, according to Ghazālī's reasoning in the preceding case. It also shows that the man was longing for death, to be closer in spirit to God, and to allow his soul to return to its source.

Although this episode may be classed as a 'response' to hearing verse recited, there are deeper causes for the response, with the man's pre-existing spiritual crisis. The man was known to be a Sufi, and thus likely to be regularly involved in spiritual or ascetic disciplines and exercises. This may explain his pre-existing altered state, that possibly he was in a threshold state where a slight stimulus was enough to precipitate a more intense alteration of consciousness or a crisis situation.

The third example in this category is of a rather different variety, involving a more creative response by the hearer answering a poetic couplet in like kind. Sarrāj relates an account from one Abū ʾl-Ḥasan b. Razʿān (d.?) that he was walking in the gardens of Basra with a friend when they heard a minstrel playing and reciting the following verses:

> O beautiful faces! you do not treat us justly,
> all our life you have all ill-treated us;
> there are duties incumbent on you to fulfil,
> since we have been afflicted in loving you –
> may you treat us justly!

Abū ʾl-Ḥasan's companion cried out and then said: 'How would it be if you were to say:

> O beautiful faces, you are destined to die,
> and your cheeks and eyes to waste away;
> afterwards you will become but an impression,
> so know this, that this is certain!'
> (*Lumaʿ* 297.13–298.1)

Sarrāj comments on the ingenuity of this answer to the reciter, and that the answer was made in an ecstatic or altered state. This is indicated in the account by his crying out aloud which may be a sign of dissociation. Sarrāj also argues that he was not perturbed by the sensuous or shameful nature of the verse. Rather the 'true' sense of the verse, the reality of the corruptibility and transience of beauty 'overwhelmed him and filled him with ecstasy', as Sarrāj comments.

What is remarkable is the spontaneity of the response. The altered state which the man experienced was evidently one of high arousal with the ensuing 'ecstatic' utterance showing high levels of conscious control and creativity. The verse couplet of the man's answer was expressed in the same poetic metre as the original, despite its apparent spontaneity! Such utterance shows a highly creative response stemming from the altered state being experienced.

Enigmatic utterances

This class of responses includes statements which are not immediately transparent in meaning, which are enigmatic or inscrutable in some way. The statements may be expressed cryptically, and the meaning needs to be uncovered in some way.

The first example of this type is recorded in Sarrāj's *Lumaʿ* and Qushayrī's *Risāla*. One Abū ʾl-Ḥusayn b. Zīrī (d.?), a companion of Junayd, would sometimes be present when there was a *samāʿ* session. If he approved of what he heard, he spread out his coat and sat down, saying: 'The poor (i.e. the Sufi) is with his heart. Wherever he finds his heart (or wherever his heart finds something) he sits down.' If he did not find it pleasing, he said: 'Listening to music is for those with hearts', and he would take up his shoes and depart (*Lumaʿ* 272.13–7; *Ris.* 341).

The second of Ibn Zīrī's sayings is more transparent than the first. The notion of listening being for those 'with hearts' means simply that certain people are able to appreciate and find benefit in *samāʿ* because of their capacity to appreciate music or poetry, or because of their spiritual receptivity and readiness for the inspiration caused by listening.

The first of Ibn Zīrī's sayings is more difficult. His statement that the poor (Sufi) is 'with his heart' may be a reference to the idiom explained above, of the capability to appreciate music and poetry. It could also allude to the person experiencing *samāʿ* being transported or overcome; thus he has 'gone' or 'flown' with his heart. Similarly, it could refer to the rapt listener being 'present' or absorbed with his heart.

The second part of this statement, 'Wherever he finds his heart, he sits down', may perhaps refer to the Sufi's quest for finding gnosis or knowledge of God, the ultimate quest of the ascetic's heart. 'Finding the heart' may mean finding the goal of the heart's quest, in this case the spiritual treasure discovered in *samāʿ*. When this is reached, he is content to suspend his quest or 'sit down' metaphorically, as well as actually.

There are many possibilities hidden in these rather cryptic and enigmatic statements. Unfortunately there is no further guidance, by way of editorial comment, on their possible meanings. Moreover, the text is itself rather ambiguous, as the alternative translation offered above suggests.

The second example in this category is the episode involving Shiblī's prayer in the mosque during the month of Ramadan. This was discussed above in Chapter 4, section E, concerning ecstatic utterances, although only the behavioural aspects of the case were dealt with there. Three sources record that Shiblī was praying once in a mosque during the month of Ramadan when a verse recited by the prayer leader caused him to cry out, change colour, and begin to tremble. He began to repeat in an automatic fashion the phrase: 'With such words do lovers converse!'[5]

The 'automatism' of Shiblī's verbal behaviour was noted in the earlier discussion; there was trance-like repetition of the same words over and over in an apparently unstoppable way. The actual import of his words, however, was not discussed previously. The enigmatic character of Shiblī's statement lies in its relation to the Qur'ān verse which prompted it. The verse is Qur.17.86: 'If We willed, We could take away what We have revealed to you, then you would find none to guard you against Us'. This is a verse of threatened punishment, the threat to withdraw God's revelation and also His mercy and protection. There is reason to suggest that verses of 'punishment' from the Qur'ān can have a dramatic effect on some hearers, causing unusual behaviours such as those recorded of Shiblī here. This may have partly caused the reactions noted here, but also the privations of food and other ascetic disciplines associated with Ramadan could well have been partly responsible.

What is noteworthy, however, is that hearing this verse of dire punishment elicited a saying from Shiblī which spoke of 'the converse of lovers', a seemingly incongruous response. The explanation lies partly in the well-attested notion of the Sufi's relation with God being that of lover and Beloved, as often expressed in poetry. Though for many this may have been only a metaphorical description, for others, among whom Shiblī must be counted, it was a more literal reality. Thus hearing this verse of punishment could be interpreted as the Beloved withholding His favours and graces, and leaving the lover in a distraught and helpless condition, a well-known motif in Sufi poetry.

Shiblī's obvious distress, therefore, could be seen in this light, and his statement then becomes more understandable. His apprehension of being denied intimacy with his Beloved leads to a reaction of fear, as indicated by his trembling, changing colour, and so on. It also leads him to state that such is the converse of lovers, where the 'capricious' Beloved can withdraw favours at any time, thus leaving the lover alone and distraught. Moreover, it can be considered a special grace from the Beloved and a sign of favourable treatment that the lover is so poorly dealt with and discriminated against. Peter Awn, for example, writes of this 'gift' in relation to Iblīs; but it is not restricted to unbelievers and enemies of God: 'It is open to those Sufis whose perfection of life allows them to cope with the paradoxical truth that God's curse, especially the curse of separation, is the ultimate goal of the mystical life.'[6]

What should not be overlooked in all these examples of the Qur'ān's intense impact is that the Holy Book was a continually intoxicating experience for these spiritual athletes. Louis Massignon reminds us that the Book was 'a rudiment of worship capable of uniting man to God: a psalmody: the recitation of the Qur'ān itself'.[7]

A third example in this category of enigmatic statements concerns a certain Jaʿfar al-Mubarqaʿ (d.?) who was once moved to ecstasy under the influence of *samāʿ*. He arose and stated: 'We are finished with disciples!' (*Lumaʿ* 287.11–12.)

Sarrāj goes on to argue that disciples ought not to be present during *samāʿ* until they have acquired certain attributes, knowledge and renunciation of desires. It may be that Jaʿfar was alluding to this in his wish to exclude disciples from his presence, particularly during *samāʿ*. Yet this is only a partly satisfactory explanation of his enigmatic statement which could have other possible references.

Jaʿfar may, for example, have been declaring his own renunciation of social companions and disciples, and his desire to retire from the world into a secluded life where he could cultivate meditative states. Other alternatives are possible, making this statement of Jaʿfar's rather ambiguous and cryptic.

Another similar example also comes from Sarrāj, concerning a certain ʿAlī b. al-Muwaffaq (d.265/878–9). At a *samāʿ* session he 'heard something' which made him say to those around him: 'Lift me up!' When they did so, he went into rapture and uttered ecstatically: 'I am the dancing shaykh!' (*Lumaʿ* 290.17–291.2.)

Sarrāj offers an explanation which is partly satisfactory, that Muwaffaq made this statement in order to conceal the real nature of his altered state. His reference to himself as the 'dancing shaykh' was meant to indicate that he had attained the state of 'beginners and disciples', according to Sarrāj, rather than his actual, higher state of 'intoxication and being absent'. This concealment was carried out due to his 'good manners', as presumably he did not wish to boast of his attainments.

Sarrāj's explanation is adequate as far as it goes, but it can only be regarded as one explanation among other possibilities. The statement 'I am the dancing shaykh' was uttered while those around Muwaffaq lifted him up in their arms. This may have referred to his perception of 'dancing' occasioned by being moved away from ground level. In his altered state he may have imagined himself as dancing while he was swaying in the arms of his companions.

An episode recorded in two and partly in a third source concerns Sahl b. ʿAbdallāh Tustarī. According to a long-time servant of his, Sahl rarely showed any emotion or ecstasy during *samāʿ*, but on one occasion he heard the Qurʾān verse (57.15) 'Therefore today no ransom shall be taken from you.' Sahl began to tremble and was on the point of falling down; when asked about this he replied: 'Yes, my friend, we have indeed become weak.' On another occasion a similar event took place with the verse 'The Kingdom that day, the true Kingdom, shall belong to the All-merciful' (Qur.25.28). In Sarrāj and Ghazālī's account, Sahl offers an explanation for his statement about becoming weak. He is asked: 'Do you mean that (the state) changes you and you tremble, and what is it that means strength of state?' Sahl replied: '(The latter is) that no condition which comes upon one (*wārid*) should arrive without its being assimilated by strength of state, and these conditions should not change one even though they are strong.'[8]

The obscurity of these statements is evident, though they all seem to hinge on the notion of 'strength of state' (*qūwat al-ḥāl*). The essence of both Sahl's replies is that by strength of will, or great presence of mind, one's composure is able to be maintained during the onset of an altered state. Such appears to be the meaning of *qūwat al-ḥāl* in this context. By maintaining that he has become weak, Sahl is referring to the failure of his presence of mind and mental strength to prevent outward signs of an altered state. Similarly, in his 'explanation' of this term, Sahl argues that one should assimilate (literally 'swallow') the onset of an altered state, and that it should not be allowed to 'change' one's outward composure, despite its strength.

As with the earlier example concerning Shiblī in the mosque, it is to be noted that the verses which prompted the reaction from Sahl were ones of threatened punishment referring to the day of judgement. It was seen in the discussions on psychology that such verses elicited unusually intense responses, anxiety or fear reactions. This may help explain the irregular nature of this particular episode.

A final example in this category of enigmatic responses again concerns Shiblī; it is recorded only in Qushayrī's *Risāla*. Once at a *samāʿ* session, Shiblī 'cried out' and went into ecstasies while remaining seated. His unusual behaviour of not rising caused those nearby to question him about this. Shiblī arose in ecstasy and replied with a verse couplet:

For me there are two types of intoxication,
for my companions there is only one;
what is something very special for me,
is only one for others.

(*Ris.* 349)

Shiblī's reply appears somewhat conceited and condescending to his companions; he claims to have a superior state of consciousness, poetically called 'intoxication', of which he experiences two types to the others' one. This 'special' experience of his seems to explain his failure to arise in ecstasy as usual etiquette would assume. Such apparent lack of regard on his part is in keeping with what is known of Shiblī's personality. He is characterised in ʿAṭṭār's *Tadhkirat*, for instance, as independent-minded, quite anti-social, and unheeding of the opinions of others.[9]

Visions of paradise

This category of responses is clearly the most ecstatic and effusive of the statements uttered by the Sufis. At the other end of the scale from plain descriptive utterances, this last category opens a window to a vision of paradise, of bliss and contentment. Such statements are rare in the prose literature of Sufism, though not in the poetic literature, where visions of wine-drinking, intimacy with a beloved, and Eden-like descriptions of nature are often found. The reason for this difference may be simply the separation of genres and a deemed propriety of occasion for speaking of such things. Often enough the more ecstatic of the Sufis are quoted as having recited verses of secular and love poetry filled with descriptions of the lover's bliss or distress. This is different, however, from actually describing a scene of paradise whilst undergoing an altered state experience.

The two examples of this category found in the sources both result from *samāʿ* in the sense of having heard sounds or verse which inspire heavenly visions of bliss and contentment, as part of the experience of an altered state.

The first example occurs in the *Kitāb al-Lumaʿ*, where Abū ʾl-Ḥusayn al-Darrāj describes the effects of *samāʿ* on his consciousness. Darrāj was reported to have said: 'Listening occupied my mind in a beautiful open field, and it made me discover the existence of the Truth as a gift. Then it gave me drink from the cup of purity, and by its means I understood the abodes of contentment, and it brought me into pleasant and spacious meadows' (*Lumaʿ* 271.17–19.)

Such a description is clearly a blissful and celestial vision occasioned by a particular type of 'listening' which is unfortunately not specified. Whether Darrāj was actually in a 'beautiful open field', as might be assumed from his opening remarks, is not clear; it may rather be a metaphor of the 'expansiveness' (*basṭ*) of his experience, as mentioned at the end of his utterance. In fact this is a common metaphor in use among Sufis and mystics when describing expansive feelings.[10]

His vision of bliss also has an 'intellectual' or knowledge component, his discovery of the existence of 'the Truth', a common goal of the mystic's quest given as a grace during moments of heightened consciousness. The drink from the 'cup of purity' alludes to heavenly experience, as referred to in the Qur'ān's visions of paradise (Qur.37.45–7; 78.34; etc.). Similarly the experience of contentment and spacious meadows is also ultimately derived from the numerous allusions to paradise in the Qur'ān.

The second example of this type comes from Hujwīrī's *Kashf al-Maḥjūb*. He relates that Ibrāhīm Khawwāṣ, who was famous for his long journeys into the desert, was once travelling in a mountain region with a companion. The companion was seized by a thrill of emotion (*ṭarabī*) and began to recite some love poetry. Ibrāhīm asked him to repeat the verses, which he did, and the companion observed that with 'affected ecstasy' (*tawājud*) he began to dance and his feet seemed to sink into the stony ground as though it were wax. Then Ibrāhīm fell into a swoon, and when he returned to consciousness he said: 'I was in the garden of paradise, and you did not see!' (*Kashf* 534.15–535.4; Nich. p.410.)

The ecstasy which overcame Ibrāhīm allowed him a vision of paradise, the content of which is not described. The reference to the 'garden' (*rauḍa*), however, suggests that vernal and natural imagery may have played a role, and it is likely that the images of his experience were derived from Qur'ānic references to paradise.

The utterances described in the four categories above help to shed some light on the nature of the experiences which overtook the individuals affected. There is no underlying pattern to these utterances, ranging as they do from plain, matter-of-fact statements to visions of paradise. What this variety of expressions does provide is a survey of the range of experiences which result from altered states. The lack of an underlying pattern or unifying theme throughout these descriptions serves to highlight the contention of this study that no single mechanism or process is operative in all these cases. The variety of utterances with which the subjects responded shows that different types of states and experiences are being manifested.

The only possible exception to this general rule is the sense of a 'retreat' or 'flight' from the world of reality to a world within or beyond, created or prompted by the altered state. It is possible to argue that in some of the responses this underlying theme or principle is involved.

Thus for Abū ʿAlī al-Maghāzalī, his state caused him to turn away from worldly concerns and to retreat from social encounter; then he made a gradual return to his usual way of interacting, with a gradual decline in his concern for renunciation. A somewhat similar situation occurred with Abū Sulayman al-Dārānī, who became suddenly transfixed as if hypnotised, retreating from reality with the sense that his reason had suddenly flown away. With Sahl Tustarī, his trance-like state meant that he was unable to communicate effectively, as he replied to his questioners that no profit could be derived from what he had to say.

As only these three examples, all from the category of 'plain' description, have this theme of retreat in common, there is probably insufficient evidence for an underlying principle involved. This theme of retreat is not unexpected, however, since the whole notion of dissociation or altered state means a transfer into a different type of consciousness which must necessarily appear as a retreat or journey away from the ordinary world.

By way of contrast, the 'enigmatic' utterances are as diverse as might be expected from this category where the sole unifying feature is the inscrutability of the statements uttered. Similarly, the 'visions of paradise' are rather different from each other, the only possible point of contact being the natural imagery used, though this is only hypothetical in the case of Ibrāhīm Khawwāṣ.

It must be concluded, then, that there is an overall diversity in these reported responses, and little in the way of unifying factors or themes. This would point to a diversity in the altered states being witnessed, that there is no one underlying state or cause operating in these examples. This conforms to the general conclusions found in the earlier discussion of the psychological effects of *samāʿ*.

Notes

1 Gerald Brenan, *St John of the Cross: His Life and Poetry*, Cambridge: Cambridge University Press, 1973, p.118.

2 *Luma*ʿ 281.18–282.5; *Ris*. 344; *Iḥyā*ʾ II.294.23–7; Mcd. p.736.
3 Abū Ḥāmid al-Ghazālī, *Al-Munqidh min al-Ḍalāl*, ed. Jamīl Salība, Beirut: Dār al-Andalus, 1996, pp.134ff.
4 *Luma*ʿ 285.20–286.18; *Ris*. 346; *Iḥyā*ʾ II.285.27–286.7: Mcd. pp.708–9; *Kashf* 533.1–3; Nich. pp.408–9.
5 *Luma*ʿ 282.17–283.1; *Ris*. 344–5; *Iḥyā*ʾ II.294.14–7; Mcd. p.735.
6 Peter J. Awn, *Satan's Tragedy and Redemption: Iblīs in Sufi Psychology*, Leiden: E.J. Brill, 1983, p.146.
7 Louis Massignon, *The Passion of al-Hallāj*, transl. H. Mason, Princeton, NJ: Princeton University Press, 1982, vol.3, p.32.
8 *Luma*ʿ 292.11–293.6; *Ris*. 347; *Iḥyā*ʾ II.300.1–6; Mcd. p.6.
9 See further, Chapter 9 below.
10 See the chapter on *qabḍ* and *basṭ* in Qushayrī's *Risāla*, 58ff; transl. Michael A. Sells (ed.), *Early Islamic Mysticism: Sufi, Qur'an, Miʿraj, Poetic and Theological Writings*, New York, NY, Mahwah: Paulist Press, 1996, pp.105ff.

8

THE RITUAL BEHAVIOUR AND ETIQUETTE OF *SAMĀʿ*

Throughout the early source texts there are scattered references to ritual behaviour, such as mass 'risings in ecstasy', other movements, dancing, or the tearing of clothes under the influence of *samāʿ*. It is only in the later texts, beginning with Hujwirī's *Kashf al-Maḥjūb*, that specific discussion on these subjects is found. Jean During argues that the earlier texts were more concerned with questions of the legality of *samāʿ*, perhaps a more fundamental issue since it affects the very existence of the practice. Questions of rules, behaviour and organisation, covered by the concept of *ādāb*, only arise later in the history of Sufism, once the practice is firmly established.[1] During also argues that this concept of *ādāb* was necessitated by the rise of spurious, debased or non-authentic *samāʿ* activities which challenged the credibility of the genuine practice.[2]

In scholarly discussion of this subject, only During's *Musique et extase* provides an adequate account, though again he mainly draws on later source works than those under consideration in the present study. The earlier texts are often overlooked, despite their witnessing important source material for the early conduct of *samāʿ* ceremonies. The main drawback with these texts, however, is their lack of organised treatment of this topic, with many brief references scattered throughout the works. It is these earliest source writings which have been the focus in the present study, and they again provide significant material for the analysis of ritual behaviour and conduct, or *ādāb*, which forms the subject of the present chapter.

Two primary concerns are maintained throughout this chapter. The first is to attempt a description of the type of *samāʿ* ceremonies practised in the early centuries of Sufism, as far as ascertainable from the source texts. This type of reconstruction may not be comprehensive, since not every aspect of the ceremonies or concerts is outlined. In fact, many of the details are gleaned from incidental references or hints which were never intended to be used for such reconstruction. It may still be possible, however, to gain a fair representation of the character of these concerts, even with a lack of completeness.

Comparison is also made with contemporary descriptions of similar ceremonies, particularly with those described in the writings of the musicologist, Regula Qureshi, whose fieldwork is the most valuable in this regard. It is undoubtedly the case that these ceremonies have altered over the centuries, from place to place, and between differing Sufi sects and orders, but some of the elements remain the same. For the purposes of this chapter, the evidence of contemporary ceremonies informs the ancient texts and the reconstruction of early Sufi rituals. It is not possible here to describe and assess the range of contemporary ceremonies.

The second concern of this chapter is more central to the subject of the book as a whole. This is to describe and evaluate the relationship between the altered states arising from *samāʿ* and their ritual expression. The section on the psychology of these states was often concerned with non-ritualised or accidental expressions of behaviour associated with 'listening'. Some of these had ritual or ceremonial implications, such as the behaviour of 'rising in ecstasy', but the non-ritual element was given focus in what was essentially a psychological study. The ritual elements, and the rules of conduct and etiquette are, on the other hand, largely social and cultural concerns. The ceremonies are always carried out in a group or social setting, often with structured hierarchies and group rules of conduct operating, and always with social implications for whatever 'individual' behaviour is carried out. The relationship between altered states and their manifestation within a group setting is a principal focus for this chapter.

As well as the source texts used previously in this study, a very important contribution to this subject is the brief polemical work of Ghazālī's brother, Majd al-Dīn, entitled *Bawāriq al-Ilmāʿ* (*Gleams of Guidance*).[3] This short 'pamphlet' is independent from his brother's more extensive writings on the subject. The author is a keen supporter of the practice of *samāʿ*, the first part of the *Bawāriq* being a spirited defence, with arguments from traditional sources, and a sustained rebuttal of opposing views. Toward the end of the work, there is a description of the conduct of a *samāʿ* session, in programmatic style with suggestions for the appropriate Qurʾānic texts to be used. This provides one of the earliest actual descriptions of such proceedings, and is an extremely valuable source of information as to their character.

Restrictions on and qualifications of participants

This question is basic to the practice of *samāʿ*, namely defining those who are suited, or allowed, to listen to concerts of music and poetry. It is an issue upon which nearly all the source writings have a view. The question is partly related to the legal issues surrounding *samāʿ*, that is, whether the practice as a whole is desirable or permissible. Most of the authors from the early period of Sufism are only moderately in favour of the practice, because of the possibility of its corrupting influence, and the pandering to sensuality which could accompany concerts. For this reason, many of the authors are keen to restrict certain classes of people from participating.

Sarrāj

There are several references scattered through Sarrāj's text concerning the qualifications of people able to listen to *samāʿ*.

The first reference has, perhaps surprisingly, more to do with aesthetics than with quasi-legal issues. Sarrāj mentions an unsourced quote that some Sufis regard *samāʿ* as

> a sweet nourishment for the spirits of those who are aware, for it is a quality finer and more subtle than other actions. It is perceived by one who has a sensitive nature, because of its sensitivity, and by the pure of heart among those who appreciate it, because of its purity and grace.
>
> (*Lumaʿ* 271.14–16)

This reference to the aesthetic qualities of *samāʿ* is not a clear statement of the qualifications for listening, but the implication is that only those with a sensitive spirit are able to appreciate the subtlety of listening. It is similar to saying that only some people have an ear for music, although there are added spiritual implications in Sarrāj's statement. In any event, this concept of sensitivity to listening and the implied suitability of the listener is emphasised elsewhere, particularly by Ghazālī (*Iḥyāʾ* II.277.23ff; Mcd. p.230).

The more usual stipulations on those who practice *samāʿ* occur several times in the course of Sarrāj's work. Bundār b. al-Ḥusayn (d.353/964–5) argues that there should be no corrupt intent, evil action, mere amusement or contravention of divine ordinances involved in listening (*Lumaʿ* 273.4–9). Such stipulations are often restated in similar form as an overriding condition of the organisation of *samāʿ* concerts (*Lumaʿ* 276.10–1; 277.11–5). Ghazālī expands on this basic stipulation by explaining the problems associated with secular poetry, for example where erotic references may occur, or where profanity or blasphemy might be expected (*Iḥyāʾ* II.279.31ff; Mcd. p.237).

One consequence of this stipulation is mentioned by Sarrāj in a statement where he frowns on the mingling of adepts with ordinary people. Such mingling might take place in what he terms 'natural (or sensual) listening' (*bi-ṭabʿhi*), where there is no restriction on those who may attend a concert together (*Lumaʿ* 278.8–9).

Another condition which Sarrāj recommends is the requirement of a meditative attitude when attending recitals of the Qurʾān. With this type of listening, Sarrāj argues the need for 'presence of heart, close consideration, thought and recollection' (*Lumaʿ* 283.2–3). In regard to *samāʿ* more generally, he suggests an attitude similar to prayer, with a collected state of mind before and after (*Lumaʿ* 293.14–15). This cultivation of a meditative attitude is formalised in the actual organisation of concerts through the recital of Qurʾān passages before and after the main recitations of the *qawwāl* or professional reciter. This feature of concerts is evidenced as early as the time of Majd al-Dīn al-Ghazālī in the early sixth/twelfth century, who describes the recital of Qurʾān verses before and after *samāʿ* concerts as a matter of course.[4] It is of interest to note that contemporary concerts also follow this order of performance. In the Indo-Muslim tradition studied by Qureshi, there is found a programme consisting of Qurʾān recitations at the beginning and ending, helping to produce a prayerful and reverential attitude in the listeners.[5]

The only remaining statement by Sarrāj on the qualifications for listening is a lengthy passage describing the prerequisites for novices to be allowed to listen (*Lumaʿ* 287.13–288.8). Sarrāj states that the novice should already understand the various divine names and attributes. Their heart should not be stained with love of the world, but rather it should be filled with praise, and they should not desire human companionship. If these conditions are fulfilled, the person can listen, provided it is not for pleasure, and that it does not become a habit which distracts them from the service of God. If these conditions are not fulfilled, they should avoid listening, except for ritual recollection (*dhikr*). A guide should be sought out, so that listening does not become an amusement, and so that one does not attribute wrongly to God and thereby blaspheme, or follow the whims of one's passions.

Qushayrī

Many of Qushayrī's pronouncements in his *Risāla* are directly attributed to his master, Abū ʿAlī al-Daqqāq. This is also the case with his views on the qualifications of people for listening to *samāʿ*. In line with Sarrāj's restrictions, Abū ʿAlī forbade ordinary people (*al-ʿawāmm*) from listening, specifically because of the continued existence of their lower or carnal natures (*nufūsihim*) (*Ris*. 340). This alludes to the possibility of such people finding in *samāʿ* a pampering of their desires or the pleasures of sensuality elicited by the music or poetry.

Abū Alī is also quoted as having taught that there are two classes of listeners, based on certain conditions attained by participants. The first is that of 'knowledge and clarity of consciousness' (*al-ʿilm wa-ʾl-ṣaḥw*) which consists of knowing the divine names and qualities. The second class depends on the 'state of consciousness' (*ḥāl*) of the participants, conditional on having 'passed beyond the lower human states, and being cleared from the effects of the passions' (*Ris*. 341).

These conditions support the earlier restriction on ordinary people from listening, as Abū ʿAlī clearly considers the activity a special prerogative of those more advanced on the Sufi path.

Ghazālī

The stipulations set out by Ghazālī prohibiting certain activities associated with 'listening' are mainly concerned with the need to avoid the cultivation of carnal desires and pleasures. This builds substantially on the rather scanty written prohibitions of earlier Sufi writers, though it is probably a case of simply codifying earlier practices. It should be kept in mind that a primary reason for the development of *ādāb*, or a code of practice, was the danger of improper and debased performances of *samāʿ* which threatened the legitimacy and respectability of the genuine practice.[6] The seriousness with which Ghazālī treats this subject, and the amount of space he devotes to it, is an indication of the gravity of this threat.

Ghazālī devotes several pages to developing the reasons for his prohibition of 'listening'. He argues that there are five basic circumstances where *samāʿ* should be prohibited (*Iḥyāʾ* II. 279.10ff; Mcd. pp.235–41).

The first is where the performer is a woman with whom it is unlawful to associate, e.g. not a family member, or where the performer is a beardless (teenage) youth. The main reason for this prohibition is the 'fear of temptation', not from the material recited or sung, but from the actual reciter or singer who may arouse unlawful desires.

The second case is where certain musical instruments are in use, namely, wind and stringed instruments and the *kūba* drum. The reason here is that these instruments are emblematic of wine drinkers and the class of singer known as a *mukhannath* ('effeminate artist'), so named because of the type of emotional songs he performed, and his being taught by women teachers.[7] Again the proximity of temptation, and even a symbolic association with unlawful actions, is uppermost in Ghazālī's thinking.

The third situation which gives rise to prohibition is where the content of the songs or poetry is offensive for various reasons. These include obscenity, ribaldry, satire or blasphemy against God and the founders of Islam, the offence in such material being clear. As well, any description of a particular woman, or of a woman with whom it is unlawful to associate, is forbidden. The reason here is obviously that of not cultivating lustful and illicit desires. Ghazālī argues carefully, however, that 'erotic' descriptions which are applicable to divine love or other metaphorical applications are not forbidden per se. The overriding principle in this is the heart and conscience of the listener: 'the thoughts which control the heart arrive first at understanding what is heard despite the actual expression' (*Iḥyāʾ* II.280.12; Mcd. p.238).

The fourth occasion develops from the former, and concerns the situation where lust has control of a person, particularly if that person is youthful. In Ghazālī's view it is Satan who is in ultimate control of such a person, and their listening which may arouse baser passions should not be allowed. It is interesting to follow the fine line drawn by Ghazālī between legitimate and prohibited or suspect *samāʿ*. The former arouses spiritual yearnings which advance the Sufi's inner life, while the latter arouses only carnal desires and passions. For those who cannot abide this subtle distinction, which has more to do with the listener's own state of mind than any more concrete circumstance, the simple answer is to prohibit all *samāʿ*. The difficulty for Ghazālī is to maintain this fine distinction, and to promote its acceptance by the Muslim community, though here his expert rhetorical skills serve him well.

The final occasion which Ghazālī sees as unacceptable is that of listening for its own sake, of taking excessive pleasure in the practice and devoting most of one's time to it. Again this is a fine distinction, since Ghazālī argues that a small amount of interest in the practice may be acceptable, while excessive devotion to it makes it unlawful. An analogy used is that a black mole on a cheek is beautiful, but a face full of moles becomes ugly; similarly, eating bread is lawful, but eating too much is gluttony.

In addition to this lengthy discussion of prohibitions, Ghazālī also has some reservations about the listening of young disciples or novices, which he includes in a section on *ādāb* at the end of the *Iḥyā'* chapter (II.298.28ff; Mcd. pp.2–3). The author outlines three types of novice for whom listening is unsuitable. The first is one who is of a practical inclination and has no 'taste' for *samāʿ*. The second is one who has a taste for the practice, but in whom there is still a residue of carnal desires and passions which has not been subdued. The third case is with one who has subdued these passions, but who has not mastered the knowledge required to practise *samāʿ* without danger of blasphemy and attributing unworthy qualities to God. Ghazālī goes on to suggest that listening is not desirable for novices whose hearts are stained with worldly love, or whose listening is merely for pleasure.

The social and ritual organisation of *samāʿ*

It should not be surprising that an activity as complex and formalised as *samāʿ* concert has an intricate organisational structure, given the large numbers of participants who often belong to 'brotherhoods' of Sufi orders. The source texts, however, are not generous in giving details of these structures, and the evidence available to us is incidental and sporadic. It is possible, though, to gain from these incidental references some picture of the structures involved, particularly concerning the central role of the shaykh or master of ceremonies.

Hierarchies

The existence of hierarchical structures is assumed in Sufi communities. Many of the authors we have discussed often write about the various 'grades' of participants in any activity, which vary from subject to subject. For example, there might be three grades of listeners: novices, a middle ranking, and adepts, while in some other capacity the grading may be different. This points to a ranked structuring, though the actual division of ranks may vary according to the criteria used. Such hierarchies are expected in religious communities where divisions among disciples and between disciples and masters can be assumed from the beginnings of Sufi organisations.

There is some incidental evidence about such hierarchical structures and their consequences available in the source texts. In the psychology chapter it was noted that the behaviour of 'rising in ecstasy' often appeared in a mass form, with whole assemblies rising to their feet all at once. It was suggested that this indicates a type of conformist behaviour consequent on strict discipline within the community: when the master rose to his feet in ecstasy, others did so as a matter of course, whether or not there was a general feeling of ecstasy.

The incident of Dhū ʾl-Nūn and his imitator is an indication of the consequent operations of a strictly hierarchical social system. In this case, the man, evidently a disciple or would-be disciple, probably felt that Dhū ʾl-Nūn was such an authoritative figure that imitation of his behaviour was desirable, however inappropriate it may have been in the situation.[8]

The incident of Nūrī and the assembly of scholars shows the operation of similar social forces, though the narrative is rather bare in details. An assembly discussing scholarly questions suddenly 'rises in ecstasy' when Nūrī unexpectedly recites verses of love poetry. The incident is probably designed to illustrate the power of recited verse, but the mass behaviour is rather exceptional in the circumstances. It suggests the operation of conformist or ritual behaviour, an outcome of a highly ordered social structure. It may be assumed that the ranking within the scholarly group prompted the mass rising: the actions of the senior and most revered members were imitated by those lower in rank.

A further example of the operation of social hierarchies is mentioned by Qureshi in describing contemporary *samāʿ* ceremonies. This involves an individual response which 'serves to express the devotee's spiritual attachment to the Sufi hierarchy and it takes the socially established form of establishing a link with a superior through an offering . . . this offering is a deferential gesture indicating the devotee's submission to the saint or confirming his attachment to his spiritual guide.'[9]

The role of the shaykh or master

Any discussion of hierarchies naturally overlaps with that of the role of members within such a structured system. The position of the shaykh or master in the Sufi system is crucially important and central to the performance ceremonies being considered here.

An incident relating to Dhū ʾl-Nūn illustrates the central role played by the master or shaykh. Four different accounts of this incident occur in the sources. There are some differences between these, but not in the essentials which affect the present argument.[10] It is recorded that Dhū ʾl-Nūn once arrived in Baghdad where he was attended by a group of Sufis among whom was a professional reciter. Despite, or perhaps because of, this new-found attachment to the famed master, they expressly asked his permission for the reciter to chant some verse. This is possibly a shorthand way of stating that arrangements were made for a *samāʿ* session to be held, though the sources convey the impression that the incident was spontaneous and informal. Dhū ʾl-Nūn grants his permission and the reciter begins to chant, whereupon the master goes into ecstasies, and other events ensue.

What is of interest here is that Dhū ʾl-Nūn's newly found band of disciples seek his permission for the performance, in deference to his authority. This is in all likelihood because of his position as a revered authority figure or their master. It is thus assumed that the shaykh will have ultimate authority over the conduct of *samāʿ* performances, as generally over the activities of his disciples.

Qureshi also points out that in contemporary practice the shaykh has effective authority over performers and musicians, for example in choice of repertoire and the style of execution.[11] That such control was maintained in earlier times could be assumed, and in this case, the poetry which caused such ecstasies in Dhū ʾl-Nūn might well have been a piece chosen by him.

The subsequent events of this incident involve Dhū ʾl-Nūn's 'rising' in ecstasy and the imitation of his behaviour by a particularly zealous disciple. At this, the master rebukes the imitator, who immediately regains his seat, thereby showing that his behaviour was not genuinely ecstatic. Sarrāj comments that for this reason masters superintend the 'states' of those lower in ranking, and they do not allow any overstepping of the mark or pretence in experiencing states which they have not experienced (*Lumaʿ* 290.9–11). Such superintendence is still a feature of contemporary *samāʿ* as witnessed by Qureshi. The shaykh is described 'not only as the one in a position of controlling the *sama* proceedings, but, more specifically, in his recognized capacity as a teacher and guide setting an example to the other listeners.'[12] Until the devotee is fully initiated, 'he is to listen under spiritual guidance and in the presence of his *sheikh* or a spiritual superior. For cultivating the spiritual delight of a mystical arousal and allowing it to progress to the point of ecstasy is a gradual process achieved only by the spiritually advanced.'[13]

A further illustration of the importance of the shaykh's supervision is provided elsewhere in Sarrāj and Qushayrī. It is related that a group were once gathered at a certain person's house with a *qawwāl* present. They were in an ecstatic or near-ecstatic state, and were being overseen by Mimshādh al-Dīnawarī (d.299/911–2). Mimshādh's supervision was perhaps not continuous, for 'when they looked at him they all fell quiet' (*Lumaʿ* 293.17ff; *Ris.* 347). This suggests that he may have been absent for a period while they began reciting and responding, or else his mood changed and they became aware of his apparent displeasure. There may be other possibilities which are not spelled out by the text, for Qushayrī's version has it that when Mimshādh looked over them, they fell silent. In any case, what this illustrates is the degree of control and authority over the proceedings exercised by the master of ceremonies. The narrative continues to relate that in fact Mimshādh was not displeased with the proceedings, since he took no notice of any sounds which might have distracted others, claiming that 'all the instruments in the world' could not distract his inner attentiveness.

The role of the shaykh as a guide and spiritual director has been mentioned above by Qureshi in regard to contemporary *samāʿ* performance. This role certainly has a long history, as indicated in a section of Sarrāj's *Lumaʿ* which outlines various reasons for the presence of elders or shaykhs at such performances. The inference to be drawn is that the elders would not otherwise be present, or that such gatherings are not a suitable place for spiritual directors to be seen.

The reasons given by Sarrāj for their presence are, first, 'the support of one of their brothers'; second, 'Their knowledge, trustworthiness, and great understanding allows them to teach others about the rules and decorum of *samāʿ*.' This role of guide extends sometimes to those outside their own fraternity, because of the elders' moral integrity and strength of purpose. Sarrāj concludes that although they may be present 'externally' or in body, they have inner detachment, and are inwardly separate (from their surroundings) (*Lumaʿ* 294.14–9). This concluding statement confirms the suggestion that *samāʿ* performances are not quite acceptable for various reasons. The inference is that inner detachment is needed to help ward off any likely 'contamination' such as sensual enjoyment from the proceedings. This appears somewhat strangely in an author who is generally in favour of the activity; however, it could be argued that Sarrāj is merely underlining the inherent dangers and temptations of *samāʿ* which are clearly spelled out elsewhere in his work.

In his *Bawāriq al-Ilmāʿ*, Majd al-Dīn al-Ghazālī describes the programme of a *samāʿ* performance of his time (late fifth/eleventh to early sixth/twelfth century). The session opens with the recital of Qurʾān verses, of which Majd al-Dīn gives some typical examples. He then relates that the shaykh 'speaks about the meaning of these verses in a manner suited to the station of mystical practices'.[14] Some typical examples of this practice are related, all of a homiletic style expounding aspects of mystical theology. This exposition of Qurʾān verses sets the mood and tone for the main part of the performance which follows immediately as the *qawwāl* begins his recitation in earnest.

Sarrāj provides an incidental, and perhaps obscure, reference to a similar practice in a rather unusual narrative concerning Abū ʾl-Qāsim b. Marwān al-Nihāwandī (d. late third/ninth century). Not being a frequenter of *samāʿ*, Abū ʾl-Qāsim was invited to a session where a certain verse of secular poetry was recited. Everyone in the audience went into ecstasies except Abū ʾl-Qāsim, who waited until the other participants had regained their usual state. He began asking their opinions about the meaning of the verse, and received various answers which were unsatisfactory to him. Then the others asked Abū ʾl-Qāsim for his interpretation, which was evidently superior to theirs (*Lumaʿ* 288.16–289.7). The purpose of the narrative as it stands has to do with the misuse of *samāʿ* as a means of attaining ecstasy without genuine knowledge. It shows incidentally, however, that discussing the meaning of recited material such as poetry was a feature of *samāʿ* sessions as early as the third/ninth century. The role of the shaykh or master is again seen to be central in such activity.

The role of the reciter

There are not many references to the role and activity of the reciter in the early sources on *samāʿ*. Despite the centrality of the reciter in all performances, it is perhaps the case that the reciter's role is not under direct scrutiny of the shaykh. This is what Qureshi suggests in regard to contemporary practice.[15] There are certainly some general ground rules on their conduct, such as those outlined above by Ghazālī regarding the content of poetry. Provided these are adhered to, it seems that the remainder is left to their own discretion within the tradition of the reciter's art.

Majd al-Dīn in his description of a typical programme outlines the importance of reciters in the proceedings. When the assembly is gathered, he writes, one who has 'the most sensitive voice' begins reciting short passages from the Qurʾān, which are then interpreted by the shaykh, as mentioned above. 'Then the *qawwāl* engages in instructive speech and a saying pertaining to the Lord';[16] the examples given by Majd al-Dīn include mystical poetry similar to the odes of the celebrated Ibn al-Fāriḍ (d.632/1235). The question of erotic poetry, discussed in detail by Majd al-Dīn's more famous brother, Abū Ḥāmid, is here dealt with summarily in a single sentence: 'Now if the *qawwāl* utters poetry in which there is a description of a cheek, a mole, and a stature, it is to be applied to the cheek, mole, and stature of the Prophet.'[17]

Following this central task of reciting poetry which will induce altered states in the listeners, Majd al-Dīn describes the reciter's equally important task of leading listeners back to ordinary consciousness, as follows:

> When their spirits receive a mystical apprehension (*ḥaẓẓ*) of the unseen states, and their hearts are softened by the lights of the divine Essence and are established in purity and the spiritual lights, they sit down, and he who chants (*muzamzim*) chants a light chant to bring them forth by degrees from the internal to the external. Then when he stops, someone other than the first reciter recites . . . [certain passages from the Qurʾān] . . . Then if there is among them anyone in whom remains the residue of a state or of absorption, the *qawwāl* repeats [what he uttered] in a lighter voice than the first; and if they remain seated, he does it a third time in a voice intermediate between the heavy and the light.[18]

In contemporary *samāʿ* performance, a similar process may be observed, as recorded by Qureshi.[19] A detailed account of a Chishti performance witnessed in Delhi includes a description of the subtle interplay between reciter and audience, particularly those in the audience responsive to the music and showing behavioural signs of altered states. The reciter is constantly adapting and accommodating the fine details of his performance to meet the needs of responsive listeners. He is heard repeating parts of verses, using varying tones of voice, interpolating fragments from other songs or poetry into the repetition of a verse, and so on. This is in order to guide the listeners' arousal and ecstasy in an appropriate way, to enhance the state of arousal, allow it to come to a peak and then subside gently. Such subtle handling of the listeners' responses is part of the skill of an expert reciter.

Majd al-Dīn's description of the reciter gently leading the listener out of an altered state shows a similarity to these contemporary practices. Qureshi's report of the Chishti performance adds some detail to the bare bones presented in the early Sufi sources, yet it appears that essentially the same process is in operation.

One of the few references by Sarrāj to the reciter's role concerns the problem of mistakes in reciting, or other mishaps which could affect the success of the performance. Sarrāj argues that the intention or purpose of the author of a poem is of no importance to the listener. In other words, the meaning of recited poetry can be interpreted variously, in accordance with the needs and state of mind of the listener. It follows that the carelessness and negligence (*ghafla*) of the reciter, resulting in mistakes or omissions, does not spoil the effect of the recitation; similarly, the 'dissonances' (*tashattut*) of the chanter in his chanting have no effect because of the alertness and 'composure' of the listeners' minds (*Lumaʿ* 296.19–297.1).

The rigorous strictures placed on Qurʾān recitation, as documented recently by Lois al-Faruqi, seem not to apply in the case of secular poetry, at least at the time of Sarrāj's writing: 'Correct pronunciation of the divine word is of course the sine qua non for good Qurʾānic chant. To recite it carelessly is regarded as blasphemy to the Qurʾān and a mark of shame on its reciter'.[20] The milder view expressed by Sarrāj may perhaps relate back to the controversial Qurʾānic verse (2.225) 'God will not take you to task for a slip in your oaths.' The word *laghw* here ('slip' or 'mistake in pronunciation') has also been understood as 'thoughtlessness' or 'carelessness'. Such carelessness or mistakes in the pronunciation of oaths may be comparable to the reciting of secular poetry, in which mistaken pronunciation is not deemed a serious offence.

Sarrāj also places the onus on the listeners to be creative participants in the performance: it is those listeners who are 'alert' or 'attentive' (*muntabihīn*) and have 'composure of mind' or 'concentration of thought' (*mustajmiʿīn*) who accommodate any problems of reciting, and allow for the assimilation of these mistakes.

Such participation on the part of listeners is echoed by Abū Ḥāmid al-Ghazālī in his discussion of behaviour at *samāʿ* performances. He writes: 'One should be attentive to what the speaker says, present in heart, turning aside little, guarding oneself from looking at the faces of the listeners and what they show of states of ecstasy, absorbed in oneself and the guarding of one's heart . . .' (*Iḥyāʾ* II.299.9–10; Mcd. pp.3–4). This is an elaboration of what is implied in Sarrāj's briefer description of the listener's attentiveness and concentration of mind. These considerations lead to the issue of the listener's role and behaviour during the experience of altered states.

Behaviour of listeners during altered state onset

In one of the few references to ritual practice in Sulamī's writings, the author mentions in his *Jawāmiʿ Ādāb al-Ṣūfīya* the value of not speaking about mystical states which have not been personally experienced. He also asserts that it is important not to claim that one has reached a certain degree of ecstasy, and that one should remain quiet when one has been overwhelmed by an ecstatic state (*Jawāmiʿ* ed. Kohlberg, pp.47,50).

The last quote above from Ghazālī's work derives from a section dealing with the behaviour of listeners during *samāʿ* performances. The author offers a categorical set of rules concerning acceptable conduct in such a situation. Following his description of what is required for close attention to the reciter, Ghazālī suggests that one ought to sit as if in thought, avoiding hand-clapping or other movements. If ecstasy overcomes one, however, the involuntary movements it engenders are excusable, but they are not to be 'enhanced' by any voluntary action (*Iḥyāʾ* II.299.11–6; Mcd. p.4).

This principle is taken further by the author's recommendation that one should not 'rise in ecstasy' or begin weeping as long as these actions are under voluntary control. On the other hand, dancing and affected weeping (*tabākā*) is allowable, provided there is no hypocrisy intended, since these activities induce joy and grief, respectively (*Iḥyāʾ* II.300.20ff; Mcd. p.8).

Ghazālī then moves to the question of the tearing of garments, which he again allows only if it is done involuntarily (*Iḥyāʾ* II.301.2ff; Mcd. pp.9–10).

With the exception of dancing and affected weeping mentioned above, the author's consistency of argument is apparent in this section. Generally speaking, involuntary actions cannot be prevented or disallowed, yet the same actions done voluntarily are to be avoided, and cannot be sanctioned.

A short but important section follows, which stresses the value of companionship and the observance of good manners during *samāʿ* performance. What Ghazālī terms the etiquette of companionship (*ādāb al-ṣuḥba*) involves the whole audience's rising in empathy with a listener who is experiencing ecstasy (*Iḥyāʾ* II.301.17ff; Mcd. pp.10–11). This mass behaviour pattern was discussed in Chapter 4, and also above in the section dealing with hierarchies. It was suggested that such actions are a type of conformism consequent upon a strictly ordered and hierarchical structure within Sufi communities, but a ritual element may also be present in these circumstances. Ghazālī's statements make these actions appear in a rather different light. Instead of simply being a function of a highly structured social order, Ghazālī suggests that these behaviours are a consequence of the close bond of companionship and harmony between members of the community. Part of their close social and spiritual connection involves empathetic action of this sort, to support and encourage their companions when they experience ecstatic reactions.

Ghazālī also appeals to the argument of custom or traditional behaviour (*ʿāda*) in explaining the actions of some listeners. One example involves discarding one's turban in empathy with a listener in ecstasy whose turban may fall to the ground (*Iḥyāʾ* II.301.19ff; Mcd. p.11). This again forms part of 'good companionship and sociability' (*ḥusn al-ṣuḥba wa-ʾl-ʿishra*), which the author justifies by the citing of a *ḥadīth* and other evidence from the actions of the Prophet's companions.

The question of dancing arises again in this context, Ghazālī arguing that one who is dancing voluntarily ought not to be encouraged by others rising in empathy. This indicates that those present are able to discriminate between actions performed voluntarily or not, in the case of dancing by the heaviness or lightness of the steps used.

The author goes so far as to quote a saying on the authenticity of ecstasy, that 'Its soundness is the acceptance of it by the hearts of those present when they are of like mind and not contrary' (*Iḥyāʾ* II.301.32ff; Mcd. p.12). This statement is an indication of the extent to which the principle of community acceptance applies; the authenticity of an altered state is not dependent on the experience of the individual concerned, but rather on whether other members of the community with a similar temperament accept it as real and genuine. In a way, this can be seen as the basic legal principle of *ijmāʿ* (community consensus) being applied more widely, not only to questions of doctrine, law, and moral behaviour, but to inner experience as well.

This should not come as anything of a surprise, however, since an individual's mystical experience always comes under the control of a spiritual master, and cannot really be regarded as autonomous and beyond outside scrutiny. In a sense, this forms part of the hegemony of mainstream religion in its supervision, interpretation, and control of 'raw' mystical experience. For the benefit of the overall religious system, mystical experience cannot be allowed to develop unchecked in an antinomian fashion. The rawness of original experience always needs a legitimising interpretation and assimilation into the structures of a particular doctrinal system. Qushayrī, one of the more conservative Sufi writers, saw in the enlightening experience of 'expansion' (*basṭ*) one of the greatest dangers, and 'an insidious deception'. This was arguably because of the potential of regarding this experience as extending beyond the confines and requirements of mainstream religion.[21]

Majd al-Dīn describes some comparable conditions in the *samāʿ* performance. He recommends that when a particular listener comes into ecstasy he should not rise until overpowered, when the others may do likewise. The same behaviours recorded in the narratives of Sarrāj's *Lumaʿ* are alluded to here in this descriptive and prescriptive passage of Majd al-Dīn's. Dance is not to be 'affected or feigned', partly in agreement with his brother's recommendations in the *Iḥyāʾ*.[22] Majd al-Dīn also mentions the practice of people leaving the assembly after the performance and returning to their homes in a state of 'absorption in ecstasy'. Some even fast for several days on account of their experience, a situation already familiar from what is recorded in the *Lumaʿ* concerning Sahl Tustarī who fasted for more than three weeks at a time.[23]

In his *Kashf al-Maḥjūb*, Hujwīrī has a detailed section dealing with these issues of behaviour and etiquette (*ādāb*) surrounding *samāʿ*. He first discusses the issue of 'dancing' (*raqṣ*), which he quite vehemently opposes as being unlawful and morally reprehensible. On closer analysis, however, one finds that he is referring to the voluntary act of dancing, not the involuntary behaviour of the listener who is overwhelmed ecstatically. Hujwīrī refers to this latter activity as *jān gudākhtan* ('purifying the soul'), which he clearly distinguishes from other forms of dance and movement. In a positive description of this activity, curiously not translated by Nicholson, Hujwīrī commends the spiritual basis and nature of this form of movement:

> The person who calls it 'dance' is far from the right path, and even further away is the person who calls it a state which does not come involuntarily from God, (the listener) bringing that movement upon himself; it is called a true

> (altered) state which 'arrives' from the Truth, and is something which cannot be explained in words: 'He who has not experienced, has no knowledge'.
>
> (*Kashf* 542.9–13)

Thus although Hujwīrī outlaws the act of dancing as such, he does not condemn the appearance of these involuntary movements which accompany altered states.

On the issue of tearing garments, Hujwīrī agrees with Ghazālī that it is allowed only if done in a state where there is loss of control of one's actions (*Kashf* 542.18ff.; Nich. pp.417–8).

Again in agreement with Ghazālī, Hujwīrī recommends that ecstatic states ought not to be forced, but should be allowed to come 'naturally' in their own time and manner. The state itself should be followed as it proceeds in its own way; 'One ought to be in a temporary state of 'seeking', allowing the dominion of that state so that its benefits may find one' (*Kashf* 545.17–546.1; Nich. p.419).

This principle of allowing the ecstasy to 'have its own way' and not to force or attempt to control its manifestation is at the basis of Hujwīrī's recommendations, which he elaborates in different guises.

An overall view of *samāʿ* etiquette

The basic assumption for the social psychology of *samāʿ* is the existence of strong hierarchical structures within the Sufi community of listeners. There is sufficient evidence in the source writings for this assumption of social rankings and highly structured relations among and between disciples and masters.

The shaykh or master has the ultimate responsibility and authority over the conduct of the performance. This is borne out in the narratives and the discursive or prescriptive sections of the source writings. He has control over the repertoire of the performers, and general oversight of the psychological states of his disciples. He is their guide and spiritual director on the matter of *samāʿ* as with other aspects of their lives. It was also seen that his role as a teacher also extends to the exposition of spiritual meaning in the texts recited during *samāʿ*.

The reciter has a crucial role in arousing and guiding the progress of altered states in listeners. This function is apparent in the earliest sources, though it is first specified in Majd al-Dīn's writing. The interplay between the reciter and his audience is apparent in the question of errors in pronunciation, or other mistakes of the reciter in which the discretion of the listener and his response becomes important.

The source writers are almost unanimous in maintaining that voluntary responses, those within the listener's power to initiate, are not acceptable as manifestations of altered states. Ghazālī is perhaps the most forthright in arguing that only involuntary responses, occasioned by the overwhelming nature of the state, should be encouraged and accepted as genuine.

Ghazālī also endorses the value of comradeship among listeners, with empathetic rising and other imitative behaviours being seen as supportive and encouraging for those experiencing these actions involuntarily. This should not be seen as a contradiction of the discouragement of voluntary actions, for in Ghazālī's view the values of supportive companionship override other considerations.

His stress on the importance of comradeship also partly undermines the view argued earlier in this study that these imitative and empathetic actions are directly the result of strict hierarchies and conformist attitudes of obedience within Sufi communities. Yet some aspects of conformism in social attitudes are seen to be operating in the argument put forward by Ghazālī that the acceptance of ecstatic states and their authenticity are a matter of community consensus, not individual experience. This notion of consensus comes very near to the basic legal principle of *ijmāʿ*, but it is difficult not to see in this an attempt also to restrain any raw experience deemed undesirable by those in authority. An important part of *samāʿ* practice is that of maintaining control by those in authority, and the rule of obedience among lesser members of the community.

Notes

1 Jean During, *Musique et extase: L'audition mystique dans la tradition soufie*, Paris: Albin Michel, 1988, pp.117–21.
2 Ibid., p.117.
3 Text and translation in James Robson (ed.), *Tracts on Listening to Music*, London: Royal Asiatic Society, 1938.
4 Robson, op.cit., p.105.
5 Regula B. Qureshi, 'Qawwālī: Making the Music Happen in the Sufi Assembly', in *Asian Music*, xviii, 1987, p.121.
6 During, ibid.
7 See Amnon Shiloah, *Music in the World of Islam: A Socio-Cultural Study*, Aldershot, Scolar Press, 1995, pp.12–13.
8 See above, Chapter 4, section D.
9 Qureshi, op.cit.
10 *Lumaʿ* 186.9–17; 289.20ff; *Ris.* 344; *Iḥyāʾ* II.291.19–25; Mcd. p.727.

11 Qureshi, '*Samaʿ* in the Royal Court of Saints: The Chishtiyya of South Asia', in G.M. Smith and Carl W. Ernst (eds), *Manifestations of Sainthood in Islam*, Istanbul: Isis Press, 1993, p.118.
12 Qureshi, 'The Maḥfil-e-sama: Ṣufi Practice in the Indian Context', in *Islam and the Modern Age*, xvii, 1986, p.151.
13 Ibid.
14 Robson, op.cit., p.105.
15 Qureshi, '*Samaʿ* in the Royal Court of Saints', op.cit., p.122.
16 Robson, op.cit., p.107.
17 Ibid., p.111.
18 Ibid., p.112.
19 Qureshi, 'Qawwālī', op.cit., pp.133ff.
20 Lois Ibsen al-Faruqi, 'The Cantillation of the Qur'ān', in *Asian Music*, xix, 1987, p.18.
21 Ris. 59. See R.C. Zaehner, *Mysticism Sacred and Profane*, Oxford: Oxford University Press, 1957 (1980), pp.86–7, for an interpretation.
22 See Robson, op.cit., p.112.
23 See above, Chapter 4, section H.

9

THE PARADIGMATIC EXPERIENCE OF TWO 'ECSTATICS', NŪRĪ AND SHIBLĪ

Many of the Sufi personalities discussed in the previous chapters are known only in a very shadowy or insubstantial way. They may be mentioned only occasionally in the source texts, often fleetingly, and sometimes anonymously. They disappear quickly back into the pages from which they momentarily arise, in which the faint memory of an episode from their lives is preserved.

There are other, better known figures who appear more frequently in the source texts, and in all writings about the early Sufis. The famed personalities of Junayd, Dhū 'l-Nūn, Sahl Tustarī, and others are well documented, and much is known of these important figures today.[1]

The two subjects of this present chapter, the third/ninth and fourth/tenth century mystics Nūrī and Shiblī, probably fall into this latter class of well-known figures. Their lives and deeds are familiar to all serious inquirers of Sufism; yet these two personalities remain further away from the centre of Islamic mysticism than is justifiable. Reading the secondary literature on the Sufis, and even at times the source texts themselves, one is left with a sense that their momentous lives have been relegated to the periphery.

The centre stage of the formative period has been occupied by the more luminous figures of Junayd, and the infamous Ḥallāj. A relative neglect of other Sufi masters may be understandable, given the centrality of these personalities to the defining period of Sunni mysticism. While Nūrī and Shiblī were both connected with their more famous associates, it is perhaps to be expected that their lives and deeds, however significant, would not match the central importance of Junayd and Ḥallāj.

Part of the explanation, though, must lie in the fact that neither of the subjects of this present chapter has left us any major writings. It is true that Paul Nwyia recently discovered a work of symbolic interpretation by Nūrī entitled *Maqāmāt al-Qulūb* (*Stations of the Hearts*).[2] Besides some poetic fragments by both Nūrī and Shiblī, however, there are no other writings by which they can be known directly. The best that is available to us is the group of sayings and ecstatic utterances (*shaṭḥīyāt*) collected in the foundational Sufi texts. The other part of their record is the tradition surrounding their deeds collected in works such as Sarrāj's *Kitāb al-Luma*ʿ and ʿAṭṭār's hagiographical *Tadhkirat al-Awliyā*ʾ.

This leads us to the heart of the matter, that both Nūrī and Shiblī are not important as theorists or teachers of Sufism, but as practising mystics for whom quality of experience is paramount. The allegorical work discovered by Nwyia is an explanation of mystical symbolism. Yet it is the raw experience of these ecstatic mystics, expressed in their fragmentary utterances, as well as in their actions, austerities, and reactions to mystical states, which are ultimately of greater benefit in understanding the essence of the Sufi path.

It is thus not surprising that both Nūrī and Shiblī have an important connection with *samā*ʿ and with the phenomena of altered states. It is the case, for example, that one of Nūrī's succinct 'definitions' of what it means to be a Sufi is given as 'one who hears the *samā*ʿ' (*Luma*ʿ 26.3–4). It is perhaps a little ironic that the apparent emotional character of Nūrī was finally played out in his death which was caused by the utter distraction of hearing *samā*ʿ. The emotional character of Shiblī is also well documented, though for him the connection with altered states sometimes came close to what we would regard today as psychosis. At other times, he certainly experienced the heightened awareness associated with those who are inspired and spiritually 'on fire'.

Both of these important Sufis were intimately connected with the famed circle of Junayd, which flourished in Baghdad in the late third/ninth and early fourth/tenth centuries. Junayd's fundamental approach was the moderate, cautious attitude and thinking characterised by adherence to *ṣaḥw*, 'sobriety' or 'clarity of mind' in all things. This contrasted with the approach of *sukr* ('drunkenness'), characterised by a more outspoken, intense and emotional attitude advocated by some Sufis.

Shiblī can be regarded with some justification as one of the 'intoxicated' Sufis of his time. ʿAṭṭār's hagiography of him often mentions the heightened, euphoric 'states' which possessed Shiblī, or his frequent states of agitation and distraction. He is also known to have adopted radical positions in matters affecting every part of his behaviour and beliefs. On his deathbed, Shiblī refused to repeat the *shahāda*, the basic creed of faith, arguing that 'since there is no other than He, how can I utter a negative?' (referring to the negative 'There is no god . . .' which comes before the affirmative '. . . but God'). This position is one that is assumed by the most radical of Sufis. His austerities and self-mortifications were legendary, as were his bizarre public ritual behaviours which led to more than one incarceration in the Baghdad asylum. This way of life seemed far from the ideal of moderation and prudence advocated by Junayd, and the tense relationship between the two was widely reported. On one occasion, Junayd said: 'Shiblī is intoxicated; were he to recover from his intoxication, he would become a leader of great value' (*Luma*ʿ 307.8–10).

Both Shiblī and Nūrī were complex and subtle personalities. This is evident from the brief anecdotes contained in a variety of sources, and from the lengthy hagiographies recorded by ʿAṭṭār. Nwyia writes of Nūrī's poetic sensibility, coupled with the audacity of a reformer; when accused of heresy, Nūrī was unafraid to confront the Caliph himself, correcting him where needed, while boldly defending his accused companions and offering up his own life to spare theirs. Junayd in the meantime had chosen to withdraw quietly.[3] Shiblī likewise displayed all the complexities of a zealous radical, and whether his 'insanity' was genuine or feigned remains debatable. He too was unafraid to confront the Caliph; as ʿAṭṭār reports, he was in a euphoric state when dragged before the authorities on a murder charge. As a result of the encounter, the Caliph himself was emotionally affected (*T.A.* II.166.20ff; MSM pp.282–3). Shiblī's deathbed narrative, as recorded by ʿAṭṭār, is a subtle interplay between the moribund central character and his attendants. A violent struggle of wills is played out between the radical, uncompromising ascetic and his more conservative companions. ʿAṭṭār also portrays the fierce battle taking place within Shiblī's body and soul, as if torn between hell and paradise, redemption and alienation (*T.A.* II.180.16ff; MSM pp.285–6).

It is clear that both these Sufis practised a radical faith which sometimes verged on the boundaries of acceptable Islam. One example centres on their connection with Iblīs: a famous narrative has Nūrī weeping in identification with Iblīs and his suffering, while

Shiblī on his deathbed expressed envy and jealousy of God's curse upon Iblīs.[4]

Of the qualities noted by his biographers, Nūrī is probably more remarkable for the compassion he shows, as in his loyalty to his companions when accused of heresy, as well as with ordinary people, illustrated by an endearing narrative about his restoring the life of a poor peasant's ass (*T.A.* II.53.15–7). His compassion is also joined with courageous action, as in his encounter with the Caliph, and again towards ordinary people, as shown in the narrative about his heroic rescue of two youths from a burning house (*T.A.* II.52.25–53.8).

What is more noteworthy about Shiblī is his intense 'inwardness', his absorption with direct inner experience. When joined with austere asceticism, the combination resulted in bizarre public behaviours and what can best be described as psychotic episodes.

The connection between these two practising (as distinct from theorising) Sufis and their experience of altered states is the subject to be addressed in this chapter. The importance of this connection can hardly be overstated, given the value both men placed on direct experience as the gateway to the mystical path. Their unmediated encounter with spiritual realities is given expression in ecstatic sayings and poetic fragments. Yet their physical and psychological reactions to the overwhelming of Reality are also worthy of investigation. This study seeks to address the experience of altered states and *samāʿ* demonstrated in the lives of these two mystics. It seeks also to investigate the importance and the consequences of this intimate connection for these two men, and for the early Sufi path more generally.

A brief life of Nūrī

Abū ʾl-Ḥusayn al-Nūrī was born around 226/840, in Khurāsān, but spent most of his life in Baghdad.[5] Little is known about his formative years, though his piety and asceticism were established early in life. This is illustrated by the narrative found in ʿAṭṭār and Qushayrī that for twenty years, when he was beginning as a Sufi, he would fast all day; those at his home thought he ate at his shop, those at his shop thought he had eaten at home. All the while, he had bought loaves of bread and given them to the poor, then worshipped in the mosque until noon, only later proceeding to his work (*T.A.* II.46.21ff; MSM p.222; *Ris.* 439). These long years of asceticism were years of spiritual struggle and formation, an account of which is given in the first person in ʿAṭṭār's *Tadhkirat.* Evidently this is based on Nūrī's own words or writings; it presents a vivid and honest account of his struggle to gain inner knowledge and the subjugation of his self. By this time he was a member of Junayd's circle, for when he imagines he has won a spiritual favour, he goes to inform Junayd, who tells him that he is deceived (*T.A.* II.47ff; MSM pp.222–3).

The best known incident in Nūrī's life centres around his being accused and condemned to death by Ghulām Khalīl (d.275/888). A strict Ḥanbalite, Ghulām accused several Sufis of heresy, and had them sentenced without trial. Nūrī impressed the executioner so much by his self-sacrificing attitude and willingness to be executed first that the proceedings were halted, and a properly constituted trial took place before the Cadi. The accused Sufis, including Shiblī, answered correctly the questions on ritual purity and prayer, and Nūrī spoke eloquently on devotion and love of God. The Cadi (according to ʿAṭṭār, the Caliph) was reduced to tears, the Sufis were freed, and the accusers were left in confusion.[6]

There are some difficulties with the details of this trial, as Carl Ernst points out in his thorough discussion of the proceedings.[7] It is interesting to note, for our present purposes, that in ʿAṭṭār's account, the initial accusations of Ghulām Khalīl were that 'a group has appeared singing songs and poetry, and dancing' (*T.A.* II. 48.5–6). Only after this does he mention that 'they speak blasphemies and heresies', as though the accusation of practising *samāʿ* was an even more heinous offence. In the strict Ḥanbalite view, of course, such singing and dancing was an odious practice. In a way, this confirms Nūrī's statement made elsewhere that a Sufi is known by his listening to *samāʿ*.

The sources seem to indicate that Nūrī was brought before the legal authorities on more than one occasion. ʿAṭṭār recounts another incident where Nūrī referred to a man's moustache as 'the moustache of God'. On being accused of blasphemy, he defends himself with a rather legalistic argument that because the man was a servant of God, his moustache really belonged to God (*T.A.* II.49.16ff; MSM pp.225–6). Sarrāj mentions a further occasion of dealings with those in authority. The chief minister of al-Muʿtaḍid (reg. 279–89/892–902) gave him a large sum of money to distribute among the Sufi community, perhaps as a recompense for earlier mistreatment. Nūrī gave the money to all who wanted it, and then remarked on the spiritual value of poverty.[8] This is consistent with a further account in Sarrāj that Nūrī was once given 300 dinars from the sale of real estate. He proceeded to drop the money piece by piece into the river Tigris (*Lumaʿ* 193.20ff).

There are many colourful incidents from his life reported by the various sources; they cannot all be recounted here. Some of these incidents, however, have a direct bearing on Nūrī's experience of altered states. ʿAṭṭār relates that on one occasion Junayd heard about Nūrī wandering around for some days and nights carrying a brick and repeating the name of God over and over. He was not eating or sleeping, but was performing the daily prayers at the right times and with due ceremony. Junayd's companions argued that this was a feigned performance; a genuine alteration of state (*fānī*) would mean total absence of awareness concerning prayer times or ritual ablutions. Junayd disagreed, however, and argued that God protects or preserves those in altered states (*dar wajd*), watching over them lest they be excluded from service at the proper time. Junayd then met up with Nūrī and asked whether his shouting was of any benefit with God, or if contentment was not better, and letting one's heart be resigned? Nūrī immediately stopped his shouting and praised Junayd for his good counsel (*T.A.* II.50.10–20; MSM pp.226–7).

This complex narrative shows very clearly the intensity of Nūrī's experience of altered states. It has certain similarities with the narrative concerning his last days: the total distraction and trance-like wandering, and the lengthy duration of this condition. It provides good evidence that such incidents were characteristic of his life, and that experiences like these were not uncommon.

The charismatic nature of Nūrī's personality is demonstrated by his ability to affect others, just as he was affected. We have noted above Sarrāj's narrative about Nūrī upsetting a scholarly assembly and turning their academic discussion into an occasion of *samāʿ*. His 'emotional' nature and his love of poetry was well known, as was his opposition to the rule of the intellect (*ʿaql*) with its inability to comprehend the transcendent.[9] These various aspects of his character are illustrated in this single narrative recorded by Sarrāj.

Nūrī practised a radical faith which verged on the borders of acceptability. The most audacious incident recorded in the sources concerns his being found sitting and weeping with an unknown person. When the other departed, Nūrī confided to his companions that this person was in fact Iblīs who was telling him about his life and the pain of separation from God (*T.A.* II.51.17–21; MSM pp.227–8). Nūrī's weeping with him shows not only the daring nature of his faith, but his deep compassion for others, including Iblīs. This is consistent with a narrative in which Jaʿfar al-Khuldī (d.?) overhears Nūrī praying for mercy on those condemned to hellfire. Actually he implores God who 'has the power to fill Hell with me'[10] to transport Hell's inhabitants to Paradise! Jaʿfar's amazement at these words subsides after he is assured in a dream that Nūrī's prayer has been heeded (*T.A.* II.51.21–52.2; MSM p.228).

His compassion extended to all people: a thief who stole his clothes; a poor man whose ass had died and who had no means of livelihood; and two young Greek (probably Christian) slaves who were caught in a fire in the bazaar. For his efforts in this latter incident, Nūrī refused to take the gold reward offered by the slave owner (*T.A.* II.52.19ff; MSM p.229).

Some of the many sayings of Nūrī will be considered later, but to end this sketch of his life, the remarkable circumstances of his last days must be reiterated. It is consistent with his character, and noteworthy for our purposes, that his death was the result of his love for *samāʿ*. According to the older sources, Sarrāj and Ghazālī, Nūrī was overcome with ecstasy at a *samāʿ* gathering, and began to wander about in a trance. He happened upon a bed of newly cut reeds, the sharp stems of which cut his feet and legs. Oblivious to the wounds, he keep wandering all night until daylight, when he was taken home, his feet swollen and bleeding. He died a few days later, presumably from septicaemia (*Lumaʿ* 290.11–7; *Iḥyāʾ* II.288.16–20: Mcd. pp.716–7).

According to ʿAṭṭār, the event which induced his ecstatic behaviour was his meeting with a blind man. The man was repeating God's name over and over; Nūrī asked him what he knew of God, and, if he knew anything, why he was still alive. This questioning of the blind man apparently induced the ecstasy. ʿAṭṭār also adds the pious detail that when Nūrī bled, the drops of blood formed the name of God in the dust (*T.A.* II.55.5–12; MSM pp.229–30). There is no mention of an association with *samāʿ* in ʿAṭṭār's account. There is, however, the implication of Nūrī being in a threshold state of consciousness, susceptible to being induced into ecstasy at any moment, given the appropriate stimulus. The implication of ʿAṭṭār's account is that Nūrī's accusation of falsehood directed at the blind man rebounded. He suddenly realised the potential and the implied meaning of his statement, which sent him into an altered state of consciousness. Ironically, in ʿAṭṭār's account, this ecstatic state led to Nūrī's own death and the 'fulfilment' of the challenge that one claiming knowledge of God should not be living.

This more colourful narrative of ʿAṭṭār's, however, has less credibility than the earlier, more trustworthy sources. It is consistent with what is known of Nūrī's character that he would have joyfully participated in *samāʿ*, as in the accounts of Sarrāj and Ghazālī. It is also in keeping with his character that this action should lead to a trance-like condition which had such a tragic outcome. His death occurred in 295/907; he was by then nearly 70 years old, and his austere life had probably weakened him physically. Junayd aptly summed up the loss of his great friend with the words: 'half of Sufism is gone'.[11]

A brief life of Shiblī

Born in 247/861 in Sāmarrāʾ or Baghdad, Abū Bakr Dulaf al-Shiblī was descended from a family originally from Transoxiana.[12] He came to Sufism late in life, at about the age of 40, having first had a career as a court official and governor of Damāwand. His first master was Khayr Nassāj of Sāmarrāʾ (d.322/934), but soon he came under the influence of Junayd in Baghdad, with whom he had a long and complex relationship.

His 'conversion' to a life of asceticism came during a visit to Baghdad accompanied by the governor of Rayy. Both officials received a robe of honour from the Caliph, but on the return journey, the governor of Rayy suddenly sneezed and wiped his nose on the robe. When word got back to the Caliph, the man was stripped of both robe and office, which set Shiblī thinking. He returned to Baghdad and resigned from his official post, proclaiming before the Caliph: 'The King of the world has given me a robe of honour, namely the love and knowledge of Him; how will He ever approve my using it as a handkerchief in the service of a mortal?' (*T.A.* II.161.3–14; MSM p.278.)

When Shiblī became a disciple of Junayd, the latter set up a series of penances and austerities lasting for several years, designed to humble the new recruit. The reason for this was to counteract Shiblī's earlier life of privilege as a court official. Hujwīrī quotes Junayd's statement to Shiblī at the outset: 'Abū Bakr, your head is full of conceit, because you are the son of the Caliph's principal chamberlain, and the governor of Sāmarrāʾ. No good will come from you until you go to the market and beg of everyone whom you see, that you may know your true worth' (*Kashf* 468.15ff; Nich. p.359). Under Junayd's regime of austerities, Shiblī was forced to be a seller of sulphur (*kibrīt*) for a year, in order to do away with his pride (*kibriyā'*). He spent a year as a beggar, and was then made to give restitution to those he had wronged as governor. After another year as a beggar, during which time his takings were distributed to the poor, he was admitted to Junayd's circle as a servant (*T.A.* II.161.15ff; MSM p.279).

By this time, Shiblī's behaviour began showing the signs of instability which were to become characteristic of him. It is difficult to say if this was a result of the austerities of Junayd's training and the extreme asceticism he came to adopt. It may simply have been part of his personality, and this appears to be how the Sufi sources accept it.

During this period of instability and unusual behaviour, he suddenly heard a voice saying: 'How long will you go about seeking the Name? If you are a true seeker, set about finding the Namer!' What ensued is one of the most remarkable incidents of altered states in the whole of Sufi literature. Shiblī suffered a full-scale psychotic episode, whose detailed and vivid description is a credit to the narrative skill of ʿAṭṭār. This episode will be dealt with in more detail later, but briefly, he became dangerously agitated and restless, tried to commit suicide by various means, and was finally chained and taken to the Baghdad asylum (*T.A.* II.162.10–163.3; MSM pp.279–80). This was the first of several episodes which led to his restraint and committal.

During Shiblī's confinement he would sometimes receive visitors with whom he would discourse rationally and with a clear mind. His lucidity on these occasions led to speculation that he was not insane at all, and that he feigned madness in order to conceal his infidelity. Shiblī himself said, in speaking of Hallāj, 'We are of one mind, but my madness (*junūnī*) saved me, while his intellect destroyed him' (*Kashf* 190.15–6; Nich. p.151).

When Shiblī was released, his behaviour on many later occasions was unusual to say the least, while his self-mortifications became increasingly austere. Some of his more bizarre actions can be regarded as symbolic or ritual in nature. Once he was seen running with a burning coal in his hand; when questioned about this, he replied: 'I am running to set fire to the Kaaba, so that men may only care for the Lord of the Kaaba!' (*T.A.* II.163.13–4; MSM p.281). This is a symbolic expression of the Sufi's disregard for outward ceremony, and his intense concern with inward spirituality. Similarly, he was observed holding a piece of wood with both ends alight: 'to set on fire hell with one end and paradise with the other, so that men may concern themselves only with God!' (*T.A.* II.163.15–7: MSM p.281.)

These symbolic or ritual aspects of Shiblī's behaviour are noteworthy in Sarrāj's account of his strange actions. It is recorded that he burned expensive clothes, perfumes and food, again claiming that these were distractions (*Lumaʿ* 400.5–11). Both Sarrāj and Hujwīrī record that he threw away large sums of money, sometimes into the river Tigris, sometimes giving it to anyone other than his family (*Lumaʿ* 400.11–5; *Kashf* 287.17ff; Nich. p.228).

These and similar actions inevitably brought censure and criticism upon Shiblī, from ordinary people and conservative scholars alike. Hujwīrī records that on one occasion, when he entered the bazaar, he was called a madman (*majnūn*), but his reply was: 'May God increase my madness and your sense!' He claimed that his madness was the result of intense love of God, while the ordinary people's 'sense' was the result of intense heedlessness (*Kashf* 196.14–9; Nich. p.156). Ḥanbalite scholars in particular criticised Shiblī's outlandish actions, his wastefulness and neglect of his family, his pretentious speech, and painful austerities.

Indeed, he was censured on numerous occasions by the more moderate Junayd for his 'intoxicated' approach to Sufism, and for public preaching and disclosure of mysteries. As with many other aspects of Shiblī's career, his public preaching was intimately connected with altered states of consciousness. ʿAṭṭār relates how Shiblī would preach publicly when 'his state was strong' (*hālat-i u quwwat qirift*), that is, when he became overwhelmed or intensely inspired. On such occasions, he would publicly disclose the intimate secrets of Sufi teachings more usually discussed at private gatherings (*T.A.* II.166.14–9; MSM p.282). Junayd's rebuke provoked this response from Shiblī: 'I speak what I hear; in both worlds what is there apart from me? Nay, for self is a word which goes from God to God, and Shiblī is not in the midst' (*T.A.* II.166.17–9; MSM p.282). This declaration of the involuntary nature of his public utterances was accepted by Junayd as proof of the genuineness of his altered state. Yet even here he was regarded by the famous Sufi master as going beyond the usual behaviour of mystics. With the moderate temperament of Junayd, Shiblī's behaviour was uncalled for; his actions were not only extreme by external standards, but by the standards of mainstream Sufis as well.

His behaviour, his beliefs and his attitudes kept Shiblī from centre stage, and relegated him to the radical periphery of Sufism. This was the region inhabited by Ḥallāj, though for differing reasons, and by other lesser known mystics of earlier and later times. Despite being away from the mainstream, however, Shiblī and the other radicals play an extremely important part in the history and development of Sufi ideas and practice. Junayd dismissed him as 'intoxicated', yet he acknowledged that were he less so, he would be of benefit to many (*Lumaʿ* 307.8–10). This presumably refers to his qualities of personality, as a teacher or master with profound ideas and deep spiritual experience.

One of the reasons preventing Shiblī from assuming this important role was the persistent distress he suffered from the onset of certain altered states. The major psychotic episode so dramatically portrayed by ʿAṭṭār has been referred to above; but there were many lesser episodes which tormented Shiblī from time to time. On one occasion, writes Hujwīrī, he was assailed by a voice while attempting to enter a mosque. Unable either to turn back or to enter in without the voice challenging him, Shiblī cried: 'O God, I implore Thee to help me against Thyself!' (*Kashf* 378.4–9; Nich. p.294.) On another occasion, records ʿAṭṭār, he went into ecstasies and began tearing his clothes upon hearing a singing voice at the Bāb al-Ṭāq gate in Baghdad. Once again he was hauled before the authorities, and when questioned he claimed to have heard: 'I stood, I stood at the Gate of Continuance! (*bāb al-bāq*)' (*T.A.* II.171.13–7). The meaningful substitution of the letter *bāʾ* for *ṭāʾ* brought on this immediate ecstatic state.

There are several other such incidents recorded in the sources showing that Shiblī was constantly susceptible to the onset of altered states. Yet what may also have prevented his playing a more important role as a teacher and leader was his deliberate rejection of worldly connections. This was partly the result of his severe asceticism, numerous examples of which are recorded in ʿAṭṭār's *Memorial.* A brief statement attributed to Shiblī found in Sulamī's *Ṭabaqāt*, however, illustrates in succinct form his radical rejection of the world which goes far beyond ascetic austerities. It is recorded that he said: 'Were all the world to accept me, it would certainly be a disaster for me; but since their drink is not mine, and their taste not mine, they have not accepted me' (*T.S.* 342.7–9).[13] This statement reveals his thinking, that he sees himself as rejected and alienated from most of humanity, but deliberately so; it is his choice not to be received by a world so utterly in opposition to his own beliefs and experience.

His final departure from the world entailed almost a rejection of the practice and belief of mainstream Islam: on his deathbed he refused the rites of the dying, and refused to repeat the *shahāda*, the basic statement of faith. His dying hours also entailed a desperate struggle within his soul. He was possessed of an urgent restlessness, punctuated by periods of quiet. At first he was envious of Iblīs' 'favoured' position in being cursed by God; later he was assailed by the opposing forces of 'His loving kindness and wrath'. He finally expired after refusing to repeat the words of the *shahāda*. He had, in his own words 'rejoined the Beloved'. His death occurred in the year 334/945, when he was well into his eighth decade.

The role of *samā*ʿ and altered states

These brief biographies demonstrate the important role played by *samā*ʿ in the lives of Nūrī and Shiblī, and the significance of altered states in their experience. Indeed it is not an exaggeration to claim that, for the mystic, the value of direct experience is paramount, and here *samā*ʿ and the apprehension of altered states are fundamental. It is perhaps true to say that for Shiblī, his experience of altered states was often accompanied by distress and unpleasant associations. With Nūrī, on the other hand, there was more a joyful apprehension of altered experience, often associated with some aspect of *samā*ʿ.

Nūrī's altered state experience

There are three principal occasions recorded in Nūrī's biography which present evidence for major episodes of altered state experience.

The first is the occasion, as mentioned above, when Nūrī was seen wandering about with a brick, neither eating nor sleeping, but performing the obligatory prayers at the correct times. The main source for this incident is ʿAṭṭār's *Memorial* (*T.A.* II.50.10–20; MSM pp.226–7), but Kalābādhī in his *Kitāb al-Taʿarruf* (*Book of Knowledge*) also has a shortened version of the narrative.[14] In Kalābādhī's account Nūrī is situated in the Shūnīzīya mosque, rather than wandering around with a brick in his hand. There is more of an emphasis on the doctrinal and theoretical implications in Kalābādhī's account, the question of 'passing away' and being 'preserved' in one's duties forming the main focus of the discussion. This may well be important, but ʿAṭṭār's version again wins out as the more full-blooded and lifelike, with less of a didactic and dogmatic underpinning.

The question which occupied Junayd and his associates was that of the genuineness of Nūrī's trance-like behaviour. Junayd argued that it was genuine, and that God 'preserves' those in altered states so that they fulfil their required duties at the right time. Some of his companions disagreed, claiming that in genuine trance there is no awareness of prayer times or ritual ablutions.

The delineation of Nūrī's condition is unclear, the accounts suggesting that at least some features of classic dissociation are present. These include the almost total distraction and trance-like wandering, the lengthy duration of the condition, and the lack of desire for food or sleep. At the same time, however, there seems to be a 'channel' of awareness open to sensory stimuli such as that required for the performance of ritual prayers. Unless one accepts a totally supernatural explanation for this aspect of Nūrī's actions, the positions argued by Junayd and by his companions can both be seen as partially correct. Some general state of dissociation was operating: the fasting, lack of sleep, distraction and involuntary shouting all point to a trance-like state. His performance of the rituals surrounding daily prayers indicates that a channel of consciousness was open to the surrounding world, this being described by Junayd as God's 'preservation' and guarding of those in a transformed state. It does not mean, as Junayd's companions argued, that Nūrī was feigning an occurrence of ecstatic behaviour. Yet the ease and rapidity with which he emerged from his trance back to everyday consciousness following Junayd's counselling suggests that Nūrī's reasoning faculties were not totally closed off. The concept of a limited channel of consciousness open to the reasoning of ordinary speech and some other stimuli best accounts for this situation. In psychology it is recognised that the symptoms of pathological trance may be reduced by environmental cues and the ministration of others.[15] In trance and glossolalia conditions, this notion of a channel appears fruitful in explaining the emergence of subjects from these altered states.[16] Junayd's companions were thus partially correct in arguing that Nūrī's altered state was in some ways 'incomplete'.

ʿAṭṭār relates that Nūrī thanked Junayd for his words of good counsel which had acted to bring him out of his trance state and back to ordinary consciousness. His immediate gratitude and praise for Junayd suggests that the condition had been one of some distress or discomfort for Nūrī, and that he was pleased to return to an everyday state. It is important to note also that there was no mention of *samāʿ* as a cause or contributory factor in this condition. Neither ʿAṭṭār nor Kalābādhī suggests any reason for the onset of this altered state. The narratives do, however, offer some clues which might point to the cause of the episode. Taken together, Kalābādhī's setting in the Shūnīzīya mosque, and ʿAttār's reference to his repeating aloud the name of God could indicate that some ritual invocation or *dhikr* might have been involved.

The second incident relating to Nūrī is wholly different in character, but there is available to us a better understanding of its cause. In fact, Nūrī himself does not undergo any transformation of state, but such is the charismatic power of his personality and his enthralling verse recitation that he entrances a whole group of people. What is even more astonishing is that the group of people involved were an assembly of scholars, meeting to discuss points of theology. This is perhaps the most unpromising group of candidates possible to be the subjects of a mass charismatic transformation of consciousness. The susceptibility of such a group of rationally focused intellectuals to the entrancing power of *samāʿ* must be very limited indeed.

It is related that Nūrī remained silent during the meeting of scholars while their discussions proceeded. Suddenly he began to recite four verses of love poetry dealing with the complaint of separation, neglect and misunderstanding. At once the whole group rose up and were induced into ecstasy (*Lumaʿ* 304.18–305.7).

The reason for Nūrī's rather daring and successful attempt at mass entrancement must surely be associated with his views on the nature of 'intellect' (*ʿaql*) and hence on those scholars who follow its guidance. His opposition to the rule of intellect is well documented, Kalābādhī noting his statement that 'the intellect is weak, and that which is weak only guides to what is weak like itself'.[17] In Nūrī's view, reason and intellect alone cannot apprehend the transcendent, nor provide direct experience or proof of divine realities (*Lumaʿ* 37.14ff).

The assembly of scholars, vainly attempting to arrive at knowledge by means of reasoning and intellect, must have struck Nūrī as an occasion of great folly deserving scorn and disdain. His mass entrancement was an unexpected breakthrough of the power of poetry and emotion to completely overwhelm the sway of uninspired intellect upon these scholars. Nūrī's love of poetry and his emotional character is shown in this somewhat humorous situation. These dry, scholarly discussions are overturned by the pure play of love poetry and its emotive consequences.

The third incident relates directly to Nūrī's own participation in *samāʿ* and his direct experience of its power. Given that one of his 'definitions' of what it means to be a Sufi is participation in *samāʿ*, it follows that he was often occupied with this activity. Furthermore, it is fitting that Nūrī's death should have resulted directly from his participation in this practice.

The events of his last days have been preserved for us in three different sources, Sarrāj, Ghazālī, and ʿAṭṭār, the earlier two being the more trustworthy accounts. The details have been recounted above in the section on the life of Nūrī, and need not be repeated here.

What does require fuller explanation is the nature of the trance which so completely overwhelmed Nūrī when he heard the recital at the *samāʿ* gathering. According to Sarrāj and Ghazālī, he arose and wandered about distractedly, repeating all night the words of the verse which had entranced him. The fact that he cut his feet and legs from stumbling onto newly mown reed beds also indicates his insensitivity to pain. The bleeding and injury evidently had no effect on his awareness. There are many similarities between the description of this trance-like state and the earlier recorded episode in which he wandered about with a brick. Such states may well have been a regular occurrence in Nūrī's life, with a similar pattern of effects in each.

The symptoms described in the sources point to a classic trance state. The action of 'rising up' (*qāma*) indicates the onset of the state initiated by his listening to verse recital, perhaps with musical accompaniment. Nūrī wandered and stumbled about involuntarily, and was heard repeating automatically the words of poetry which had initiated his state. Such highly stereotyped and patterned behaviour is also a classic feature. Insensitivity to pain, and being oblivious to one's surroundings and to the passing of time is also symptomatic of a trance state.

The conclusion of Nūrī's state is also of interest, since the sources leave some ambiguity as to the cause of his death a few days later. The most likely cause is the suppuration of his legs and feet, their swelling and wound injuries, which would have led to septicaemia. That this occurred over several days is a likely outcome. The sources do not state specifically the course of events, however, merely referring to his being carried home where he died some days later. It is possible that his trance state continued for these remaining days, and that he did not recover from its effects.

Before moving on from Nūrī's experience of altered states, it would be worthwhile to consider some of his many sayings on the subject, and his own descriptions of such states.

The source texts are peppered with snatches of verse attributed to Nūrī and attesting to his renown as a poet and lover of poetry. The episode recounted above of his disrupting the scholars' gathering with verses of love poetry attests to this renown. Some of the verse attributed to him is of a very high order of poetry. The following lines are translated rather expansively by Arberry, but they manage to convey something of the subtlety of the original:

So passionate my love is, I do yearn
To keep His memory constantly in mind:
But O, the ecstasy with which I burn
Sears out my thoughts, and strikes my memory blind!
And, marvel upon marvel, ecstasy
Itself is swept away: now far, now near
My lover stands, and all the faculty
Of memory is swept up in hope and fear.
(*Doctrine of the Ṣūfīs*, p.106)

The kernel of Nūrī's thought here is that contemplation or love of the Divine is so overwhelming that the very contemplation (*dhikr*) itself is made nought in the process. This is a basic tenet of the notion of *fanā'* (passing away from ordinary consciousness) in Sufism, but is here expressed in terms of its experiential characteristics, of being overwhelmed in the act of contemplation or remembrance.

This experiential reference to being overwhelmed also has a direct bearing on *samā'* and the actions and behaviours which accompany it. At another point in Kalābādhī's *Kitāb al-Ta'arruf*, Nūrī is quoted as saying that 'Ecstasy is a flame which springs up in the secret heart, and appears out of longing, and at that visitation (*wārid*) the members are stirred to joy or grief' (*Doctrine*, pp.116–17). The notion of ecstasy as a flame of fire arising from the 'secret heart' appears also in Ghazālī's description found in his *Iḥyā'* (II.266.16ff; Mcd. p.199). The direct result of this 'ecstasy' for Nūrī, however, is its behavioural manifestations, its stirring of the body to action of an unusual sort. This is a reference to the type of event which overcame Nūrī in his experience of altered states, and in his trance-like behaviours.

In a statement about the nature of 'ecstasy' (*wajd*) recorded in 'Aṭṭār's *Memorial*, Nūrī stresses its paradoxical ineffability: 'By God, how incapable is the tongue in describing its reality, and how dumb is eloquent erudition in describing its essence, for the experience of ecstasy is among the greatest of experiences.' He goes on to say that 'no pain is too painful for the cure of ecstasy' (*T.A.* II.54.11–14).

This linking of *wajd* ('ecstasy', or 'intense experience') with illness and the suffering of pain is apposite, since Sulamī records an incident where both Nūrī and Junayd speak eloquently of their experience of illness. On one occasion, both Sufis became ill; for Junayd, it is an opportunity to speak of his experience of pain, but Nūrī, on the other hand, chooses to keep silent. When questioned about this, he admits that he has suffered pain, but goes on to express his feelings in verse:

> If I was worthy of illness,
> then you (illness) are worthy of praise;
> It is pleasant, and the heart remains no longer,
> it says to illness: 'Stay a while!'
> (*T.S.* 167.11–168.5)

When Junayd heard what Nūrī had said, he replied that he too wished to 'reveal something of the essence of the power within us', and similarly began to recite verse:

> I exalt what came from you,
> for it was more glorious than you;
> And in the intimacy of my heart, you
> are more glorious than can be imagined;
> You obliterated me from all I was,
> so how can I take heed of the cause?
> (*T.S.* 168.6–10)

This verse of Junayd's is difficult and elusive, though it appears to speak of the experience of *wajd* and *fanā'*. Nūrī's verse is perhaps more understandable, as he seems to welcome the experience of illness and pain. He speaks of it as having a similar effect on the heart as that of ecstasy and *fanā'*, the experience of 'passing away'.

It was mentioned earlier that Paul Nwyia recently discovered a work attributed to Nūrī which describes mystical experience in symbolic language. Nwyia claims that his discovery of the *Maqāmāt al-Qulūb* is an advance on our former reliance on anecdotes and small fragments in the hagiographies.[18] He also claims that this image-based work of Nūrī's is not 'studied' or developed to any degree, and that it deals with the level of experience, rather than that of concepts and thought. These claims by Nwyia cannot really be upheld upon reading Nūrī's *Maqāmāt al-Qulūb*.[19] The promise of an experiential description of mystical states is not fulfilled; rather what is presented is a work of symbolic interpretation and allegory quite removed from the level of experiential data.

It is this raw data, expressed so often in fragmentary utterances and snatches of narrative, that gives us a clearer picture of Nūrī's situation. Such is the experiential description which has been attempted here, drawing upon the diverse source texts with their scattered fragments of information about his life, actions and sayings. The picture which this leaves us is one of an intense, spiritually aware man who had a passion for direct experience of the divine, and for expressing what he felt in a variety of ways. He clearly enjoyed the activity of *samāʿ*, though this indulgence eventually led to his death. He was fond also of poetry, and had almost charismatic powers in conveying his passion for recited verse. Nor was he a stranger to the unusual effects of *samāʿ* and the experience of altered states of consciousness.

Shiblī's altered state experience

The first documented episode of Shiblī being subject to altered states comes fairly late in his life, following his 'conversion' to Sufism at about the age of 40 and a period of austere training as a disciple of Junayd's. It is arguable that the severity of his discipleship, the years of fasting, begging and menial tasks, led to some mental instability. Shiblī's earlier life was that of a privileged member of a high social class, and the easy life which this would have entailed contrasted greatly with his new life as a Sufi acolyte. Perhaps this contrast was too great for him to bear; or perhaps his instability was present all along, particularly since there is no detailed account of his earlier life. Whatever the preceding circumstances, it is clear that unusual behaviours and states of mind soon became manifest once Shiblī finished his early discipleship (*T.A.* II.162.10–19; MSM, pp.279–80).

ʿAṭṭār details the most formidable of the episodes which seemed to occur with some frequency in Shiblī's later life, and which led to frequent committals to the Baghdad asylum. This important episode is a classic case of psychosis, and it is brilliantly and sympathetically portrayed by ʿAṭṭār. It shows all the author's narrative skill and is a fine example of pre-modern writing describing the symptoms of a particular psychological condition (*T.A.* II.162.20–163.3; MSM, pp. 280–1).

Shiblī had been showing signs of an unusual state of mind, and some strange behaviours. Distributing lumps of sugar or money to children who repeated the name of 'God', he felt a sudden change of heart and unleashed a sword, threatening to kill anyone who uttered the name of God unheedingly. He then went around inscribing the divine name wherever he could, until suddenly he 'heard' a voice saying to him: 'How long will you go about seeking the Name? If you are a true seeker, set about finding the Namer! (or the Named)'. This audition began for Shiblī a remarkable altered state experience, though his preceding actions and state of mind might also be included in this. The 'voice' had such an effect on him that he lost his composure, 'love's power took hold', as ʿAṭṭār describes, and he became distracted, overwhelmed and agitated. The state which overtook Shiblī made him become suicidal, and he attempted various means of killing himself: throwing himself into the Tigris, self-immolation, seeking out hungry lions, and throwing himself off a mountain top. Each of these means proved unsuccessful, the forces of nature rebuffing his various attempts in a kind of benign conspiracy to protect him from danger. The river cast him back upon the shore, the fire did not burn him, the hungry lions ignored him, and so on. This benign 'conspiracy' only frustrated Shiblī and made his agitation worse, compounding the distress he already suffered by not allowing him to be delivered from his torment. His anxiety and agitation increased so much that he had to be restrained and committed to the asylum where he apparently recovered after some time.

The proximate cause of the episode is given as Shiblī's hearing a 'voice' which urged him to stop seeking the Name, and to seek the Namer (or the Named). The source of this voice is not clearly stated, though it is often the case in ʿAṭṭār's writing that such voices are assumed to be divine in origin. Perhaps this is not clearly stated in the present case because of the obvious negative outcome of hearing this voice. While there may be some ambiguity here, in modern medical terms there would be little doubt about the psychotic quality of such an audition.

There are several major symptoms of psychosis present in this description of his condition. First, he is overwhelmed by anxiety and restlessness, though described in rather general terms by ʿAṭṭār. The Persian word used is *bī-qarārī*, which has a wide range of meanings including 'instability, restlessness and disturbance'. The picture given is that of a generalised and severe agitation of body and mind, a derangement which robs the individual of all composure and equilibrium. When Shiblī was thwarted by natural forces in his attempts at suicide, his agitation increased 'a thousandfold', as ʿAṭṭār states in hyperbolic fashion. His failure to commit suicide clearly compounded his frustration and anxiety, which was already severe.

A second clear sign of the pathological nature of the episode is Shiblī's attempt at suicide. The message of the 'voice' drove him to distraction, and we can surmise that his intense anxiety and inner torment caused him to seek deliverance from his suffering by ending his life. There are many parallels here with a psychotic illness where auditory hallucinations and the accompanying anxiety states lead many sufferers to attempt deliverance through suicide. It is also clear that this was no temporary state or momentary process; his varied attempts at suicide indicate a lengthy and deliberate process of journeying to mountains and to areas where wild lions roamed, and so on.

This points to a third sign of disturbed behaviour, namely his distracted wandering and journeying in his attempts to commit suicide. This is probably best seen as a directedness of behaviour akin to what may be seen in trance states. Some of the qualities associated with trance may be seen in Shiblī's behaviour, such as an inner orientation and directedness, obsession and lack of regard for consequences.

The result of this episode in Shiblī's life was a period of committal to the Baghdad asylum, where his health eventually improved and he was released. At first he needed restraint with chains and bonds, an evident sign of insanity in an age when very little treatment was available. ʿAṭṭār also relates that the Caliph appointed someone to oversee his treatment, and to administer medicine to him. It is noted that they needed to do this by force as he was unwilling to accept treatment voluntarily. Shiblī remarked: 'Do not take such trouble, for this is not such an illness that yields to medicine' (*T.A.* II.163.8–9; MSM, p.281). During his stay in the asylum, he was allowed visitors. On one occasion some visitors called him a madman, which prompted a very lucid retort from Shiblī: 'In your eyes I am mad and you are sane (*hushyār*); may God increase my madness and your sanity so that I may be brought nearer (to Him) by that means, and you may be driven further away (from Him)' (*T.A.* II.163.4–7; MSM, p.280). On another occasion some people claiming friendship with him came to visit, but he threw stones at them, making them run away. He disowned their friendship, seeing that stones could so easily drive them apart (*T.A.* II.163.9–13; MSM, p.281). There is no indication of the duration of Shiblī's stay in the asylum. We can only assume that it was lengthy, because of the severity of his condition and the lack of available treatment.

This episode remains the most dramatic and important of Shiblī's altered state experiences. It is a case where the more negative and distressing aspects of altered consciousness come into play. In Shiblī's case, it could be argued that this major episode had profound implications for his life afterwards. He probably never recovered fully, as there were other lapses into strange states and behaviours recurring for the rest of his life.

It also provided him with a legitimate excuse for outlandishness, not only in behaviour, but also in speech and belief, which he could rely on in times of persecution and heresy trials. His lucidity when visited in the asylum could mean that his insanity was not real, that he was feigning madness for other reasons, such as the concealment of unconventional beliefs. Yet the fact that people suffering psychoses often have periods of lucidity is no argument against the reality of their illness, and this applies fully in Shiblī's case. There is some truth to the suggestion, however, that his madness insulated him from harsher consequences meted out by the legal and religious authorities. Referring to the fate of Ḥallāj, he commented that 'We are of one mind, but my madness saved me, while his intellect destroyed him' (*Kashf* 190.15–6; Nich. p.151). At Ḥallāj's execution scene, Shiblī was one of the accusers who denounced him. His motive for doing so cannot be other than his wish to save his own life. Yet it can be argued that his frustration and disillusionment must have grown intense at seeing the message preached by Ḥallāj so utterly rejected and denounced by his fellow believers. What other recourse was there except madness and bizarre behaviour for one so committed to the truth of radical mysticism as Shiblī was? When he was inspired, he would go about preaching and disclosing secrets heard only behind closed doors. This was exactly what Ḥallāj had done, and for this Shiblī earned the wrath of Junayd (*T.A.* II.166.14–9). Was there any other avenue left for one such as Shiblī apart from the refuge of madness?[20]

Michael Dols, however, argues that it was in fact Shiblī's intelligence which saved him, while Ḥallāj's madness destroyed him, to paraphrase Hujwīrī's statement.[21] His simulation of madness due to his real intelligence accounts for his rejection of Ḥallāj at the gallows, where he was showing wisdom and prudence.

Perhaps his madness was not genuine, but a ruse to protect his unconventionality. There is at least some truth in this, yet Shiblī himself testified to his insanity, as does any independent scrutiny of his behaviour and state of mind. In the end it would be unwise to ignore both his own testimony and the evidence of objective analysis. Yet while most psychotic episodes must be seen as destructive of the personality and utterly distressing for the person concerned, this is not the case with Shiblī's period of psychosis. The evidence of his own words to his visitors in the asylum is illustrative of a surprising attitude toward his altered state experience. He asked God to increase his madness, because by this means he was brought near to the divine presence; the corollary was that he asked for 'normal' people to have their normality increased, for by this means they moved further away from the divine presence. These are not the words of one who is regretful, fearful or distressed by his experience, wishing for it to depart and to leave him in peace. Rather he welcomes what by any realistic criterion is destructive and negative; in fact he seeks its increase! It is the reality of spiritual experience and nearness to the divine presence which is his ultimate goal, even if the means to this experience involves intense suffering. By the criteria of mysticism this goal and quest is the ultimate, the most prized, and in the end the only goal worth seeking.

There are several other, shorter episodes of Shiblī's altered state experience recorded in the sources. Not all of them were as distressing as this first major episode. For example, Sarrāj records that Shiblī would imitate a rapturous state whenever he heard a particular verse of secular love poetry; evidently his feeling for poetry was similar to that of Nurī's (*Luma*ʿ 292.1–3). On one occasion, Sarrāj mentions that in a similar rapturous state Shiblī expressed the sentiment that 'Only He knows what is in my heart', a confirmation of the intimate link he felt between himself and God (*Luma*ʿ 304.7–9).

A more extended and profound episode occurred once during the month of Ramadan, as recorded in three of the sources. Sarrāj, Ghazālī and Qushayrī all relate an incident which occurred during Ramadan prayers in a mosque. When the prayer leader recited a certain verse, Shiblī cried out and turned green (or red, according to Ghazālī) and began trembling uncontrollably, repeating over and over: 'With such words do lovers converse!'[22] The features of this altered state have been discussed in Chapter 4 and need not be repeated here.

Shiblī's major episode of psychosis was apparently activated by his 'audition' of a voice. This was not an isolated occurrence, as the sources record two other, less traumatic episodes of altered state which were activated by the same means. The first of these cases involved his 'mishearing' the voice of a singer at the Bāb al-Ṭāq gate in Baghdad. It is reported that Shiblī lost consciousness and began tearing his garment upon hearing the poetry of a street singer. He was taken before the authorities and was asked for an explanation. Shiblī answered that he 'heard' the singer recite 'I stood, I stood in the Bāb al-Bāq (the gate of continuance)', whereas everyone else had heard the singer recite 'Bāb al-Ṭāq' (a place name) (*T.A.* II.171.13–7). The reason for Shiblī's being overwhelmed was the apparent reference of the singer to his standing in the 'gate of continuance'. The word *bāq* is cognate with *baqā'*, the complement of *fanā'*, which taken together indicate the ultimate state of ecstatic experience in Sufism.

Hujwīrī relates a narrative which involved Shiblī in the audition of a more threatening voice with paranoiac elements which left him in a distressed and bewildered state. In a chapter dealing with purification, Hujwīrī relates that Shiblī once purified himself and went to enter a mosque. A voice within himself began assailing him, asking whether he was so pure as to enter Our house with such boldness. Shiblī began to turn back whereupon the voice asked 'Do you turn back from Our door? Where will you go?' Caught in an impossible situation, Shiblī let out a cry to which the response came: 'Do you revile Us?' But even his standing silent brought a rebuke: 'Do you intend to endure Our affliction?' In desperation he exclaimed: 'I implore God to help me against Yourself!' (*Kashf* 378.4–9; Nich. p.294.) This is a rather strange account of being assailed by a 'voice' from within, though undoubtedly meant to be taken as divinely instigated, and the impossible situation in which Shiblī is placed by its taunts. The high demands it places on his every action, and the challenge to his every move appears like the projected conscience of an extreme ascetic. It is as if his own scrupulous standards of purity have finally come to haunt him after years of meticulous formation and the imposition of innumerable austerities.

In this narrative, Shiblī's inner conscience has reached the level of almost paranoiac persecution and attack on the subject, with his every move or lack thereof challenged and threatened by this demanding master. The likelihood that the roots of this 'voice' were in Shiblī's own ascetic conscience provides an explanation which fits well with what is known of his life and character.

The possibility of the voice being psychotic in nature also conforms to Shiblī's character. All the classic elements of a paranoiac audition are present: the threatening and overwhelming voice, the subject being rendered helpless from decisive action, the hostility of the voice toward the subject, and so on. Even the text hints at the voice's subjective nature with the mention of it arising from within his inner self.

Neurologically, such auditions can be seen as the invasion by secondary circuits of the primary ego/consciousness circuit, the neural mechanism which allows ordinary cognitive functioning and data processing. This overflow or disruption by secondary circuits is usually prevented in ordinary consciousness as the latter resonates with the external world. People suffering from psychosis, however, may not be able to distinguish themselves clearly from the outside world because many of their secondary pathways are accessible to their primary ego circuit, and they are thus susceptible to hallucinated voices.[23]

What is clear from this narrative is that the earlier psychotic episode was not an isolated occurrence. It is likely that several such disturbing events beset Shiblī during his long life.

A further occurrence of altered state experience recorded by ʿAṭṭār had direct implications for Shiblī's relations with fellow Sufis and with the world at large. This relates to his career as a roving 'preacher', ʿAṭṭār noting that 'when his state (*ḥāla*) was intense' he would go about preaching in public (*T.A.* II.166.14–9; MSM p.282). This evidently refers to his being overwhelmed by divine inspiration or spiritual fervour which impelled him to go about spreading the Sufi message to all hearers. There is clearly the notion of an altered state involved here, with reference to the intensification of his 'state' and the sense of urgency and the involuntary impulse to preach. Shiblī says as much himself in his reply to Junayd's reproach to him for preaching secrets and 'mysteries' heard only behind closed doors. He declares the involuntary nature of his actions and public utterances in replying to Junayd: 'I speak what I hear; in both worlds what is there apart from me? Nay for self is a word which goes from God to God, and Shiblī is not in the midst' (*T.A.* II.166.17–9; MSM p.282). Junayd's reproachful attitude toward Shiblī for proclaiming mysteries in public is assuaged by this statement which he accepts as indicating the forcefulness and impulsion behind Shiblī's state of inspiration.

Shiblī's experience of altered states shows a more dramatic, intense and darker quality than does the parallel experience of Nūrī. This must obviously stem from their differing personalities. The warmer, more poetic and outward-looking Nūrī met with experiences which were more benign and exhilarating. Shiblī's more intense, ascetic and inwardly inclined personality shows itself in the darker and more threatening character of what he encountered. That the character of the individual is reflected in their encounter of *wajd* is already mentioned by some of the Sufi authors, notably Sarrāj and Ghazālī. It does not mean that their experience is nothing but a subjective encounter; rather, in Ghazālī's words, 'when the heart is moved, there is manifested what it contains' (*Iḥyā*ʾ II.266.19; Mcd. p.199).

It is also noteworthy that there is little mention of *samā*ʿ relating to Shiblī's experience of altered states. It is not that he was opposed to the practice, as there are several accounts of his involvement in the activity. It may be more that his response to *samā*ʿ was unlike that of Nūrī, that he was not as positive and receptive to its influence. For Shiblī, the experience of altered states was more associated with the darker forces of his personality, with his own encounter of the twilight world which borders on insanity.

The importance and consequences of *samā*ʿ and altered states

The importance of *samā*ʿ and the experience of altered states can hardly be overstated in relation to the lives of these two mystics. For Nūrī, the practice of *samā*ʿ was part of the definition of what it meant to be a Sufi. As Nūrī was an enthusiastic champion of its practice, it is natural that he should embrace it in such an overwhelming way, and with such a joyous spirit of poetry and play. For him it was more important to disrupt the dry discussion of the academic gathering, and to replace it with the sheer joy and rapture of *samā*ʿ by the recital of secular love poetry.

The most important aspect of *samā*ʿ and altered state experience is that these form part of the direct 'taste' (*dhauq*) or apprehension of divine Realities. This immediate experience is the very goal and reason for the Sufi's existence. It is not a minor pastime or diversion, an activity to amuse novices, but one of the most significant of all the mystic's activities, which leads most directly to the divine presence. Nūrī expressed this notion most eloquently in the poetic fragments which were discussed above. In fact, it was also the pain deriving from bodily illness which allowed an apprehension of ecstatic feeling not unlike that associated with *samā*ʿ. In a related way, Shiblī's major psychotic episode allowed him to approach the divine presence, and for this reason he wanted his insanity to increase!

His apprehension of a psychotic state, for most people threatening, distressing and unwelcome, allowed him to 'taste' the nearness of God, and to achieve a means of approach not otherwise possible.

The consequence of participation in *samāʿ* was for Nūrī a genuine life and death choice. His entry into a trance state, and the consequent injury he suffered due to a lack of pain sensitivity, led directly to his death. This is indeed a high price to pay for his participation in this otherwise ecstatic and joyful activity.

For Shiblī the consequence of his cultivation of altered states through intense asceticism was a descent into madness and his committal to an asylum. It is clear that he deliberately sought a more intense experience of the divine presence through years of strict ascetic practices and austerities. He did not shun the psychosis which was one of the results of this approach to spiritual Reality, but rather he welcomed the new insight this offered. A cultivation of altered states also led to his being inspired to go about publicly preaching mystical secrets not otherwise divulged. This impulsive inspiration led to conflict and disagreement with the more cautious Junayd. What is more, it led to Shiblī being open to the charge of unconventionality in belief and practice. His retreat into madness may have been due to a desire to veil the unconventionality of his belief, and to prevent his being accused of heresy. But his bizarre public behaviours coupled with his acknowledged psychotic state led to suspicions and doubts about the soundness of his beliefs and practice. Shiblī was prepared to accept the charge of infidelity, and even to be put on trial for heresy, as occurred once in association with Nūrī. He was prepared to accept life as an outcast, indeed he relished the opportunity to live in a state of rejection from a world so opposed to his uncompromising beliefs. He could do this knowing that his real goal as a Sufi was for a deeper appreciation of the divine presence and an experience of the state of grace that this allowed.

It is clear that this yearning for direct appreciation of religious experience was one of the main driving forces behind Nūrī's and Shiblī's lives as mystics. It is also clear that neither man was important as a theoretician or teacher; their importance was in their practice of the mystical path. In this, the quality of their experience of the divine was paramount. The isolated utterances recorded in the source writings and the narratives of their actions best express the raw experience they encountered. For these two ecstatic mystics, the experience of *samāʿ* and altered states was the key direction of their upward journey.

Notes

1 See, for example, studies such as Gerhard Böwering, *The Mystical Vision of Existence in Classical Islam*, Berlin, New York, NY: Walter de Gruyter, 1980; and Ali Hassan Abdel-Kader, *The Life, Personality and Writings of Al-Junayd*, London: Luzac, 1976.
2 See Paul Nwyia, *Exégèse coranique et langage mystique*, Beirut: Dar al-Machreq, second edition, 1991, pp.316–48.
3 Nwyia, op.cit., pp.316–17.
4 See Peter J. Awn, *Satan's Tragedy and Redemption: Iblīs in Sufi Psychology*, Leiden: E.J. Brill, 1983, pp.172, 176.
5 See article *al-Nūrī* by Annemarie Schimmel in *E.I.*, vol.8, p.139.
6 See Nwyia, op.cit., p.317; Carl W. Ernst, *Words of Ecstasy in Sufism*, Albany, NY: State University of New York Press, 1985, pp.97–100; T.A. II.48.4–49.16; and A.J. Arberry, *Pages from the Kitāb al-Lumaʿ of Abū Naṣr al-Sarrāj*, London: Luzac, 1947, Arabic section pp.5–6.
7 Ernst, ibid.
8 *Lumaʿ* 195.3–8; but see Ernst, ibid., for a different interpretation.
9 See Schimmel, op.cit., and Nwyia, op.cit.
10 The text is unambiguously 'me', not 'men' as in Arberry's translation (MSM, p.228), though this may be a typographical error.
11 Schimmel, op.cit.
12 For biographical details, see article *al-Shiblī* by F. Sobieroj in *E.I.*, vol.9, p.432.
13 The semantic range of the key word *dhauq* ('taste, experience') is fully exploited in this saying.
14 Abū Bakr al-Kalābādhī, *The Doctrine of the Ṣūfīs*, transl. A.J. Arberry, Lahore: Ashraf, 1966 reprint, pp.143–4.
15 See *Diagnostic and Statistical Manual of Mental Disorders*, fourth ed., Washington D.C.: American Psychiatric Association, 1994, p.728.
16 See Felicitas D. Goodman, *Speaking in Tongues: A Cross-Cultural Study of Glossolalia*, Chicago, IL and London: University of Chicago Press, 1972, pp.64, 136.
17 Kalābādhī, op.cit., p.51.
18 Nwyia, op.cit., pp.319–20.
19 Paul Nwyia, 'Textes mystiques inédits d'Abū-l-Ḥasan al-Nūrī' in *Mélanges de l'Université Saint-Joseph* (Beirut), xliv, 1968, pp.117–154.
20 See Asʿad E. Khairallah, *Love, Madness, and Poetry: An Interpretation of the Mağnūn Legend*, Beirut: Franz Steiner, 1980, p.20, etc., for an expansion on this.
21 Michael W. Dols, *Majnūn: The Madman in Medieval Islamic Society*, Oxford: Clarendon Press, 1992, p.385.
22 *Lumaʿ* 282.17–283.1; *Ris.* 344–5; *Iḥyāʾ* II.294.14–17; Mcd. p.735.
23 See Eugene D'Aquili and Andrew B. Newberg, *The Mystical Mind: Probing the Biology of Religious Experience*, Minneapolis, MN: Fortress Press, 1999, p.64.

10

CONCLUSIONS

The experiences associated with the practice of *samāʿ* were important to the Sufis of the second/eighth to the sixth/twelfth centuries. These practices formed part of a larger group of ascetic exercises and spiritual disciplines which were in a process of development.

The variety of practices associated with 'listening' in a broader sense is illustrated by the numerous accounts recorded in the source texts. It is clear that the more formal and ritual practice of *samāʿ* seen in later centuries was still in the process of evolution. The precise history of these practices may be difficult to chronicle, and it was not the task of the present work to attempt this. Nor was it possible to give a detailed account of the ritual ceremonies from these formative years, beyond the bare outlines offered incidentally by the source texts.

The main contribution of the present study was in examining the psychology associated with these practices. The behaviours, ecstatic sayings and states of experience witnessed in ritual *samāʿ*, and in more casual 'listening' situations, were discussed in a phenomenological framework. Such an approach has been made possible in recent years with the emergence of altered state research and cross-cultural psychology studies.

The physical reactions and behaviours evoked by ritual *samāʿ* and by other listening situations are multifaceted. There are a wide variety of reactions in many different situations, involving a number of different individuals of varying status and background. Equally, there appear to be a variety of causal factors, and a variety of precipitating conditions, such as fasting or other ascetic deprivations. It cannot be concluded that there is a single response or condition evoked; nor is there a single causal or contributory factor.

Some of the reactions indicate a dissociative cause from deep within the psyche; this is especially evident in trance-like and epileptiform reactions. The evidence suggested, however, that such dissociative reactions were present in only a minority of cases. Many of the reactions indicate more casual factors operating: everyday causes such as anxiety or fear reactions, emotional release and other more familiar explanations. Physiological factors were also seen, including the effects of ascetic practices, the deprivations of fasting, and hyperventilation caused by repeated chanting.

Gilbert Rouget's work, *Music and Trance*, has been the only previous study which suggested an explanatory model for these behavioural and consciousness changes. Rouget suggested a distinction between 'ritual' *samāʿ*, which resulted in a culturally sanctioned trance state, and 'non-ritual' *samāʿ* which resulted in a crisis outcome beyond the bounds of cultural acceptance. The difficulty with this explanation, apart from being a circular argument, is its uncritical adoption of mainstream religious prescriptions for the practice of *samāʿ*. While this distinction may hold for the performance of ritual *samāʿ* ceremonies, it does not adequately explain much of the evidence from the texts of the early Sufi period. Even within religiously sanctioned practices, there are often 'crisis' outcomes, to which Rouget's theory does not apply. Outside the formal practice of *samāʿ* this explanation is even less plausible as there are many 'non-crisis' outcomes beyond sanctioned ritual.

Two important considerations emerged from our discussion. The first related to the factors causing trance or altered states among a number of individuals. It was clear from the texts that in several situations episodes of altered states occurred with very little prompting or evocation from external stimuli. This suggests that the individuals concerned were experiencing 'borderline' states of consciousness, and that these were an everyday part of their lives. Altered states sometimes arose from insignificant triggers, such as the misheard cry of a street vendor, or a chance encounter with a reciter or singer. This suggests that the person involved was psychologically prepared by means of deprivation, ascetic practices, chanting, and so on. The occurrence of these episodes in everyday situations meant that this preparedness extended well beyond a ritual environment where susceptibility is likely to be greater. In these cases, a seemingly small trigger was required to alter the person's everyday, ordinary perceptions to a changed reality where special meanings were perceived in otherwise insignificant stimuli.

The second consideration which arose from our discussion of altered states involves the connection between the explanations of mainstream psychology, and the understanding of the early source writers. Until very recently, the consensus of psychology, with the inbuilt bias of Western sciences, was to regard these phenomena as abnormal, dysfunctional or pathological. This may have been one reason for the lack of attention to this area of Sufi and Islamic studies. In recent years, however, with developments in the area of consciousness studies, and cross-cultural psychology, the bias of seeing these states as abnormal and pathological has changed. It has been recognised, for example, that ritual or institutionalised forms of trance occur in around 90 per cent of societies studied ethnographically.[1] The near universality of this phenomenon means that it cannot be regarded as abnormal, despite Western bias, and despite the lack of thorough psychological explanations.

For the Sufi authors studied here, the integration of these unusual behaviours and states into a cohesive religious and social framework was never really in question. The conduct of the majority of Sufis who encountered these states was accepted and tolerated, and seen as part of their living religious experience. This is the case even with the sober and cautious writing of Sarrāj, whose apologetic purpose was to explain and integrate Sufi teaching and conduct into mainstream Sunni Islam. That he writes of these phenomena with such candour and openness is a witness to their acceptance and tolerance as part of legitimate religious experience. An example of this is that Sarrāj includes in his work several chapters devoted to a commentary on the more questionable sayings and actions attributed to Abū Yazīd al-Bisṭāmī. Even here, the author's purpose is one of inclusion and harmonisation of unusual mystical experience with the bases of Islamic belief and practice.

Certainly there were conservative critics of the Sufi path, particularly critics of their more extravagant and unusual behaviours. It is for this reason that authors such as Sarrāj and Qushayrī wrote their apologetic works.

Equally, there were a number of radical or outspoken Sufis whose behaviour and beliefs often stretched the bounds of acceptability. Our discussion in Chapter 9, dealing with the lives and experience of Nūrī and Shiblī, shows this quite conclusively. As we have seen, Shiblī spent time in the Baghdad asylum recovering from psychosis, being considered outside the social convention of sanity. Yet he himself saw his psychosis as divinely inspired, furthering his development as a seeker of unitary experience. He integrated what would otherwise be a disruptive and terrifying episode into his life's journey of seeking nearness and encounter of the Real (*al-ḥaqq*). Shiblī's own understanding of his situation is reflected in the writings which recorded his words and actions for later generations. If an integral understanding was possible then, how should abnormality and pathology explain his condition now? If his experience was part of a life quest for wholeness, why should we regard it as dysfunctional and pathological?

The emergence of new understandings in psychology over the last few decades has made this integrative argument tenable. This also gives more legitimacy to the Sufis' own understanding of these states, exemplified in the texts studied here. It is true that one must accept the underlying assumptions of the Sufi world-view to concur fully with their psychology. Yet, even if this is not possible, the Sufi writers' psychology still makes an important contribution. The inclusion and acceptance of unusual states and behaviours within the prevailing religion and culture is valuable and exemplary. This acceptance of non-ordinary states of consciousness is only now being given credence in contemporary Western sciences.

Apart from the unusual states and behaviours discussed in this study, there were also the sayings of the Sufis during their encounters with altered consciousness. A range of different types of sayings were found; some purely descriptive, some more cryptic sayings, some ecstatic outbursts, or lyrical and poetic fragments. With this range there was also found a variety of possible causal factors. Carl Ernst has done research on the slightly different phenomenon of ecstatic sayings or *shaṭḥīyāt*, published in *Words of Ecstasy in Sufism*, and other writings. This is certainly one area where more inquiry would be fruitful, particularly on the literary side, for example with the poetry of Shiblī or Nūrī, which could not be attempted in this present study.

A further area where future inquiry would be profitable is in the documentation of ritual ceremonies associated with *samāʿ* among contemporary Sufi communities. There already exists the excellent fieldwork of Regula Qureshi, which has been relied on for the purposes of the present study. Most contemporary performance seems to involve traditions and customs which developed later than the period under study in this book. The survival of rituals from prior to the seventh/thirteenth century is a topic which needs addressing. There have been no studies which correlate contemporary performances with these early textual sources; such inquiry would have taken the present work beyond manageable limits.

It was possible, however, to glean from the early texts a number of details concerning social aspects of *samāʿ* performance and the social framework of Sufi groupings. The organised structures of Sufi orders which are observable from later periods are represented rather more loosely in the earlier texts. In many instances, the whole social organisation of the Sufi 'community' was none other than a group of personal followers of a revered master or teacher. The ceremonies or rituals carried out by that community were thus portrayed in the texts as quite spontaneous and informal gatherings or performances, rather than the structured and formal ceremonials of a larger religious order. By this means, the texts allow us to observe something of the early stages in the development of ritual and ceremony.

In the last chapter of the study, the lives of two important 'ecstatic' Sufis were considered, particularly in regard to the role of *samāʿ* and altered states in their religious experience. This biographical survey sought to exemplify many of the issues dealt with more abstractly in previous chapters by applying these issues to the life histories of Nūrī and Shiblī. The importance of *samāʿ* was seen particularly with Nūrī, who was an enthusiastic practitioner, and of whom many incidents in his life related to its performance and enjoyment. It was fitting, though somewhat ironic, that his death was also caused as a result of his participation in a *samāʿ* performance. Shiblī, on the other hand, was better known for his frequent encounters with darker altered states. Yet at other times his experience was of a more benign nature, where he was animated and awakened by a spirit of intense religious fervour.

Most importantly for these two ecstatic personalities, altered state experience formed part of their direct 'taste' (*dhauq*) or apprehension of divine Reality. This direct knowledge was the principal reason for their religious journey, and the goal of their lives. Scattered references in varying sources allow us to piece their lives together and form a coherent picture of their deeds and sayings. These diverse accounts provide the most direct approach to their experience which it is possible for us to gain.

Given the admitted limitations of the present study, further research in this area will surely produce more fruitful outcomes. We can look forward to a greater understanding of this fascinating area of Sufism, and of human behaviour generally.

Note

1 See Richard J. Castillo, 'Culture, Trance, and the Mind-Brain', in *Anthropology of Consciousness*, 6, 1995, p.17.

BIBLIOGRAPHY

Abdel-Kader, Ali Hassan (1976) *The Life, Personality and Writings of Al-Junayd*, London: Luzac and Co.

Affifi, A.E. (1979) *The Mystical Philosophy of Muhyid Din Ibnul Arabi* (reprint), Lahore: Ashraf.

American Psychiatric Association (1994) *Diagnostic and Statistical Manual of Mental Disorders*, fourth edition, Washington DC: American Psychiatric Association.

Arberry, A.J. (1937) 'Did Sulamī plagiarize Sarrāj?', *Journal of the Royal Asiatic Society*, pp.461–5.

—— (1947) *Pages from the Kitāb al-Lumaʿ of Abū Naṣr al-Sarrāj*, London: Luzac and Co.

—— (1950, reprinted 1979) *Sufism: An Account of the Mystics of Islam*, London: George Allen & Unwin.

ʿAṭṭār, Farīd al-Dīn (1905–7) *Tadhkiratu 'l-Awliyā*, ed. R.A. Nicholson, 2 vols, London: Luzac and Co., Leiden: E.J. Brill.

—— (1966, reprinted 1979) *Muslim Saints and Mystics: Episodes from the Tadhkirat al-Auliyaʾ*, translated by A.J. Arberry, London: Routledge and Kegan Paul.

Awn, Peter J. (1983) *Satan's Tragedy and Redemption: Iblīs in Sufi Psychology*, Leiden: E.J. Brill.

Badawī, ʿAbd al-Rahman (1993) *Tārīkh al-Taṣawwuf al-Islāmī*, Beirut: Dār al-Qalam.

Baldick, Julian (1989) *Mystical Islam: An Introduction to Sufism*, London: I.B. Tauris.

Bennett, T.L. (ed.) (1992) *The Neuropsychology of Epilepsy*, New York, NY and London: Plenum Press.

Blois, François de (1994) *Persian Literature: A Biobibliographical Survey, begun by the late C.A. Storey*, vol.5, Part 2, London: The Royal Asiatic Society of Great Britain and Ireland.

Blum, S. et al. (eds) (1991) *Ethnomusicology and Modern Music History*, Urbana, IL and Chicago, IL: University of Illinois Press.

Böwering, Gerhard (1980) *The Mystical Vision of Existence in Classical Islam*, Berlin and New York, NY: Walter de Gruyter.

—— (1993) 'Ideas of Time in Persian Sufism', in L. Lewisohn (ed.), *Classical Persian Sufism: From its Origins to Rumi*, London: Khaniqahi Nimatullahi Publications, pp.199–233.

Bowker, John (1970) *Problems of Suffering in Religions of the World*, Cambridge: Cambridge University Press.

Brenan, Gerald (1973) *St John of the Cross: His Life and Poetry*, Cambridge: Cambridge University Press.

Browne, E.G. (1921, reprinted 1962) *Arabian Medicine*, Cambridge: Cambridge University Press.

Burckhardt, Titus (1959, reprinted 1973) *An Introduction to Sufi Doctrine*, translated by D.M. Matheson, Lahore: Ashraf.

Burgel, J.C. (1980) 'Musicotherapy in the Islamic Middle Ages as reflected in Medical and Other Sources', *Studies in History of Medicine*, 4, pp.23–8.

Cambridge History of Arabic Literature, The (1990) *ʿAbbasid Belles-Lettres*, ed. Julia Ashtiany et al., Cambridge: Cambridge University Press.

Cambridge History of Arabic Literature, The (1990) *Religion, Learning and Science in the ʿAbbasid Period*, ed. M.J.L. Young et al., Cambridge: Cambridge University Press.

Campbell, Donald (1926, reprinted New York: AMS Press, 1973) *Arabian Medicine and its Influence on the Middle Ages*, vol.1, London.

Carrington, Patricia (1986) 'Meditation as an Access to Altered states of Consciousness', in B.B. Wolman and M. Ullman (eds), *Handbook of States of Consciousness*, New York, NY: Van Nostrand Reinhold, pp.487–523.

Castillo, Richard J. (1995) 'Culture, Trance and the Mind-Brain', *Anthropology of Consciousness*, 6, pp.17–34.

Clarke, John H. (1983) *A Map of Mental States*, London: Routledge and Kegan Paul.

Critchley, M. (1977) 'Ecstatic and Synaesthetic Experiences during Musical Perception', in M. Critchley and R.A. Henson, *Music and the Brain*, London: William Heinemann, pp.217–32.

—— (1977) 'Musicogenic Epilepsy (1) The Beginnings', in M. Critchley and R.A. Henson, *Music and the Brain*, London: William Heinemann, pp.344–53.

—— and Henson, R.A. (1977) *Music and the Brain*, London: William Heinemann.

D'Aquili, Eugene and Newberg, Andrew B. (1999) *The Mystical Mind: Probing the Biology of Religious Experience*, Minneapolis, MN: Fortress Press.

Davies, Paul (1992) *The Mind of God: Science and the Search for Ultimate Meaning*, London: Simon and Schuster.

Deschēnes, B. (1992) 'The Dynamogenic Impact of Music', in R. Spintge and R. Droh, *Music Medicine*, Saint Louis, MO: MMB Music, pp.232–40.

Dols, Michael W. (1992) *Majnūn: The Madman in Medieval Islamic Society*, Oxford: Clarendon Press.

Dozy, R. (1881) *Supplément aux dictionnaires arabes*, 2 vols, Leiden: E.J. Brill and Paris: Maisonneuve and Co.

During, Jean (1988) *Musique et extase: L'audition mystique dans la tradition soufie*, Paris: Albin Michel.

—— (1992) 'What is Sufi Music?', in L. Lewisohn (ed.), *The Legacy of Medieval Persian Sufism*, London: Khaniqahi Nimatullahi Publications, pp.277–87.

—— (1993) 'The Sacred Music of the Ahl-i Haqq as a Means of Mystical Transmission', in G.M. Smith and C.W. Ernst (eds), *Manifestations of Sainthood in Islam*, Istanbul: Isis Press, pp.27–41.

—— (1960–) 'samāʿ', *E.I.*, vol.8, p.1018.

Encyclopaedia of Islam, The (1960–) new edition, ed. H.A.R. Gibb et al., Leiden: E.J. Brill.

Ernst, Carl W. (1985) *Words of Ecstasy in Sufism*, Albany, NY: State University of New York Press.

—— (1992) 'Mystical Language and the Teaching Context in the Early Lexicons of Sufism', in Steven T. Katz (ed.), *Mysticism and Language*, New York, NY: Oxford University Press, pp.181–201.

Farah, Caesar E. (1990) 'The Prose Literature of Sufism', *The Cambridge History of Arabic Literature: Religion, Learning and Science in the ʿAbbasid Period*, ed. M.J.L. Young et al., Cambridge: Cambridge University Press, pp.56–75.

Farmer, Henry George (1952) 'The Religious Music of Islām', *Journal of the Royal Asiatic Society*, pp.60–5.

Al-Faruqi, Lois Ibsen (1987) 'The Cantillation of the Qurʾān', *Asian Music*, 19, pp.2–25.

Fischer, Roland (1986) 'Toward a Neuroscience of Self-Experience and States of Self-Awareness and Interpreting Interpretations', in B.B. Wolman and M. Ullman (eds), *Handbook of States of Consciousness*, New York, NY: Van Nostrand Reinhold, pp.3–30.

Forman, Robert K.C. (ed.) (1990) *The Problem of Pure Consciousness: Mysticism and Philosophy*, New York, NY: Oxford University Press.

Fraser, George A. (1994) 'Dissociative Phenomena and Disorders: Clinical Presentation', in R.M. Klein and B.K. Doane (eds), *Psychological Concepts and Dissociative Disorders*, Hillsdale, NJ: Lawrence Erlbaum Associates, pp.131–51.

Gardet, L. (1960–) 'ḳalb', *E.I.*, Vol. 4, pp.486–8.

Al-Ghazālī, Abū Ḥāmid Muḥammad (1939) *Iḥyāʾ ʿUlūm al-Dīn*, 4 vols, Cairo: Matbaʿa Mustafā al-Bābī al-Halabī wa-Ulāda bi-Misr.

—— (1996) *Al-Munqidh min al-Ḍalāl*, ed. Jamīl Salība et al., Beirut: Dār al-Andalus.

Gifford-May, Derek, and Thompson, Norman L. (1994) '"Deep States" of Meditation: Phenomenological Reports of Experience', *Journal of Transpersonal Psychology*, 26, pp.117–38.

Godwin, J. (1986) *Music, Mysticism and Magic*, London: Routledge and Kegan Paul.

Goldman, Alvin I. (1993) 'Consciousness, Folk Psychology, and Cognitive Science', *Consciousness and Cognition*, 2, pp.364–82.

Goldman, J.S. (1992) 'Sonic Entrainment', in R. Spintge and R. Droh, *Music Medicine*, Saint Louis, MO: MMB Music, pp.194–208.

Goodman, Felicitas D. (1972) *Speaking in Tongues: A Cross-Cultural Study of Glossolalia*, Chicago, IL: University of Chicago Press.

Gramlich, Richard (1990) *Schlaglichter über das Sufitum: Abū Naṣr as-Sarrāǧs Kitāb al-lumaʿ* eingeleitet, übersetzt und kommentiert, Stuttgart: Franz Steiner Verlag.

Gribetz, Arthur (1991) 'The samāʿ Controversy: Sufi vs. Legalist', *Studia Islamica*, LXXIV, pp.43–62.

Hakīmī, Ismāʿīl (1992) *Samāʿ dar Taṣawwuf*, fourth edition, Tehran: University Publications.

Halm, H. (1960–) 'al-Ḳushayrī', *E.I.*, Vol. 5, pp.526–7.

Halperin, Daniel (1996) 'Trance and Possession: Are They The Same?', *Transcultural Psychiatric Research Review*, 33, pp.33–41.

Handel, S. (1989) *Listening: An Introduction to the Perception of Auditory Events*, Cambridge, MA: MIT Press.

Harrer, G. and Harrer, H. (1977) 'Music, Emotion and Autonomic Function', in M. Critchley and R.A. Henson, *Music and the Brain*, London: William Heinemann, pp.202–16.

Haywood, John A. (1965) *Arabic Lexicography: Its History, and its Place in the General History of Lexicography*, second edition, Leiden: E.J. Brill.

Hilgard, Ernest R. (1992) 'Divided Consciousness and Dissociation', *Consciousness and Cognition*, 1, pp.16–31.

Hodges, Donald A. (ed.) (1980) *Handbook of Music Psychology*, Dubuque, IA: Kendall Hunt.

The Holy Quran (1938, reprinted 1977) Text, translation and commentary by Abdullah Yusuf Ali, Lahore: Ashraf.

Hosain, Hidayet (1960–) 'Hudjwīrī', *E.I.*, vol.3, p.546.

Al-Hujwīrī, Alī b. ʿUthmān al-Jullābī, *Kashf al-Maḥjūb*, ed. V.A. Zhukovski, Tehran: Amīr Kabīr, 1336 a.h.s. (repr.).

—— (1911, reprinted 1982) *The Kashf al-Maḥjūb*, translated by R.A. Nicholson, Leiden: E.J. Brill and London: Luzac and Co.

Hussaini, Syed Shah Khusro (1970) 'Bund Samāʿ (or Closed Audition)', *Islamic Culture*, XLIV, pp.177–85.

Idel, Moshe (1988) *Kabbalah: New Perspectives*, New Haven, CT: Yale University Press.

James, William (1960, reprinted 1982) *The Varieties of Religious Experience*, Glasgow: Collins.

Jennings, Jerry L. (1986) 'Husserl Revisited; The Forgotten Distinction between Psychology and Phenomenology', *American Psychologist*, 41, pp.1231–40.

Jilek, Wolfgang G. (1989) 'Therapeutic Use of Altered States of Consciousness in Contemporary North American Indian Dance Ceremonials', in C.A. Ward (ed.), *Altered States of Consciousness and Mental Health: A Cross-Cultural Perspective*, Newbury Park, CA: Sage Publications, pp.167–85.

Al-Kalābādhī, Abū Bakr (1935, reprinted Lahore: Ashraf, 1966) *The Doctrine of the Ṣūfīs*, translated by A.J. Arberry, Cambridge: Cambridge University Press.

Katz, Steven T. (ed.) (1992) *Mysticism and Language*, New York, NY: Oxford University Press.

Khairallah, Asʿad E. (1980) *Love, Madness, and Poetry: An Interpretation of the Mağnūn Legend*, Beirut: Franz Steiner.

Kildahl, John P. (1972) *The Psychology of Speaking in Tongues*, New York, NY: Harper and Row.

King, Don W. et al. (1993) 'Convulsive Non-Epileptic Seizures', in A.J. Rowan and J.R. Gates (eds), *Non-Epileptic Seizures*, Boston: Butterworth-Heinemann, pp.31–7.

Kirsch, Irving (1997) 'The State of the Altered State Debate', in W.J. Matthews et al., *Current Thinking and Research in Brief Therapy*, 1, pp.91–112.

Klein, Raymond M. and Doane, Benjamin K. (eds) (1994) *Psychological Concepts and Dissociative Disorders*, Hillsdale, NJ: Lawrence Erlbaum Associates.

Koran Interpreted, The (1964, reprinted 1991) translated by A.J. Arberry, Oxford: Oxford University Press.

Lambek, Michael (1989) 'From Disease to Discourse: Remarks on the Conceptualization of Trance and Spirit Possession', in C.A. Ward (ed.), *Altered States of Consciousness and Mental Health: A Cross-Cultural Perspective*, Newbury Park, CA: Sage Publications, pp.36–61.

Lane, Edward William (1984) *An Arabic-English Lexicon*, London: Williams and Norgate, 1863–93, repr. 2 vols, Cambridge: Islamic Texts Society Trust.

Lathers, Claire M. and Schraeder, Paul L. (eds) (1990) *Epilepsy and Sudden Death*, New York, NY: Marcel Dekker.

Lewisohn, Leonard (ed.) (1992) *The Legacy of Medieval Persian Sufism*, London: Khaniqahi Nimatullahi Publications.

—— (ed.) (1993) *Classical Persian Sufism: from its Origins to Rumi*, London: Khaniqahi Nimatullahi Publications.

Lings, M. (1990) 'Mystical Poetry', in Julia Ashtiany et al. (eds), *The Cambridge History of Arabic Literature: ʿAbbasid Belles-Lettres*, Cambridge: Cambridge University Press, pp.235–64.

Locke, Ralph G. and Kelly, Edward F. (1985) 'A Preliminary Model for the Cross-Cultural Analysis of Altered States of Consciousness', *Ethos*, 13, pp.3–55.

Lukoff, David (1985) 'The Diagnosis of Mystical Experiences with Psychotic Features', *Journal of Transpersonal Psychology*, 17, pp.155–81.

Macdonald, D.B. (1901/02) 'Emotional Religion in Islam as affected by Music and Singing, Being a Translation of a Book of the Iḥyā ʿUlūm ad-Dīn of al-Ghazzālī with Analysis, Annotation and Appendices', *Journal of the Royal Asiatic Society*, 22 (1901), pp.195–252 and 705–48; and 23 (1902), pp.1–28.

—— (1930–1) 'The Development of the Idea of Spirit in Islam', *Acta Orientalia*, 9, pp.307–51.

Malamud, Margaret (1994) 'Sufi Organizations and Structures of Authority in Medieval Nishapur', *International Journal of Middle East Studies*, 26, pp.427–42.

Malony, H. Newton and Lovekin, A. Adams (1985) *Glossolalia: Behavioral Science Perspectives on Speaking in Tongues*, New York, NY: Oxford University Press.

Ibn Manẓūr, Muḥammad b. Mukarram (1955–6) *Lisān al-ʿArab*, Beirut: Dār Sādir, Dār Bayrūt, 15 vols.

Marcel, A.J. and Bisiach, E. (eds) (1988) *Consciousness in Contemporary Science*, Oxford: Oxford University Press.

Markoff, Irene (1993) 'Music, Saints, and Ritual: Samāʿ and the Alevis of Turkey', in G.M. Smith and C.W. Ernst (eds), *Manifestations of Sainthood in Islam*, Istanbul: Isis Press, pp.95–100.

Massignon, Louis (1954) *Essai sur les origines du lexique technique de la mystique musulmane*, Nouvelle éd., Paris: J. Vrin.

—— (1963) 'Le temps dans la pensée islamique', *Opera Minora*, vol.2, Beirut: Dar al-Maaref-Liban, pp.601–12.

—— (1982) *The Passion of al-Hallāj: Mystic and Martyr of Islam*, translated by H. Mason, 4 vols, Princeton, NJ: Princeton University Press.

—— (1984) *The Passion of al-Hallāj*, abridged edition, translated by H. Mason, Princeton, NJ: Princeton University Press.

Mojaddedi, Jawid A. (2001) *The Biographical Tradition in Sufism: The ṭabaqāt genre from al-Sulamī to Jāmī*, Richmond: Curzon Press.

Molé, Marijan (1963) 'La danse extatique en Islam', *Les danses sacrées*, Sources orientales VI, Paris: Editions du seuil, pp.145–280.

Nasr, Seyyed Hossein (1971) 'The Influence of Sufism on Traditional Persian Music', *Islamic Culture*, XLV, pp.171–9.

—— (1978) *An Introduction to Islamic Cosmological Doctrines*, London: Thames and Hudson.

Nelson, K. (1985) *The Art of Reciting the Qur'an*, Austin, TX: University of Texas Press.

Netton, Ian Richard (2000) *Sufi Ritual: The Parallel Universe*, Richmond: Curzon Press.

Nicholson, Reynold A. (1975) *The Mystics of Islam* (reprint), New York, NY: Schocken Books.

Nurbakhsh, Javad (1992) *The Psychology of Sufism*, London: Khaniqahi Nimatullahi Publications.

Nwyia, Paul (1968) 'Textes mystiques inédits d'Abū-l-Ḥasan al-Nūrī', *Mélanges de l'Université Saint-Joseph* (Beirut), tome XLIV, fasc.9, pp.117–54.

—— (1991) *Exégèse coranique et langage mystique*, second edition, Beirut: Dar el-Machreq.

Oxford Companion to the Mind, The (1987) ed. by Richard L. Gregory, Oxford: Oxford University Press.

Pattison, E. Mansell and Kahan, Joel (1986) 'Personal Experience as a Conceptual Tool for Modes of Consciousness', in B.B. Wolman and M. Ullman (eds), *Handbook of States of Consciousness*, New York, NY: Van Nostrand Reinhold, pp.199–245.

Pattison, E. Mansell et al. (1986) 'Trance and Possession States', in B.B. Wolman and M. Ullman (eds), *Handbook of States of Consciousness*, New York, NY: Van Nostrand Reinhold, pp. 286–310.

Peters, Larry G. and Price-Williams, Douglass (1983) 'A Phenomenological Overview of Trance', *Transcultural Psychiatric Research Review*, 20, pp.5–39.

Pickworth, Wallace B. et al. (1990) 'Stress, Arrhythmias and Seizures', in C.M. Lathers and P.L. Schraeder (eds), *Epilepsy and Sudden Death*, New York, NY: Marcel Dekker, pp.417–46.

Poché, Christian (1978) 'Zikr and Musicology', *The World of Music*, 20, pp.59–71.

—— (1983) 'David and the Ambiguity of the Mizmar according to Arab Sources', *The World of Music*, 25, pp.58–73.

Poliakova, E.A. (1987) 'Some Problems of Sufi Studies', *Islamic Culture*, LXI, pp.73–89.

Porter, Rojer J. (1993) 'Epileptic and Non-Epileptic Seizures', in A.J. Rowan and J.R. Gates (eds), *Non-Epileptic Seizures*, Boston, MA: Butterworth-Heinemann, pp.9–20.

Pouzet, Louis (1983) 'Prises de position autour du <samāʿ> en orient musulman au VIIe/XIIIe siècle', *Studia Islamica*, LVII, pp.119–34.

Pressing, Jeff (1980) 'Musical Experience, Altered States of Consciousness, and psi', in A. Gabay (ed.), *Proceedings of the Psychic Orientation Conference*, Melbourne: La Trobe University, pp.43–54.

Price, Reese (1987) 'Dissociative Disorders of the Self: A Continuum Extending into Multiple Personality', *Psychotherapy*, 24, pp.387–91.

Al-Qāshānī, ʿAbd al-Razzāq (1991) *A Glossary of Sufi Technical Terms*, translated by Nabil Safwat, London: Octagon Press.

Quen, Jacques M. (1986) *Split Minds/Split Brains: Historical and Current Perspectives*, New York, NY: New York University Press.

Qureshi, Regula Burckhardt (1988) 'Listening to Words through Music: The Sufi Samāʿ', *Edebiyāt* (New Series), 2, pp.219–45.

—— (1986) 'The Mahfil-e-sama: Sufi Practice in the Indian Context', *Islam and the Modern Age*, XVII, pp.133–65.

—— (1986) *Sufi Music of India and Pakistan: Sound, Context and Meaning in Qawwali*, Cambridge: Cambridge University Press.

—— (1987) 'Qawwālī: Making the Music Happen in the Sufi Assembly', *Asian Music*, XVIII, pp.118–57.

—— (1991) 'Sufi Music and the Historicity of Oral Tradition', in S. Blum et al., *Ethnomusicology and Modern Music History*, Urbana and Chicago, IL: University of Illinois Press, pp.103–20.

—— (1993) 'Samaʾ in the Royal Court of Saints: The Chishtiyya of South Asia', in G.M. Smith and C.W. Ernst (eds), *Manifestations of Sainthood in Islam*, Istanbul: Isis Press, pp.111–27.

Al-Qushayrī, Abū ʾl-Qāsim ʿAbd al-Karīm (1969) *Arbaʿ Rasāʾil fī ʾl-Taṣawwuf*, ed. by Qāsim al-Samarrāʾī, Baghdad: Al-Majmaʿ al-ʿIlmī ʾl-ʿIrāqī.

—— (n.d.) *Al-Risālat al-Qushayrīya fī ʿIlm al-Taṣawwuf*, ed. by Maʿrūf Zarīq and ʿAlī Balṭajī. Beirut: Dār al-Jīl.

Reynolds, E.H. and Trimble, M.R. (eds) (1981) *Epilepsy and Psychiatry*, Edinburgh: Churchill Livingstone.

Ritter, Hellmut (1960–) 'ʿAṭṭār', *E.I.*, vol.1, pp.752–5.

Robson, James (ed.) (1938) *Tracts on Listening to Music, being Dhamm al-malāhī by Ibn abī ʾl-Dunyā and Bawāriq al-ilmāʾ by Majd al-Dīn al-Ṭūsī al-Ghazālī*, London: Royal Asiatic Society.

Rouget, Gilbert (1985) *Music and Trance: A Theory of the Relations between Music and Possession*, Chicago, IL: University of Chicago Press.

Rowan, A. James and Gates, John R. (eds) (1993) *Non-Epileptic Seizures*, Boston, MA: Butterworth-Heinemann.

Roy, Alec and Barris, Madeleine (1993) 'Psychiatric Concepts in Psychogenic Non-Epileptic Seizures', in A.J. Rowan and J.R. Gates (eds), *Non-Epileptic Seizures*, Boston, MA: Butterworth-Heinemann, pp.143–51.

Rychlak, Joseph F. (1997) *In Defense of Human Consciousness*, Washington DC: American Psychological Association.

Sacks, Oliver (1985) *The Man Who Mistook His Wife for a Hat*, London: Picador.

—— (1995) *An Anthropologist on Mars*, Sydney: Pan Macmillan.

Al-Sarrāj al-Ṭūsī, Abū Naṣr ʿAbdallah b. ʿAlī (1914, reprinted 1963) *The Kitāb al-Lumaʿ fī ʾl-Taṣawwuf*, ed. by R.A. Nicholson, London: Luzac and Co.

Schimmel, Annemarie (1960–) 'al-Nūrī', *E.I.*, vol.8, p.139.

—— (1993) 'Abū ʾl-Husayn al-Nūrī: Qibla of the Lights', in L. Lewisohn (ed.), *Classical Persian Sufism: From its Origins to Rumi*, London: Khaniqahi Nimatullahi Publications, pp.59–64.

Scott, D.F. (1977) 'Musicogenic Epilepsy (2) The Later Story: Its Relation to Auditory Hallucinatory Phenomena', in M. Critchley and R.A. Henson, *Music and the Brain*, London: William Heinemann, pp.354–64.

Scotton, Bruce W. et al. (1996) *Textbook of Transpersonal Psychiatry and Psychology*, New York, NY: Basic Books.

Sells, Michael A. (ed.) (1996) *Early Islamic Mysticism: Sufi, Qur'an, Miʿraj, Poetic and Theological Writings*, New York, NY Mahwah: Paulist Press.

Sharpe, Eric J. (1986) *Comparative Religion: A History*, second edition, La Salle: Open Court.

Shay, Anthony (1995) 'Dance and Non-Dance: Patterned Movement in Iran and Islam', *Iranian Studies*, 28, pp.61–78.

Shehadi, Fadlou (1995) *Philosophies of Music in Medieval Islam*, Leiden: E.J. Brill.

Shiloah, Amnon (1977) 'The Role and Nature of Music in the Practice of the samaʿ', *International Musicological Society Report of the twelfth Congress*, Berkeley, CA: IMS, pp.425–8.

—— (1993) 'The Epistle on Music of the Ikhwān al-Ṣafā', in A. Shiloah, *The Dimension of Music in Islamic and Jewish Culture*, Aldershot: Variorum, pp.3–73.

—— (1993) 'Ibn Hindū, le médecin et la musique', in A. Shiloah, *The Dimension of Music in Islamic and Jewish Culture*, Aldershot: Variorum, pp.447–62.

—— (1995) *Music in the World of Islam: A Socio-Cultural Study*, Aldershot: Scolar Press.

Shorter, Edward (1992) *From Paralysis to Fatigue: A History of Psychosomatic Illness in the Modern Era*, New York, NY: The Free Press.

Shorter Encyclopaedia of Islam, The (1953, reprinted 1974) ed. by H.A.R. Gibb and J.H. Kramers, Leiden: E.J. Brill.

Smith, Grace Martin and Ernst, Carl W. (eds) (1993) *Manifestations of Sainthood in Islam*, Istanbul: Isis Press.

Smith, Margaret (n.d.) *Al-Ghazali The Mystic*, reprinted Lahore: Kazi Publications.

Sobieroj, F. (1960–) 'al-Shiblī', *E.I.*, vol.9, pp.432–3.

Søndergaard, Svend (1990) 'al-Sarrādj's Use of Triads in Kitāb al-Lumaʿ', in E. Keck et al. (eds), *Living Waters* (F. Løkkegaard festschrift), Copenhagen: Museum Tusculanum Press, pp.347–52.

Spintge, R. and Droh, R. (1992) *Music Medicine*, Saint Louis, MO: MMB Music.

Steingass, Franz (1892, reprinted 1977) *Persian-English Dictionary*, London: Routledge and Kegan Paul.

Al-Sulamī, Abū ʿAbd al-Rahmān (1960) *Kitāb Ṭabaqāt al-Ṣūfiyya*, Texte arabe avec une introduction . . . par Johannes Pedersen, Leiden: E.J. Brill.

—— (1969) *Ṭabaqāt al-Ṣūfīya*, ed. by Nūr al-Dīn Sharība, second edition, Cairo: Maktaba 'l-Khānijī.

—— (1976) *Jawāmiʿ Ādāb al-Ṣūfiyya and ʿUyūb al-Nafs wa-Mudāwātuhā*, ed. by Etan Kohlberg, Jerusalem: Academic Press.

—— (1981) *Kitāb al-Arbaʿīn fī ʾl-Taṣawwuf*, second edition, Hyderabad: Majlis Dā'ira ʾl-Maʿārif al-ʿUthmānīya.

Tart, Charles T. (1986) 'Consciousness, Altered States, and Worlds of Experience', *Journal of Transpersonal Psychology*, 18, pp.159–70.

Temkin, Owsei (1994) *The Falling Sickness*, Baltimore, MD: Johns Hopkins University Press.

Thapa, Komilla and Murthy, Vinoda N. (1985) 'Experiential Characteristics of Certain Altered States of Consciousness', *Journal of Transpersonal Psychology*, 17, pp.77–86.

Trimble, M.R. (1981) 'Hysteria and Other Non-Epileptic Convulsions', in E.H. Reynolds and M.R. Trimble (eds), *Epilepsy and Psychiatry*, Edinburgh: Churchill Livingstone, pp.92–112.

Trimingham, J. Spencer (1971) *The Sufi Orders in Islam*, Oxford: Clarendon Press.

Vullers, Ioannis Augusti (1962) *Lexicon Persico-Latinum Etymologicum*, 3 vols, reprint, Graz: Akademische Druck-u. Verlagsanstalt.

Waley, Muhammad Isa (1993) 'Contemplative Disciplines in Early Persian Sufism', in L. Lewisohn (ed.), *Classical Persian Sufism: from its Origins to Rumi*, London: Khaniqahi Nimatullahi Publications, pp.497–548.

Walsh, Roger (1995) 'Phenomenological Mapping: A Method for Describing and Comparing States of Consciousness', *Journal of Transpersonal Psychology*, 27, pp.25–56.

Ward, Colleen A. (ed.) (1989) *Altered States of Consciousness and Mental Health: A Cross-Cultural Perspective*, Newbury Park, CA: Sage Publications.

Watt, W. Montgomery (1960–) 'al-Ghazālī', *E.I.*, vol.2, pp.1038–41.

Wehr, Hans (1976) *A Dictionary of Modern Written Arabic*, ed. by J.M Cowan, third edition, London: Harrap.

Wensinck, A.J. (1936–88) *Concordance et indices de la tradition musulmane*, Tomes I–VIII, Leiden: E.J. Brill.

Whinnery, James E. (1997) 'Psychophysiologic Correlates of Unconsciousness and Near-Death Experiences', *Journal of Near-Death Studies*, 15, pp.231–58.

Whiteman, J.H.M. (1986) 'The Mystical Way and Habitualization of Mystical States', in B. Wolman and M. Ullman, *Handbook of States of Consciousness*, New York, NY: Van Nostrand Reinhold, pp.613–59.

Wilcox, Lynn (1995) *Sufism and Psychology*, Chicago, IL: Abjad.

Wilkes, Kathleen V. (1988) '____, yìshì, duh, um, and consciousness', in A.J. Marcel and E. Bisiach (eds), *Consciousness in Contemporary Science*, Oxford: Oxford University Press, pp.16–41.

Williams, D. (1981) 'The Emotions and Epilepsy', in E.H. Reynolds and M.R. Trimble (eds), *Epilepsy and Psychiatry*, Edinburgh: Churchill Livingstone, pp.49–59.

Wolman, Benjamin B. and Ullman, Montague (eds) (1986) *Handbook of States of Consciousness*, New York, NY: Van Nostrand Reinhold.
Zaehner, R.C. (1957, reprinted 1980) *Mysticism Sacred and Profane*, Oxford: Oxford University Press.
—— (1969) *Hindu and Muslim Mysticism*, New York, NY: Schocken Books.
Zainuddin, Roquiya (1995) 'Altered States of Consciousness and Sufism', *Journal of Indian Psychology*, 13, pp.33–9.
—— (1995) 'Spiritual States: Sufism and Psychology', *Islam and the Modern Age*, XXVI, pp.49–57.

INDEX